E

POINT

ENTRY POINT

TOWARDS
CHILD THEOLOGY
WITH
MATTHEW 18

Haddon Willmer

Keith J White

WTL PUBLICATIONS

Published 2013 by
WTL Publications Ltd
10 Crescent Road, South Woodford, London E18 1JB, UK

ISBN 978 095647573 2
Published 2013
Revised and reprinted 2014
10 9 8 7 6 5 4 3 2 1 0

A catalogue record for this book is available from the British Library

Design by Tony Cantale
Printed in UK by Lightning Source

For further copies of this book or information
call +44 20 8504 2702
email enquiries@wtlpublications.co.uk
or visit wtlpublications.co.uk

Contents

To Nathaniel

For some, there is no God.

For some, God is a vague shadow around the edges of life

For some, God is a tremendous presence, filling life,
silencing speech

For some, God is found in the Bible and in the church

For some, God is named the Rock, the God of Israel,

For some, God is the Father to whom Jesus taught us to
pray

For some, God is in Christ reconciling the world to
himself.

Some know God confidently in some form, under one
name or another

Some seek God with all their heart, some in occasional
bursts of longing

Some believe and some pray, I believe, help my unbelief

Some look for God in solitude, others in company, others
in service

Some look for God as consolation for suffering, others in
coming of new Jerusalem on earth

There are many who take God seriously, one way and
another.

There are many who talk with themselves about God,
seeking and finding, grieving and celebrating.

There are some who talk with one another, like the women
John Bunyan met, sitting on their doorsteps in Bedford,
talking about the things of God.

There are, in short, many theologians in the world.
There are many who talk theology all their lives even if
    they never know it.

God, we can see in the Bible, is a theologian too.
God talks God in his Word,
Through whom he creates all things,
So all things are there for his speaking,
Words for the Word

And the Word was made flesh
And speaks in life, a particular life,
In meaningful action, humanly chosen

God speaks God in the Spirit, sharing the Son
With those he chooses and holds on to
Those who know his voice and follow him.

God speaks God in all things
And in all things God is hard to follow,
Speaking God in what is not God
Truth in indirection
The word of God in human mouth

And God the Word puts into our argument
Sometimes a special word,
Clue and lever:
Child

HADDON WILLMER

*A*T THAT TIME *the disciples came to Jesus and asked, "Who is the greatest in the kingdom of heaven?"*

He called a little child and had him stand among them. And he said: "I tell you the truth, unless you change and become like little children, you will never enter the kingdom of heaven. Therefore, whoever humbles himself like this child is the greatest in the kingdom of heaven.

And whoever welcomes a little child like this in my name welcomes me. But if anyone causes one of these little ones who believe in me to sin, it would be better for him to have a large millstone hung around his neck and to be drowned in the depths of the sea.

Woe to the world because of the things that cause people to sin! Such things must come, but woe to the man through whom they come! If your hand or your foot causes you to sin, cut it off and throw it away. It is better for you to enter life

*maimed or crippled than to have two hands or
two feet and be thrown into eternal fire. And if
your eye causes you to sin, gouge it out and throw
it away. It is better for you to enter life with one
eye than to have two eyes and be thrown into the
fire of hell.*

*See that you do not look down on one of these
little ones. For I tell you that their angels in
heaven always see the face of my Father in heaven.*

*What do you think? If a man owns a hundred
sheep, and one of them wanders away, will he not
leave the ninety-nine on the hills and go to look
for the one that wandered off? And if he finds it,
I tell you the truth, he is happier about that one
sheep than about the ninety-nine that did not
wander off. In the same way your Father in
heaven is not willing that any of these little ones
should be lost."*

MATTHEW 18:1-14

This scripture text is from the NIV Anglicised version. Elsewhere in the book
we have used a variety of translations including, on occasions, our own.

Introduction

THIS BOOK IS the outcome of a sustained conversation on the text of Matthew 18:1-14. It is however neither a critical commentary nor pure exegesis. It is rather an essay, venturing ideas; our daring is greater than our competence.

Our antennae, as we pondered the text, have been focused by questions about the relation of theology and child. Each subject, child and theology, is in itself a complex enterprise, bristling with thought-provoking issues. When they are brought variously together, the potential lines of thought and action multiply. To escape bewilderment, we need to identify just one or two lines that we can follow usefully. We have taken a distinctive line, and make no claim to its being a comprehensive account of theology and/or children. An image that has seemed in some ways appropriate has been that of a borehole through the earth's strata. It is not a geological map: just a record of what is found in a sample taken by drilling in one direction with limited equipment.

Three Elements

On reflection there are probably three main elements that have gone into producing this essay on Matthew 18.

▓ God in Jesus

We have lived with the story of Jesus' placing a child in the midst of the disciples (Matthew 18:1-10) for over a decade. To write this book we have meditated on it, individually and in conversation without any conscious framework or intention save that of seeking to do some justice to the text. But this description of what we have attempted gives too much prominence to our activity. What is more important and exciting is the sense of being in the presence of Jesus, hearing him speak, being under the pressure of what he is saying and doing. Let us be clear about this: Jesus has not appeared to us. As we have been reading the gospel story, it has become the place where we have encountered Jesus.

We have not merely heard and received a report of a Jesus enclosed in the story, separated from us as a museum specimen behind a glass wall. Had that been so we could have acted as though Jesus were available to us as a resource, we ourselves being the controllers and directors. That is inevitably the outward form of this, and any other book: we are doing the writing, not Jesus. But the book has its roots for us in the fresh experience of Jesus who, through the witness to his words and action, comes to us as the living Lord. Over the years we have found that Jesus enters into conversation with us through this story. We still do most of the talking, but he drives, shapes and gives it substance. The authority is his.

▓ Child Theology Movement

Early in our work together on this essay, which is for us an attempt at doing Child Theology[1], we discarded other ways of exploring the relation between child and theology and committed ourselves to this text from Matthew's Gospel. It has been our prime source and companion in this project, but we have not been left alone with the text. A major sustaining, encouraging, often impatient context for our work has been the Child Theology Movement (CTM).

Hundreds of Christians engaged with children at risk throughout the world met in a Cutting Edge conference in Holland in 2001.

Keith White argued that the massive activism represented there needed deeper theological roots. There was a lively response to his paper, including hundreds of recorded comments and questions, and he was charged to do something about it. After taking soundings he organised a consultation in Penang in June 2002, out of which has come the Child Theology Movement.[2] Since then, CTM has held many consultations and taken part in many developing networks. The key aspiration of CTM is expressed in the formula: "No child related activity without theological reflection; No theology without the child in the midst." There is, however, no CTM orthodoxy, and CTM is not a powerful organising agency. It is rather a loose fellowship where people who have some interest in both children and theology stimulate, encourage and challenge one another in serious and friendly conversation. Its aspiration is to become a community of scholars. Sharing in the developing life of CTM has helped us enormously in writing this book, but it is not the "book of the movement".

Different directions of travel

CTM, in the context of the many global Christian movements concerned with children, includes ways of thinking not encompassed by our reading of Matthew 18. There is significant tension between different ways of relating children and theology. In this context, we are neither censors nor teachers: we may be gadflies. We do not seek to turn difference into polarised opposites: it can be the source of conflict or of fruitful meeting.

To illuminate the difference, think of our home cities of Leeds and London. From frequent journeys over a period of ten years, we know they are linked by road and rail. Some journeys go from London to Leeds, some from Leeds to London. Likewise the connection between children and theology can be made in one direction or another. Some look to theology to give grounding and support to the care and welfare of children. Here the direction goes from theology to child. Theology is asked to stimulate and guide so that the child is placed in the midst of caring attention. Natural products here are "theology of childhood" and theology as "advocacy for children".

The other direction runs from child to theology. It is not so obvious or popular, and may even seem to some shocking and dangerous, but it is to be risked. What difference does it make to theology if the child is placed in the midst? How does it change anything we say about God if the child is there? One product here may be theology which, even when it does not mention children, talks of God in a changed way because the child has somehow influenced it.

In practice these two different directions get mixed up: traffic is two-way between Leeds and London. When the direction runs from theology to child, there are always some hints and gestures in the other direction. This book mainly travels in the child-to-theology direction, but that does not mean it eliminates some traffic on the other carriageway. That becomes particularly obvious in Chapters Six and Seven. "Child-to-theology" implies and shapes "theology-to-child".

By concentrating on the movement from child to theology, doing theology with child in the midst, an unusual view emerges. Only as it gains visibility can it be evaluated and have a chance to carry conviction.

Anything called Child Theology attracts people concerned with care, education of, advocacy for, and ministry to children, and with the training of carers. We know this from our experience in CTM. Those whose professed primary concern is with theology, in the academy or the pulpit, tend to leave work with children to children's specialists. Their work as theologians is informed from many sources and has many concerns so that the child is easily lost, unnoticed in the crowd. Sometimes theologians talk amongst themselves about questions which only they are equipped to deal with: what use is the child then? At other times theology aims to speak to people outside their guild, but the child is only one in a variegated audience.

There are some good reasons why traffic from the child to theology is thin.[3] We want to increase the flow, overcoming the weight of tradition and professionalism which makes the child marginal to theology. There are some hopeful signs that in some academies the child is being put into the midst of the study of theology, not as the object of care by theology, but as a source of critical and constructive light for theology.

The shape of the book

As indicated already, the passage from Matthew 18 provides the overall framework for our exploration, but we have not attempted to produce a commentary. The shape, as represented by the seven chapters, has been more fluid and dynamic than that.

The Gospel gives us our starting point: a **CHILD**[4] whose only known distinguishing characteristic is that he or she (*paidion*) was placed in the midst of the disciples by Jesus.

The disciples were talking about greatness in the **KINGDOM** of God. That kingdom was the great concern of Jesus, the perspective within which he lived all his life, the presence and promise he proclaimed.

TEMPTATION: kingdom is always tempting because it stimulates ambitions and anxieties. In human experience generally, and richly for Israel, kingdom is a focus of hope and disappointment, of power in use and abuse. Here the hopes and fears of all the years meet. There are good kingdoms and bad; the kingdom of God is not truly and fully realised and present even in the best kingdom in the world and it is contradicted by the worst. Temptation means that people can miss the good and choose evil. Any encounter with the human project of kingdom puts people to the test. What are we seeking? What kind of people are we? What treasure do we value? What cause are we serving with our lives? What Lord do we trust?

In his own life, Jesus persistently discerned and chose the kingdom of God in a world confused by competing kingdoms. He called people to be his **DISCIPLES**, to be with him in the service of the kingdom of God in the terms in which he signed and proclaimed it. He warned them that people who were anxious and ambitious for greatness could not enter the kingdom of God. The entry point Jesus offered was to "deny self, take up their cross and follow him." The disciples had heard this call but it seems they did not understand it or follow it closely in spirit and action. When Jesus showed them the child, was he giving them a different way, more suited to their incapacity to follow him in the way of the cross? Is the child the foundation image of an alternative, gentler religion centred on the child-loving rather than the crucified Christ? We do not think so. Rather, by placing a child in the midst of the disciples, Jesus was reiterating his demand that disciples deny themselves, take up their cross and follow him. The child is another way of inviting us into the way of the cross. Our vision of discipleship, in its promise, cost and grace is not diluted, but enlarged and earthed.

That the child reiterates the call to discipleship can be seen in the meanings Jesus gives to the child placed in the midst. Denying self, radically symbolised by the cross, is a way of **HUMILITY**. We follow Jesus on a path that goes down into the depths, not to end in the abyss, but rather to enter the kingdom of God. It is a way of hope, to joy through sorrow, to life through dying, to love together through loneliness and rejection. The cross and humility are both off-putting to people whose ambition and anxiety is to be great in some form: rich, successful or happy. But the kingdom of God with its inexhaustible generosity, its self-giving in littleness and its coming in fullness, gives encouragement and joy to those willing to stoop and take the path of humility.

The child given to the disciples is more than a model of a spiritual quality (as humility is often seen) which they should imitate and make their own. The child is to be received. **RECEPTION** is real many-sided action. It is natural: it is what mothers do bodily from the beginning. It is transcendently spiritual, for each child confronts us with the mystery of personhood, to be respected and cherished. Receiving the child is an action typical of what makes and keeps human society human. And it is an eloquent reflection of, and participation in, the way God receives all people and all things in Christ, valuing the little, gathering in the alienated, forgiving the sinner. To receive a child in Christ's name is to receive him and the one who sent him and thus to share now in his missionary service of the kingdom of God.

This raises the question of whether reception is practised or even practicable in the world. The truth is that little ones are despised. Millions of children have a rotten time. They are not received into a life that is anything like the kingdom of God or even on the way to it. Is there a real rule of God which is effectively for goodness, love, life and joy all over the world? Or do the facts of the world not only dispose of little ones, but speak against God? Is the gospel of the kingdom of God as proclaimed by Jesus credible? The gospel has no easy path to credibility. God is despised along with all the despised of the earth, squeezed out of the world on to the cross. For those who follow Jesus in his way, this crisis of faith is what they find at the cross he called them to. If there is any hope, goodness, life and joy worthy of a kingdom of God, it can only be convincingly realised if the seeds of it have enough vitality to germinate and grow in this place of death, as life springing from the dead, and as the affirmation of the despised defying the regnant power of darkness. Thus the **FATHER** is faithful to the Son, raising him as the first-born of all creation and so the pledge and power of its rescue and vindication.

This last chapter about the depth of despising is not to be avoided. The kingdom of God is not to be sought as the icing on an earthly cake that is already tasty and satisfying enough. Rather we pray for God's kingdom to come as salvation and fundamental reversal, as resurrection life and the light of the glory of God in and upon God's darkened creation. We need it because following Jesus leads us to the place where all is lost unless God proves resourceful and faithful.

NOTES

1   We hope that the book will illustrate how one type of Child Theology might work in practice, but have not attempted to define the term either prescriptively or systematically. The term was first used in writing in a paper delivered by Keith J. White: *Child Theology is Born*, read to the Annual Forum of the Christian Child Care Forum in London on 5th February 2002. By then Haddon and he had met to discuss Keith's 2001 paper and make plans for the Penang Consultation. The term was used at Penang One in June 2002, and it was there that the idea of a book on Child Theology arose with Haddon and Keith suggested as the authors.

2   For information about Child Theology and the Child Theology Movement, see www.childtheology.org.

3   They include: a sense that the needs of children are so great and pressing that theological reflection is a luxury that cannot be afforded; a tendency in theology to have a stereotypical adult in mind thus overlooking the presence and gaze of children; a belief that this is dealt with in specialist disciplines in the academy such as "Christian education" or "child development" so that mainstream theology can get on with its primary tasks without reference to the child.

4   In this outline of the book, the words in bold capitals correspond to the titles of chapters.

Chapter One

Child

*"Jesus called a little child
and had him stand among them ..."*
MATTHEW 18:2

CTM starts with placing a child in the midst

WHEN THE CHILD THEOLOGY MOVEMENT began, and we embarked on the first outline of this book, the phrase "the child in the midst" was not a common catchword or *leitmotif*.[1] The phrase had not been picked out from the much-read story to be found in varying forms in Matthew 18:1-10, Mark 9:33-37, and Luke 9:46-48. In the run-up to the first Child Theology consultation at Penang and in the months after it,[2] the phrase came to have weight with us, because we wanted to be dealing with real children. The actual child can get lost in statistics, stereotypes, ideal types, in theory and in organised advocacy and action, even in sentimentality and nostalgia. How could these traps be avoided?

Someone suggested that the Penang consultation should begin with our sharing and comparing the theologies of childhood we were bringing to the table. Others resisted this method. Although a generalised concept of childhood seemed an appropriate focus for our theological reflection we sensed it might lead us into theoretical talk, which, however well-intentioned, would go around and even past the real child. We needed rather to find ways of attending to the child who might actually upset our existing theologies and assumptions. If we simply compared and synthesised the theories we were bringing to the table, we could be lulled into thinking that we were already sufficiently in touch with the child. Armed with our theories, we could make ourselves invulnerable to the child and not be shaken up by the gospel of God in Christ which places a real child (not a theology of childhood) in the midst as sign and provocation.[3]

No doubt, this distinction between "child" and "theologies of childhood" is not as simple as it might sound.[4] We cannot do without theory, but it is always necessary to look for protection against the dangers of theory. Within theory, we can become too confident, too enclosed, too attracted, or too combative, alienated progressively from reality. Talk can drive out listening, and theory can overwhelm seeing. Both the Bible and Jesus can be absorbed into theology and made impotent: we speak about God, and do not hear what is being said to us. It is not enough to add quotations from the Bible to our theory: proof-texts in support of theory merely become another level of theory.

The Bible and Jesus, as well as the child, resist being theoretically absorbed, but they do so not by any commanding or magical power. Rather they stand at the door and knock,[5] pleading for a hearing.[6] They try to squeeze through chinks in our theoretical armour. They are like David who refused to wear Saul's battle gear and went as he was to meet Goliath. He had the confidence of a shepherd boy trusting God, knowing how to defeat the formidably armed professional soldier with no more than his shepherd's crook, his skill with a simple sling, and a sense of what kind of stone would do the job.[7] Jesus and the Bible invite us to acquire a critical distance in relation to our established, highly developed ways of thinking, however necessary, prudent and solid they seem.

Taking real children seriously in actual situations and contexts does not, however, free us for action without theory. It rather helps to improve thinking: both stimulating wonder and imagination and keeping it close to reality and practice. Jesus and the Bible call us to humility in theorising, recognizing there may be much that our theorising is insensitive to or excludes; theory always needs to be refreshed by new encounters with reality. The presence of a child does not have a good effect on thinking in theology in any automatic or one-sided way. The thinker has to be open to the child, and receive her without imposing preconditions on the encounter.

When we are confronted by Jesus, and are listening out for the Word of God, the Spirit of God works on the side of the hearing as well as the speaking. The Spirit of God opens up the human spirit to receive the word. God gives the hearing ear. But the Spirit operates mysteriously, not coercively. There is a conversation of Spirit with spirit,[8] often characterised by striving, but never the elimination of the human by the divine. Looking to the Spirit to help us in our receiving of the Word of God does not save the Word from being like sheep among wolves, looking for a reception but not always finding it. So the Word is always vulnerable.

As Christians, whether individually or as a group, we should not imagine that we have heard and received the Word fully and unreservedly so that the Word finds untrammeled freedom and space in our hearts and communities.[9] It is not only outside the church that the Word is unreceived. We need rather to take heed how we hear and to be aware that our receiving the Word may be partial and distorting. We have a calling and responsibility, in penitence and sensitivity, to learn to hear anew and more fully and plainly what God says.[10]

The Church is not so much the community which has heard, possesses and is unfeignedly faithful to the Word of God, but a community where there is, at best, a sustained attempt to hear that Word. It is committed to a constant humble critical quest to hear more truly: changing and growing to give space and freedom to God, rather than expecting God to fit into what we are and have. Such a church will engage in critical dialogue with the Word, as the disciples did with Jesus. It is a church recognising that its hearing is compromised by past mishearing, so that if the Word is to be heard in the present, there needs to be a liberation, a turning, an uncluttering of accrued baggage. When Jesus places a child in the midst, a church of this sort will not let obsessive debates about theories of childhood cushion the shock that the real, un-theorised child may bring.[11]

The first CTM consultation was a tentative move in the direction of placing a child in the midst of our discussion; later this method was deliberately developed. We found that the gospel story gave us concrete help. Instead of beginning by sharing our theologies of childhood, we were led by the single action of Jesus who placed a child in the midst. This action, as we shall see, is a potent seed of theory[12] including theologies of childhood but, in itself, it invites us to pause and attend to the child who is standing in the midst, to be quiet and learn at a root-point before any theology of childhood appears.

How then did we seek to bring the real child into the midst of our processes of developing child theology together? We chose not to place an actual child in our circle.[13] One reason was that this was likely to be boring and even abusive for the child. Secondly, having a child present in her own body would not have prevented our reading our ideas into her, thus substituting the child by theorising. That is a natural, virtually unavoidable human practice: it starts with loving parents who nurture the child they envision rather than the child they have actually been given.

Everyone round the table brought known children with them in their hearts and minds. It only needed some imaginative work and story telling for them to be present. Anyone who has lived at all has met many different children, in and beyond the family; no one is short of supply when invited to place a child in the midst. But doing that requires a two-fold disciplined act: first to search out the child from our memory-store and then to bring her to view in the centre, and secondly, to draw back and let the child be there, confronting us with something strange in her integrity.

Thus a child, imagined from actual children we have encountered, may stand impressively in the midst. The imagination at work here is not primarily creative, or masterful; it does not treat the child as its creature. It is rather respectful and curious, humble and trusting: operating by giving space to the other and then waiting to see what the other gives. In CTM consultations, the exploratory drama of placing a child in the midst is an important moment in which to pause and notice. With a child thus welcomed into the group, we go on to find out what difference she makes to our theologising.[14]

Through this experimental reflection, we have a strong sense that the gospel story takes us beyond our theories of children and childhood because it puts the child in the midst in a special way. The child we have in view is in the hands of Jesus, and that limits our freedom to interpret her so that she becomes a carrier of our ideas. The child is a sign of the kingdom of God which we have yet to enter, and thus is a child that eludes us in important ways. This child is not, primarily, the child we think we can manage and understand because we care for him. The child with Jesus is the child we glimpse from time to time, a mystery,[15] an Other, an invitation to transcend our self by being transcended.

Attending to the gospel story made us pause in the moment when the child first stood amongst the disciples, in a silence before anything was said. This method is powerful in generating new vivid discussions, which centre on children in their reality as they have encountered us in the world. We have perhaps been overconfident in assuming that this process adequately translates into our contemporary situation and context what Jesus was seeking to do and communicate with his disciples.[16] It is vital that the gospel story keeps its independence, even over against experiments that are rooted in the story.

The child in the midst quite apart from Jesus

Having been highlighted by CTM, the isolated phrase "the child in the midst" has acquired considerable popularity since 2002 and has been used without reference to its biblical source and the theological reflection shaped by those roots. It has emotive and appealing power, like charity pictures of children in distress.[17]

Our history poses a question. It took time for us to see that there is an important difference between "the child in the midst" and "the child placed by Jesus in the midst". Given that "the child in the midst" is such a popular idea with immediate appeal, why should we swim against the tide, contending for the significance of the less catchy, explicitly Christian phrase, "the child placed in the midst by Jesus"? This is the question for the rest of this chapter.

The child can be "in the midst" quite apart from Jesus. There are two main reasons for this, which can be labeled loosely as anthropological and historical, or nature and culture.

Nature

When a baby arrives, the child naturally steps into the centre of life and transforms it: a woman becomes a mother, a couple becomes a family, and their settled pattern of life and expectations are disturbed by an unpredictable newcomer. This is elegantly described by Niall Williams in his novel, *As It Is in Heaven*, when a baby is born to a couple, Stephen and Gabriella: "She became the clock of the cottage. Her wakes and sleeps dictated the rhythms of their days and nights."[18]

In a sense children are present by "natural force": they take up space, social and physical. They have their being without being asked whether they want it; they do not need deliberately to strive for or contrive it. They wield power by being themselves.[19] They can suck power out of others as well as inspiring it. In them are invested the hopes of parents, or the fears of people about the future, and children live from that investment. Loved or unloved, they cannot be overlooked or avoided. Loved, they are a focus of delight and care. Even unloved and regarded as a nuisance, they are somewhat protected by the reverence for life; within whatever space they find in the world, they make their own way if they have to. Empowered by the brute necessity of life, they are opportunistic, resilient and creative.[20]

Children have the power of life, but it is insufficient to serve their best interests. Some orphaned or abandoned children have to grow up too quickly, becoming streetwise to survive the urban jungle; some have parental responsibility for siblings thrust upon them, when, for example, parents have died from HIV. Such children do not have the secure leisure to enjoy life; they must graft and fight for basic necessities and often are badly hurt and disadvantaged in the process. Whether their life is good or bad, easy or difficult, they show the power of resilient life. The child thus comes naturally into the midst of life.

The child in her own being claims more than physical space: she claims respect and attention. The child muscles in, with charm or insouciance, grabbing moral and spiritual space without regard to the existing occupiers, putting them under pressure to make new choices about what sort of human being they will be. They can grow to be hospitable to the newcomer or they can harden themselves by drawing a boundary against the child. The child forces parents, and others, to grow in one way or another. So over years, parents not only live under the challenge of responding to the growing child, but also become aware of who they are, through reflecting on the way they have lived with the child. Some parents may end up having good reason to be pleased with what they have become through living with their children, some may be complacent about their achievement only because they are insensitive, while others may be sad and defeated, disappointed both for the child and about themselves. Regrets incurred in parenting may be too painful to give voice to.

Adults can resist the attraction and claims of the child, thereby doing violence to themselves as well as the child, leaving them ashamed, or hardened against shame, and either way, diminished as persons. They may flee from the child to take comfort with other hardened people, even seeking refuge in views of the world which serve to justify their exclusion of the child. They may grow old regretting their failures in parenting too late. Once a child comes, these choices and dangers are inescapable for parents and carers.[21]

Thus the child coming into the midst is an alarming challenge. But that is not all. The child rewards welcome. Smiling at a baby evokes a smile. The child gives joy, not by intention, but simply by being and growing. There is not a great separation between the demand the child makes and the reward the child gives: the reward is rooted in the caring, because the caring has to be intimate, continuous, reliable and sensitive. So it leads to a deep knowing of the mystery and wonder of the child, and amazement at the simultaneous otherness and closeness of the child. The child is in the midst not merely through urgent demand but by attraction of life answering life in person.

All this can only be said in relation to "the child", not children in general. It is not a group which comes into the midst as transforming enlivening mystery.[22] As the child grows by relating intensively with one or a few carers, so adults can only be affected deeply by attending to a child in her particularity. It is happily possible to parent several children simultaneously, but usually, there is a space between their births, and each has her initial moment to come into the midst of the family. A child can be pushed into the background in a large busy family, but a big family can be good, so that each child has love and respect effectively focused upon her. This is what makes birthday parties so important and valuable. Then the child is like the younger son in the parable of the Prodigal Son, for whom a feast is made, because he is alive, or like the older brother who is always with the father, sharing all he has (Luke 15:11-32). So the child as challenge and reward is imperfectly but really met in the relatively small circle of the family, nuclear and extended; it is hard for managers of services to hundreds or thousands of children, like CEOs of large children's organizations, to avoid being distanced from the child by their work for children.

Does focusing on the child "in the midst" make for an artificial isolation from the nexus of relationships that comprise kith and kin?[23] Is that implied in the story of Jesus' placing a child in the midst? That child seems to be alone there, at least for the moment.

There is no hint of an anxious or proud parent standing by. Yet there is no reason to think this was an abandoned child and it was not an idealised child existing without family. The family, with its intimate small-scale parenting and sibling relationships, is a special setting in which the significance of child can become evident. Here, it is possible for the individual child, however small, to come into the spotlight and enjoy a relation with carers who have, or are learning, sensitive appreciation of the child. Then, seeing and celebrating the child is part of the substance of living: it gives life meaning. The child in the midst automatically and implicitly brings into play a complex web of relationships. A child bereft of all such relationships is either a strange figment of the imagination or much to be pitied as a victim of abuse or neglect, and in need of immediate care.

The child is naturally "in the midst" in relation to parents and kin. That is true in profoundly personal and spiritual ways. But it is also a relation which is inescapably bodily and earthly. The child is in the midst of attention and care for prudential, practical reasons, such as concern for the human future on earth. Children are a basic natural pension plan for parents who will grow old. Even when there are other pension arrangements, children answer the "legacy" worries of mortals, who want to be remembered and to die feeling their life has not been futile.[24] The child thus meets anxieties which are deep rooted in human being. Are these anxieties wholly wrong? Some children feel restricted by the expectations of parents, burdened by a sense of obligation to them; but this can be a healthy and helpful ingredient in the process of growing up. To live in such a way that parents are glad about their children is part of what it means to honour father and mother. It can be a spur to living well.

The child is also "in the midst" of a wider society than the family, serving all sorts of necessary and unnecessary economic and political interests. The family small-holding or other business, like the corner shop, needs workers now and in the future; the government must have soldiers and tax-payers; sellers must have markets; producers must have consumers; and the media must have audiences. The power of the clan and other collectives depends on producing children: "Like arrows in the hand of a warrior are the sons of one's youth. Happy is the man who has his quiver full of them. He shall not be put to shame when he speaks with his enemies in the gate."[25] Conversely, Rachel's inconsolable sadness when her children "are no more"[26] reminds us that the loss of children is devastating, unless of course we happen to be armoured with Herod's fearful calculating self-concern.

There are so many ways in which the child is "in the midst".

History

In recent times, cultures have been refocused by a deliberate and value-laden concern for children. The meaning of "the child in the midst" is historically conditioned.[27] From the Romantics in the 18th century to Dr Spock, Save the Children[28] and the UN Convention on the Rights of the Child, (UNCRC, 1989), poetry, art, storytelling, the science of child care and education, political action and humanitarian sensibility have all been putting the child in the midst in various new, deliberate, complex ways. With systematic awareness, education has become professedly, if not always effectively, "child-centred". Children are educable, not to be written off merely because they are at present socially troubled and troublesome. In law and childcare it is explicitly insisted that the "best interests of the child" are paramount in every situation.[29] As the view grows that human beings, enlightened with all-round intelligence and good will, can parent effectively, the waste of children becomes more scandalous. The decline in infant mortality strengthens the sense that the suffering of children is avoidable; the death of children cannot be accepted as inevitable natural wastage.

Romanticism discovered and celebrated the child in a way which changed visions of what it is to be human. Childhood was seen as representing humanity in its innocence and spontaneity, and so inspired adult dreams and attempts to be more fully human by preserving or recovering child-likeness. This approach some-times had a melancholic downside, as it led people to regret adult-hood. Instead of the older (Augustinian) view that children are born in sin, implying that sin is universal, people now were seen as beginning in innocence before growing up into the loss of inno-cence and freedom.[30] Idealised childhood was invented and pro-longed. Education struggled to distinguish itself from work and servitude: sometimes, it was humanised by being child-centred, not being afraid or dismissive of play as though it were wasteful, learning with the child rather than imposing on the child.[31] This high regard for the child, a fascination that is both wistful and car-ing, stimulated more scientific observation of children in the quest for more effective care of children.[32]

The positive attraction of the beautiful child has been a driver of modern child-friendliness. Another is an ethically and reli-giously-based hope and concern for the "ugly child"[33] or, simply and comprehensively, the child in any kind of distress. The child in distress evokes sympathetic and urgent responses for several inter-locking reasons. If adults are, or want to think of themselves as sensitive, compassionate or just, they cannot ignore the needs of anyone in distress. When they have a sense of the essential worth, goodness and beauty of the child, they react to any violation of the child. The loss of children, either in early death or in the breaking of spirit and the stunting and misdirection of potential, is judged to be unacceptable.

Hope is integral to the being of the child, because growing is natural in a child. The child has become a concrete universal symbol of hope. For this reason the child can be the focus of a com-munal quest, moving towards universal humanity. The child moves people. In our better moments we are inspired, individually and collectively, when we think primarily of children. In the UK, the television programme *Children in Need* raises millions of pounds each year. The basic underlying assumption is that every-one who is genuinely human will respond to the cries of a suffer-ing or hungry child. But there is more to the process than the fact that individuals are moved. The child brings people together in communities of care and hope, local, national and international as a sign of hope for humanity and human civilization.

Child-friendliness?

For reasons such as these, the concept of the "child in the midst" has a wide appeal.[34] We might discern an implicit religion of the child in the midst, which encompasses, inspires and mobilises politics, organisations, education, and social work at every level. The UNCRC is formally a legal instrument, guiding practice; but it also symbolises the much broader claim of the child upon loyalty and service, and extols her worth and meaning for all. The child crystallises and represents humanity for many people and organisations. If God makes a preferential option for the poor, it might be said that some today make a preferential option for the child. Child-friendliness is a significant characteristic of contemporary culture, including humanism and Christianity.

But whatever is meant by "child-friendliness", it is tragically obvious that it is far from being universally realised. The neglect and suffering of children is unbearable. A billion people live on one dollar a day; not surprisingly, many children are undernourished. Many lack safe water and other simple necessities and so die of preventable diseases. Many live with HIV/AIDS and over 15 million have been orphaned by the disease. Hundreds of thousands of child soldiers represent the terrible extreme of what war does to children, intensifying poverty, disrupting education, corrupting the spirit. Hundreds of millions of children work, often in unhealthy and cruel ways, enslaved, trafficked, unprotected. Millions are trapped in sex trades like prostitution and pornography. Maybe 100 million live on the streets, with no parents or friendly society to care for them: gangs are a poor substitute.[35] Even affluent children suffer by growing up "rich in things and poor in soul," with stuff instead of personal affection, a gross distortion of humanity.[36] Education as mere induction into consumerism or employability is abusive.

The evil disclosed in the varied sufferings of children belongs to us all and is not in any way to be minimised: it cannot be made tolerable.

The world is not consistently child-friendly. Many children are neglected, not wanted, disposed of. Targeted by abusers and exploiters, they are in the midst of enemies. John Saward argues that the modern world is hostile to children. The 1890s were in his view a "very dark night", when the attack on Christianity was, above all, "an onslaught on childhood."[37] The world has not got better since: "Modern men and women seem to have declared war on their children. In societies dedicated to the pursuit of unrestrained sexual pleasure, the child has become an obstacle to be circumvented, even an enemy to be destroyed. The dominant contraceptive mentality is intrinsically contra-child, for the contracepting person wills a child not to be." Thus Saward attempts to portray the world today as systematically hostile to children.

This sweeping generalization is, however, contentious and dangerous. The wrongs children suffer in this fallen world are not to be minimised or excused, but it is not helpful to condemn the whole world "outside Christianity" as systematically hostile to children or to see it in terms of an apocalyptic moral war between Christianity and the world, between the Lamb, the Woman and Child and the Devil (Revelation 12:1-12).[38] Saward says, "Throughout Western Europe and North America there are well-endowed societies for the prevention of cruelty to children, but better funded by far, backed by governments and international agencies, are bodies for the prevention of children." The remark is striking, suggesting that the forces of child-friendliness are vastly outweighed by systematic hostility to children. His calculation may be overly pessimistic, but even if it is not, it bears implicit witness to the fact that some organised child-friendliness is at work. Even if it is in a minority, it is not a small or lethargic minority. Child-friendly people must avoid being intimidated by the forces of child-hostility with their rampant power to inflict misery: instead let them respond to this terrible situation with courage, freedom of spirit and constructive hopefulness sustained by love and trust in God. Cursing the darkness is no virtue: let us light a candle, even if it is only a little one, and add ours to all the candles already shining.

Child-friendliness goes much wider than Societies for the Prevention of Cruelty to Children: it includes many ordinary, unpretentious, frail, fallible but serviceable families. The contraceptive mentality has not stopped people choosing to have children out of love. There is a lot of faithful long-term "good enough"[39] parenting, too easily taken for granted and undervalued.[40] Saward's is not the only exaggerated criticism of the way things are, which, extrapolating from the extensive and deep-rooted sufferings of children, ends with an overall judgment on the contemporary world as hostile to children.

By contrast, a commitment to children will try to generate more sustained, patient, practical action for children; it would build on whatever actual and potential child-friendliness it can find rather than demonizing the world.

Without overestimating the power or achievement of manifold personal, family and organisational child-friendliness, its reality and significance is therefore to be affirmed. It is an invitation to all of us to join, hopefully and sacrificially, in being as fully child-friendly as we can. Child-friendliness is real, in spite of its limits. This means that we do not theorise a world shaped and dominated by hostility to the child, making judgmental ideological generalisations and engaging in a holy war against the world, but rather follow a vision growing from seeds of child-friendliness.[41]

So for both Christians and non-Christians, it is good that the child today is anthropologically and historically in the midst. "The child in the midst" is common ground, a shared concern that brings us together to respect the child for all the child is worth.

The child placed in the midst: and the Jesus who places the child

This book is concerned with the child as placed by Jesus in the midst. In addition to the child in the midst it is also concerned with Jesus and his action in the placing of the child. While considering this text, the difference between the meanings of the "child in the midst" and the "child placed by Jesus" has become a key question for us. What is the difference between an independent, solitary child, and a child placed by someone or something other than itself? What is the difference between the child as placed by Jesus and the child placed by, say, Tom, Dick or Hannah? What is the difference between the phrase "the child in the midst" as a free-ranging slogan and the phrase, "child placed by Jesus", which is rooted in the gospel narrative?

The child who is in the midst by virtue of nature and history has great moral and cultural power. This child symbolises a real but limited and fragile child-friendly context which shapes action, thought and relationships. This context affects our perceptions of Jesus' placing of the child. Is Jesus' placing of the child superfluous so long as the child is naturally in the midst? Is his action no more than an ancient, culturally restricted and subordinate instance of the child placed in the midst?

The child in herself is familiar to all; but Jesus is known only to a minority. The child is a practical costly concern to many; a costly engagement with Jesus is less common. The child is universally and visibly present in the human community; Jesus is not universally present in the same way. We know the child in what we remember of ourselves and what we do as parents and carers or abusers and exploiters; we have a more distant, even ethereal, sense of Jesus, mediated to us by thought, history and ritual. The child in the midst is a convincing reality; the ideas people have of Jesus have a variable capacity to persuade and grip them.

Yet the child placed by Jesus in the midst has significance. We hope to testify to that significance, not by unveiling a totally new discovery but by responding to what has for long been waiting for us in the gospel. Today, we come to know and live with the significance of the child placed by Jesus in the context of the child in the midst apart from Jesus. Before reading the gospel more closely, we make observations about some ways of finding the meaning of the child placed by Jesus in the cultural context where the child is naturally in the midst. Without taking critical notice of our context we would have a recipe for futility, like leaving a seed unplanted, because we feared putting it in the ground to die (John 12:24).

Those who will let themselves be guided by Jesus who placed a child in the midst cannot avoid some kind of theological work. How this child theology converses with its context, especially the child in the midst apart from Jesus, involves taking into account diverse forms of theology, and a range of attitudes Christians take towards them. We do not attempt a complete taxonomy, but rather highlight examples.

▓ Relativising Jesus and his placing of the child

Jesus did not oppose child-friendliness; Jesus resisted those who were unfriendly to children. He would probably have gone along with today's diverse child friendliness, at least on his principle that "whoever is not against us is for us" (Mark 9:40). Like many other child-friendly people, he would be critical of some of the ways in which the child is now put in the midst. He might, for example, make a new version of his story of the rich old fool. Could it have gone like this, we wonder? "There was once a child overwhelmed by induced acquisitiveness, stimulated by targeted advertising. One day, the child is hit by the question: "I have all this stuff, but what am I coming to?" A child's life does not consist in the abundance of his possessions. Young or old, he "who lays up treasure for himself and is not rich toward God" is a fool". (Luke 12:13-21) Such criticism is not a sign of hostility to children; rather it is but an element of the wisdom essential to a genuine child-friendliness. It is attacking the ravening wolves who conceal themselves in false child-friendliness.[42]

Jesus in his teaching and example does not have the cultural power to define or ground or guide modern child-friendliness in its totality. Today his is one of many voices and examples within it. He makes a contribution, sitting within its relativizing context. We can ask what that contribution is, and what value it adds, and how necessary it is.

Jesus takes his place now with child-friendly people, as he did in his life on earth, entering freely and easily into the company and concerns of ordinary people who, without dogma or historical scholarship, respond to him. Today's child-friendliness is often compatible with Jesus, because Jesus is child-friendly. He is an ancient symbol and a practising teacher of child-friendliness: he embraced the children and told us to welcome them. When we welcome children, we are close to him in spirit. It is comforting to know that. Working with Jesus for the children means we share the heart of the matter with him. We do not have to satisfy the requirements of the religions that have been built by the professed followers of Jesus over the centuries. In child-friendliness we find the spiritual essence of what he was about in a most practical, down-to-earth, life-enhancing way.

To be liberated into this way with Jesus is easy: it requires little study or theological labour. The Gospels do not take long to read and are not obscure on this point. To seek for the child-friendly Jesus we do not have to be lonely Bible-students thinking intensely against the cultural tide. In many places, the child-friendly Jesus has already been found and popularised in modern times.[43]

In the context of contemporary child-friendliness, there is nothing which necessarily prevents child-friendly people from finding significance in Jesus and his placing of the child. The context is not necessarily philistine or intolerantly secularist.

Inclusive secular child-friendliness tends to place Jesus where he can be simultaneously respected and disempowered. In this comfortable indifference, Jesus is both valued and scaled down; either way, he gives no trouble. Jesus symbolically endorses the good already espoused, but adds nothing to it.

There is opportunity and threat here for child-friendly Christians. They find open space where they can work for children with people of other faiths and none. To a large extent, Christians can express and develop their faith-identity through serving and caring for children. But there is also a threat to that identity from those who directly attack Christian faith and want it curtailed; and from child-friendliness which is peacefully indifferent to Jesus.[44]

Christians respond to this ambivalent situation in various ways which we now consider.

Christian child-friendly activism

Activism is good. Every community, every family, every enterprise needs practical people, who see what has to be done and are committed to getting it done. Christians engage for and with children on a massive scale throughout the world with whatever skills and resources they have.[45] They are moved by compassion for children in need and by commitment to their fulfilment in life. Obvious and basic needs show them where to start work. They are spared Hamlet's reflective hesitation.[46] At its bluntest, the activist approach was asserted by Bob McClure, one of the greatest missionary surgeons of the twentieth century, when he was visiting a conservative Christian hospital under war conditions in China. In the operating room, with the patient ready on the table, the Christian staff followed their normal practice of praying at length. McClure, who always prayed succinctly before operating, waited impatiently for them to finish. When the Amen sounded at last, he said: "Now that we've cut the cackle, let's cut the patient."[47] The activist expresses his faith in works and has little patience with talk, which is often seen as a delaying tactic. Like Nehemiah, he will not let talkers distract him from the work (Nehemiah 6:3).

There is a danger that activism becomes a workaholic fanaticism, despising and rejecting anything not directly useful to the project. Lacking reflection, it risks getting imprisoned within existing habits and perspectives.[48] The child in the midst is enough to move Christian action for children. Christian activism is often devoted to Jesus, but sees little need to reflect theologically on the One who is a Friend and Partner in the work. In the light of this it is hardly surprising that the concept of "the child placed by Jesus" stirs little curiosity.[49]

The tendency to drop and fade Jesus and theology

Child friendly Christians take every opportunity to work with and for children. They build and run confessedly Christian projects and organisations. They also work in secular organisations where Christian faith can only be implicit. Since resources are limited, Christians make practical compromises to achieve pluralist cooperation. In Britain organisations that have Christian origins often give up or blur their Christian identity. They move with the times from having a Christian basis, often laid down in Victorian times, to affirming respect for "Christian values", then going on to the point where there is no reference to Christianity at all. In this way they set themselves free to employ anyone who is committed to children and to win funds more easily, because there is nothing in their mission statement which could raise the suspicion that their service might fail to be non-discriminatory and universal. Dropping Jesus sets us free to do more for children.

Individually, Christians who work in such conditions may retain a personal Christian identity and be strongly and intelligently moved by Christian vision and commitment. But they know that Christian vision is not shared by others they work with; it can only rarely and on the personal margins be quoted as a source of wisdom and encouragement for the work. Along with others Christians do all the good they can within the limits set, and they learn how to fit in with them positively and graciously, because they are there for the children, not for sharing their faith. They are Christians incognito. Sometimes, this practical distinction between the child and the faith becomes a policed principle of separation. Marking out faith in God in Christ, as distinct from the interests of children, may be a stepping stone to viewing the visible faith of the carer as somehow dangerous to children.

Christians may come to terms with this separation, accepting it as inevitable and normal. With more or less unease, they assimilate to the ideology intrinsic to the work, which is without a religious or theological dimension. Spirituality may be valued for workers and clients, but it is acceptable in secular contexts because, unlike Christian faith, it is without a defined and organised identity. Spirituality is what each person seeks and finds about their own deep meaning, strengths and satisfaction.

The accommodation the Christian makes with the secularity of the work may in time feed back into his own mind and spirit. He may find that he can do quite well without theology; sermons and the kind of arguments that blow up in churches cease to be of interest and come to irritate by their futility. Within these conditions, many people move from explicit Christian commitment to a wider spiritual search or drift into indifference. The child in the midst continues to be a meaningful spiritual symbol, but the child as placed by Jesus requires a kind of attention to the text of the Bible and its theological interpretation which is not encouraged in this environment.

▨ Fighting for Christian faith as public truth[50]

Sometimes Christians do not easily accept the silence and loss of confessed Christian identity that the pluralist secularity of society encourages, even when it is not prescribed. They are aware of the danger of being impoverished as people of faith if concessions to the pressures of a privatising culture or legal order lead them to give up holding and presenting Christian faith as public truth, as faith for all. Those who know God in Christ have a responsibility to go on sharing what they know: God is God not just for those who believe but also for those who deny or ignore or do not know God. God is creator of all the earth, not just a religious segment of it.

So it is good that Christians wish to present Christian faith as public truth. That commits them to sharing the gospel as good news for all the world, bringing reality to light. It commits them to thinking the gospel with respect for truth in every direction and to speaking in ways which are intelligible to outsiders.[51] In under-standing Christian faith, they cannot then cultivate a merely private or sectarian view, but must witness to One who is God for all, including those who are and remain outside the community which confesses faith.

This is a difficult and dangerous task. The universality of the truth of God is not to be achieved by somehow imposing a partisan opinion on everyone, whether by force, tricks of communication or education of the young. The task of the witness is not to be an elite controlling public opinion or shaping culture. Rather witnesses need to think and live with others even when they remain outside the community of faith. The gospel needs to be spoken not as "my truth I am giving you" but as "God's truth which is waiting for all people wherever they are." To witness is to bear good news as truth for the other person. The witness may sometimes not understand the message he carries or it may strike him as strange, because it is not primarily for him, but for the other. The witness makes his being available as the medium for a stretching, sacrificial translation.

The aim is not to transfer to someone else the truth as it is possessed by the witness, so duplicating it in a new territory; it is rather to serve the coming to light, or perhaps a coming to birth, of a truth that enlightens and liberates both the messenger and the one who receives it. Before the Word of God, both are forever learners, always, as Luther put it in his last written words, "We are beggars."[52] Paul in his masterfulness wanted his converts "to become as I am, for I also have become as you are," but the serving Apostle did not seek to clone many little Pauls: "My little children, with whom I am again in travail *until Christ be formed in you*." (Galatians 4:12,19). The witness contributes soundwaves, words and ideas, but, through the Holy Spirit, what is heard is God speaking to each *in their own tongue* (Acts 2:8-11; 1 Corinthians 9:19-23). Witness and mission of this sort is far beyond our ordinary capacity; in practice we only come near to it in occasional moments, which often take us by surprise. But it is an intelligible goal worth aspiring to; it is certainly to be accepted as a criterion by which to test practice. It implies openness to others and to the world where Christians are witnessing and serving; waiting and learning and experimenting humbly in the hope of being able to offer something which is simultaneously true to the gospel of God in Christ and in a language which others find as their own.[53]

Fighting for any good cause brings the danger that the fighting itself will corrupt the goodness and betray the cause. Any form of fighting to win space for explicitly Christian action for children in a secularising society needs to be disciplined and transformed continually by the renewing of the mind. Where Christian faith is deliberately marginalised or is whittled away by indifference, Christians face the temptation to defend faith by attacking the opposition. That means making enemies rather than friends. Christians may get trapped into making a merely fearful defence of Christian space against what is perceived as persecution. The persuasive defence of Christian faith in situations where it is not already welcomed or at least culturally latent is not to be made by attacking unbelievers, by argument, or by legal restrictions, let alone by blows. It has to be ventured by positive and faithful representation of faith, as an invitation to all, as a light for life, as a goodness to be tried out. Christ did not die *against* anyone, but *for* all, including the godless and those who crucified him.[54]

It is right for Christians to contend for freedom, their own and other people's. But any resistance to the curtailment of Christian freedom needs to be rooted in living and cheerful faith in God.[55] We need to find ways of consistently witnessing to the grace and love of God, whose coming kingdom brings life for all. To make even a little faltering start on living like that depends on the fullness of the gift of the generous resilient forgiving Spirit of God in Christ. One part of that gift, only a small part, is the will and courage for theology of a kind which bears the word in ways that give the Spirit the freedom for translation. Discerning how to live in tight situations, and how to be true to truth which is not popularly supported requires Christians to think as wisely as serpents, even while, trusting in God, they are as simple, as peaceful and friendly, as doves.

Jesus places a child in the midst

The trajectory of a secularising society such as Britain today[56] carries us from confessedly Christian child-activism to the assimilation of many Christians to a largely de-christianised child-friendliness. Once there, Christians can resist being made invisible or marginal, by fighting to maintain the traditional status and privileged space for Christianity, or seek for ways to be faithful to the gospel, sharing share it as public truth with humility and openness.

Within this secularised cultural context, the child's being *placed by Jesus* has no significance. The child is important in his own right and Jesus adds nothing of value.

Assimilated Christianity makes no protest. In its Bible reading, theology and life may make much of Jesus in general, but little of Jesus who placed the child in the midst. In recent years and round the world there has been a significant growth in Christian thinking and writing about the child, in church, mission and academy. Much of it has a practical concern for children in need and at risk, for child development, evangelism, catechesis and the spirituality of children. Children are increasingly the theme of intentional scholarly work.[57] The child is sometimes seen as the source of knowledge of God apart from the revelation in Christ. A kind of natural theology is derived from the child who in herself images God and thus leads us to God; so the child can be in the midst of theology and spirituality, without being placed there by Jesus, who is "passed by".[58] Jesus placing the child has occasionally been noticed by scholars working on the Gospels, but insights from biblical studies are often only slowly taken in by systematic or practical theology.[59]

What would be added if we were to pause to notice Jesus placing a child in the midst of disciples who have their minds on other things? That is the leading question in this book.

NOTES

1   While ancient commentators take this text seriously and in some ways leave us little to say about it (e.g. Matthew Henry), we have not found much evidence that theologians and spiritual teachers have latched on to the "child in the midst" as a focus and guiding inspiration for their interpretation of Christian faith. George MacDonald in *Unspoken Sermons* (1886) is a rare, dated and not altogether persuasive exception.

2   Matthew 18:1-5 was the text of a sermon preached in Penang by Haddon Willmer before the first consultation there, in 2002. The report of the consultation shows that the text of Matthew 18 was already floating in the conversation: it says, for example, that our task was to rethink theology "taking account of what Jesus might have meant when he took a child and placed it (him or her) 'in the midst' of the disciples" (p. 2). But the concept and text did not shape the vast agenda we envisaged nor the book project then discussed. The report of the Cape Town consultation in February 2004 shows that Matthew 18 was by then the framework of this book and it provided the basis of the first experiment in CT; in Houston (May 2004) Matthew 18 is mentioned again but did not shape the consultation; in the second Penang consultation (June 2004) there is a longer treatment of Matthew 18 and Child Theology (pp. 10-12); in Cambridge (Sept 2004) it played a much larger role in shaping the consultation, but did not prove to be very persuasive.

3   Karl Barth, *The Christian Life*, 1981, pp. 267-271, 203

4   Quite apart from the relation between real children, past and present, and theology, we are of course aware of the sociological problematics associated with the concepts of child and childhood. For example, Julia Brannen, "Children and Agency in Academic and public Policy Discourses", in *Children and Social Exclusion*, ed. Keith J. White 1999, pp. 15-29

5   Revelation 3:20

6   For example, Matthew 11: 28-30

7. 1 Samuel 17:38-40

8   This insight is pivotal in the work of James E. Loder, and forms a basis for *The Logic of the Spirit*, 1989. See 1 Corinthians 2:10-16, which is quoted by Loder at the beginning of Chapter 1, p. 3.

9   The Word is essentially the Word of God in Christ (John,1:1-18ff) which is witnessed to in the Bible. It is God speaking. Human beings speaking and hearing in human language and ways can usurp or displace the Word which God speaks with living and free and manifold voice; but human speaking may also be serve the Word, carrying it with humility and reverence for what is before and beyond human speaking, and yet free and willing to be carried and pointed to, however inadequately.

10 This was one of the emerging themes of the *Now and Next Theological Conference* on Children, held in Nairobi in March 2011. See pp. 6-10.

11 Parents often know how they are going to bring up their first child: they are confident until they have the real child to live with, a child who lives her own life in her way. Parents may rightly be grateful for good theorists, like Dr Spock, who help them in their perplexities. But woe betide them if they submit to managing theorists (like Truby King) and impose rigid patterns of care upon the child. The goodness of Spock was in large part that he said to parents, "Trust yourself: you know more than you think you do." And he encouraged people to "have children and to love them" and to let the child lead them. http://www.bbc.co.uk/news/world-us-canada-14534094 (Compare: http://women.timesonline.co.uk/tol/life_and_style/women/families/article2490406.ece)

12 Keith J. White, "Child Theology as a Seed" in *Toddling Forward*, 2010, pp. 11-22

13 The back cover of the Report of the Penang Consultation Report has, significantly, a real child in the midst, and this child was with us throughout the gathering, though thankfully for him, he was not obliged to attend any of the discussions.

14 Haddon Willmer, *Experimenting Together: One Way of Doing Child Theology*, 2007

15 Martin Marty: *The Mystery of the Child*, 2007

16 It is not wise to linger at this point, but CTM has continued to wrestle with the question of how far the action of Jesus of placing a child in the midst in his own time and context, produces the same effects and meaning for us so many centuries later. Another way of coming at this has been to ask what action he might have taken to produce the same effect in today's world.

17 For example: http://www.childinthemidst.org/ (Lois and Tom Lofton); http://blog.compassion.com/a-child-in-the-midst/#comments
It is the title of the regular newsletter sent out by the Church of England National Children's Adviser. See also the Viva Prayer Diary for 2010 which used this slogan as its organising principle. Googling "Child in the midst" yields many other examples.

18 Niall Williams, *As It Is in Heaven*, 1999, p. 288

19 A famous example of this is Augustine's description of his infancy in *Confessions* (1.6.8): "I flung about at random limbs and voice, making the few signs I could, and such as I could, like, though in truth very little like what I wished. And when I was not presently obeyed (my wishes being hurtful or unintelligible), then I was indignant with my elders for not submitting to me, with those owing me no service, for not serving me; and avenged myself on them by tears." (Trs: E.B. Pusey)

20 Respectable fearful society may speak of them pejoratively as "feral", but it would be good to remember that all wild animals (fera in Latin) are God's creatures and by their mere being, they witness to God's gift of life and call us to care for it in loving faith which "hopes all things". God's last appeal to Jonah was in the footnote, which added to the little children "also much cattle" (Jonah 4:11).

21 Such issues are raised in Rowan Williams, *Lost Icons*, 2003, chapter One, notably pages 36-38. See also:http://www.guardian.co.uk/lifeandstyle/2012/jan/01/parenting-france-britain

22 "Although we need labels to order and make sense of the ways in which we work, we also need to take care that we do not lose our children in the process. One of the greatest challenges in the field of transforming lives (our own as well as the children's) is to hold on to the person beyond and within the process and the procedure. ... We need to be still enough to find the child within the pulsating pressures of our times." Keith White and Jo-Joy Wright, "Theoretical Frameworks Defining Risk and Resilience, in *Celebrating Children*, ed. G. Miles and J-J Wright, 2003, p. 117

23 This was an issue specifically raised at the Cambridge CT Consultation (Report, 2004, p. 7) by Professor Adrian Thatcher, author of *Theology and Families*, 2006; http://www.adrianthatcher.org/data/resources/families%20-%20oxford%20291111.pdf
A rare picture by Thomas Stothard of the child placed in the midst of the disciples includes an anxious or proud mother, but her presence is not mentioned by the Gospel writer: http://www.tate.org.uk/art/artworks/stothard-christ-teaching-his-disciples-and-holding-a-child-t10055

24 J. Moltmann, "Child and childhood as Metaphors of Hope", *Theology Today*,

Volume 56, No 4, January 2000 pp. 593-603

25 Psalm 127:3-5

26 Jeremiah 31:15; Matthew 2:18

27 There are many competing narratives of this process starting with Philippe Aries, *Centuries of Childhood*, 1965. Two useful summaries are Hugh Cunningham's *The Invention of Childhood*, 2006, and M. Woodhead and H. Montgomery's *Understanding Childhood*, 2003.

28 Clare Mulley, *The Woman who saved the Children*, 2009

29 John Darling, *Child-Centered Education and its Critics*, 1994, seeks to trace the history of modern educational theory from Rousseau's writing, notably *Emile*. The UK Children Act 1989 (Section 1(1)) makes the interests of any child the paramount concern of the court in all proceedings.

30 William Wordsworth's Ode: *Intimations of Immortality from Recollections of Early Childhood*,1804 is probably the most famous and influential example:

> *"Our birth is but a sleep and a forgetting:*
> *The Soul that rises with us, our life's Star,*
> *Hath had elsewhere its setting,*
> *And cometh from afar:*
> *Not in entire forgetfulness,*
> *And not in utter nakedness,*
> *But trailing clouds of glory do we come*
> *From God, who is our home:*
> *Heaven lies about us in our infancy!*
> *Shades of the prison-house begin to close*
> *Upon the growing Boy,*
> *But He beholds the light, and whence it flows,*
> *He sees it in his joy ... "*
> (lines 58–70)

Compare also Charles Finney, *The Oberlin Evangelist*, 1852, "The Child-Like Spirit an Essential Condition of Entering Heaven", (http://www.gospeltruth.net/1852OE/520526_child_like_spirit.htm)

31 For example Dickens against Gradgrind and his obsessive confidence in "facts" in *Hard Times*, 1854

32 William Buchan, *Advice to Mothers*, 1803, is an early example of the expert trying to improve parenting: "A mother may blunder on, as most of them do, until she has killed a number of children, before she is capable of rearing one". Quotation displayed in Kirkstall Abbey Museum, Leeds

33 The contrast of the beautiful and ugly child is fundamental to George MacDonald's argument, and makes it open to question (see note 1).

34 The strapline for Barnardos, the largest children's charity in the UK as we wrote this was "Believe in Children" www.barnardos.org.uk (accessed 5th April 2012)

35 The statistics come from the Action International Website, www.actionintl.org. dated 29th January 2009. The sources of information are listed as following: (1)UNICEF, *The State of the World's Children 2008*, 21. (2) Ibid. (3) Sylvia Foth, *Daddy Are We There Yet?* (Mukilteo, WA: Kidzana Ministries, 2009), 84. (4) UNICEF, "Child Labor," www.unicef.org (accessed June 20, 2007). (5) Sylvia Foth, *Daddy Are We There Yet?* (Mukilteo, WA: Kidzana Ministries, 2009), 88. (6) UNICEF, *Annual Report 2007*. (7)United Nations Office on Drugs and Crime, "Briefing Note 8: Statistics on Human Trafficking in South Asia," *UN-GIFT – Global Initiative To Fight Human Trafficking*, www.giftasia.in (accessed August 11, 2008). (8) "Fast Facts: Faces of Poverty," UN Millennium Project 2006,

www.unmilenniumproject.org. (9) Sylvia Foth, *Daddy Are We There Yet?* (Mukilteo, WA: Kidzana Ministries, 2009), 90. (10) "Street Children and Homelessness," CYC Online, 68 (September 2004).

36 David A Sims *The Child in American Evangelicalism and the Problem of Affluence*, 2009

37 John Saward *The Way of the Lamb*, 1999, pp. 12, 17, 23, 151ff. Saward, p. 3, quotes Hans Ur von Balthasar, *Das Ganze im Fragment*, 1990, p. 282: "everywhere outside of Christianity the child is automatically sacrificed".

38 Graham Kendrick's hymn, for example, *Who can sound the depths of sorrow in the Father heart of God?*, is a Western/Christian lament for the children " ... we have sacrificed on the altar of our Gods".

39 D. W. Winnicott, *The Child, the Family, and the Outside World*, 1973, p. 17 and p. 44

40 PACE, Parents Against Child Sexual Exploitation (formerly CROP) is the only charity in England which supports parents whose children are being groomed and exploited. It has worked during the last decade with over 600 affected families, where parents are actively engaged on behalf of a child affected by sexual exploitation. It is commonly held that children who are sexually exploited come from dysfunctional or chaotic families, or have been abandoned by families. The implication is that parents have failed them and are irrelevant to the work of helping exploited children. The evidence of PACE counts against that view. There are many who have not been bad parents and yet their child is exploited. When the child is trapped by exploiters, many parents are persistent and resourceful and sacrificially committed to restoring the child to life. They, with many others, provide evidence for the view that there is much ordinary faithful parenting which is overlooked, undervalued, under supported and even despised.

41 Isaiah 11:1-9, 65:17-25

42 See CTM Houston Report, Keith J. White "Media and Children" pages 34-36. Also David Sims, *The American Affluent Evangelical Child.*

43 Consider the popular work of Harold Copping (1863-1932), especially his 1915 painting, The Hope of the World, http://bibleillustration.blogspot.co. uk/2008/01/my-favorite-bible-artist-5.html; http://www.ingentaconnect. com/content/berg/mar/2005/00000001/00000001/art00005: Sandy Brewer, "From Darkest England to The Hope of the World: Protestant Pedagogy and the Visual Culture of the London Missionary Society," *Material Religion: The Journal of Objects, Art and Belief*, Volume 1, Number 1, January 2005, pp. 98-124(27)

44 On the tension between identity and relevance of faith, see J. Moltmann, *The Crucified God*, 1974, chapter 1.

45 Patrick McDonald's guestimate in 2003 was that there were at least 25,000 projects reaching 2 million children with full time care, and 100,000 fulltime Christian workers, supported by more than a thousand mission and parachurch agencies in more than 192 countries. *Celebrating Children*, 2003, p. 153.

46 W.Shakespeare, *Hamlet*, Act III Scene 1:
> *Thus Conscience does make Cowards of us all,*
> *And thus the Native hue of Resolution*
> *Is sicklied o'er, with the pale cast of Thought,*
> *And enterprises of great pitch and moment,*
> *With this regard their Currents turn awry,*
> *And lose the name of Action*

47 Munroe Scott, McClure: *The China Years*, 1977, p. 328

48 Patrick McDonald, *Celebrating Children*, 2003, p. 160: "the evangelical movement has had a fairly marginal input in the areas of research and analysis."

49 Bill Prevette *Child, Church and Compassion*, 2012, pp. 319-326.

50 Karl Barth, *Letter to a Pastor in a Marxist Land*, 1959; L. Newbigin, *The Gospel in a Pluralist Society*,

51 1 Cor14:19-25

52 http://www.iclnet.org/pub/resources/text/wittenberg/luther/beggars.txt

53 V. Donovan, *Christianity Rediscovered*, 2003.

54 Haddon Willmer, "The Justification of the Godless: Heinrich Vogel and German Guilt", 1990, pp. 327-346. Matthew 5:43-48; Romans 12:14-21.

55 Haddon Willmer, "Ant and Sparrow in Child Theology", *Faith and Thought*, April 2013, pp. 20-31, Victoria Institute.

56 It is impossible in an essay like this to speak in terms of the many different societies in the world, even if we were competent to do so. While we know a little about some other societies, we have been formed in England and work daily through the issues it presents to us. So long as we say as clearly as we can what we have to say, we can confidently leave it to our readers to sift and interpret this essay and take from it what is useful.

57 The bibliography, which does not claim to be exhaustive, may be given in evidence here. The volumes edited by Marcia Bunge are leading examples of this literature.

58 G.A. Studdert Kennedy "When Jesus came to Birmingham, they simply passed him by ... " from his poem, "Indifference"

59 Judith M Gundry "Children in the Gospel of Mark ... " in M. Bunge (ed.) *The Child in the Bible*, 2008, pp. 143-176; Joyce Ann Mercer, *Welcoming Children*, 2005, pp. 43-70. Surprisingly, many major treatments of Jesus make little of children and of his placing them in the midst.

Chapter Two

Kingdom

*"The disciples were discussing who was the greatest
in the kingdom of heaven"*

MATTHEW 18:1

A theological discussion

C HILD AND JESUS go together in having theological significance in this story. Jesus placed the child, so Jesus is
behind and in what child does to make a difference. To
appreciate the difference made by the child with Jesus and Jesus
with the child, we must consider where the child was placed by
Jesus.

The child in the ordinary course of things naturally gets into
the middle of many places and situations. Alice got herself into
Wonderland and Lucy into Narnia without anyone organising it for
them. But this child only got into the circle of disciples of Jesus, as
a hinge-turner in a tense theological argument, through being put
there by Jesus.

The child is not placed by Jesus into a neutral space, or on to a
pedestal, but in the middle of a group of men. And they are not in
the process of passing the time of day by playing or drinking, or in
a reflective mode praying or contemplating life in general. They
are arguing about greatness in the kingdom of heaven.[1] Matthew
presents them as disciples asking their rabbi a question, hoping to
receive definitive guidance, whereas Mark and Luke suggest that

they were personally engaged, perhaps with anger and certainly to their own shame, in the competition to be the greatest.[2] It is customary to read this story in terms of moral character: the disciples showed what sort of people they were by competing to be greatest and Jesus seeks to improve them. This reading is not untrue, but is unbalanced, for it obscures the explicit theological element in the story, the question: What is the kingdom of God?

The term, Child Theology, is not a vague label for any kind of religious concern for children. The word, theology, is deliberately chosen, in full awareness that theology is often unpopular, difficult, and shunned by many Christians, including many who give children priority. We may be grateful that Jesus did not practise theology in some of the off-putting forms we know. Theology is always shaped and coloured by its media and contexts and motives. So it can be unattractive or flawed in many different ways. Jesus did not deal in books and publishing, schools and universities, or in churches and sermons, so his theology was different from ours. But no one who speaks seriously of the kingdom of God, as Jesus did, can avoid some kind of theology.

Theology is speaking and thinking about God, or better, speaking from, towards, with, perhaps for, but not as, God. We do not help ourselves by imagining that Jesus had found a way of speaking of God without engaging in theology. It would be better to accept that Jesus engaged in theology, and so to let ourselves be encouraged and challenged to look for better ways of doing it. We can see from Jesus that theology calls for more than books and a computer, a lectern and an examination system. A child in the midst, like other realities outside ourselves capable of signing God and the kingdom, will be helpful, but that child in the midst does not make for a theology-free zone.

A discussion about the kingdom of God is unavoidably theological, but that does not mean the talk will inevitably be friendly, peaceful, or illuminating. Theology is done by human beings, with interests and passions and frailties. Theology does not merely bring God into view through speech; theology plays out and reveals what is in human beings. As a species human beings are not merely often out of tune with God, distant from God so their talk of God is taking the Name in vain; they are aggressive, devious and lacking in self-awareness as they set out to use God for their own purposes. We aim to serve God, maybe sincerely and passionately concerned for the glory of God, but we easily infect talk of the peace of God with our unrest, the purity of God with our confusions, the generosity of God with our self-concern.

This means that theology may be an intense and conflictual activity. Anyone who observes what goes on in theology is oftentimes likely to be perplexed and dismayed. For the sake of God and humanity it may seem right to abandon the sort of theology which is so unpleasantly practised. Being disciples and companions of Jesus did not ensure their theological activity was good. It grieved and annoyed Jesus. It made the disciples ashamed when they were brought to look at how they were behaving. Down to the present day, theology (that is, Christians and others arguing about the central realities of faith) has not stopped being a fallen human activity.

That Jesus put a child into this distasteful, heated, apparently unedifying argument may show what risks he would take and how far he would go in talking about God and his kingdom; and how committed he was to working with the disciples to help them to enter the kingdom of God which they so little understood. He knew their condition and he worked with them as they were. He did not merely inform them about the kingdom of God, as though it were a simple matter of fact, or a question of conduct on which they could be instructed. He argued to unravel the tangle they had got themselves into.

The subject matter of theology, God and the kingdom of God, is hard to grasp, and actually brings us into tangles, so theology has an obligation to help us through the tangles that it has brought us into. Thus theology itself involves spiritual conversion as well as purely intellectual enlightenment. This is a kind of turning which is unimaginable before it happens, alarming when it happens, and always a mystery to us when we have some experience of it. The enlightenment in view here is not a few incremental steps in knowledge, like going on in England from GCSE to A level. It is akin to the transformation from being mortal to immortality that Paul speaks of in his first letter to the Corinthians.[3]

It is not surprising, then, that as we talk on the way which we hope will take us into the kingdom of God, our talking and our direction of travel may go astray together. It is with such disciples that Jesus engaged, by placing a child among them. Just as Jesus invented parables to get under the defences of resistant hearers, so he placed a child to get through a theological blockage. The child in the midst is thus a sign of the concern of the Lord for the disciples in and through theological argument. The theological was not detached from the everyday human practice and character of the disciples.

Admittedly, this conversation does not conform to common expectations of theology. It is not academic (in either a good or bad sense of the word). It is not dispassionately intellectual, though the thinking is tough and imaginative. It is not peaceful, anaemic and irrelevant. It is flecked with anger and anxiety because it engages with the most serious realities of life. Here people grapple with each other and with God across gulfs of misunderstanding and even hostility. When theology is done with raised voices, it is often told to shush, because rowdiness is evidently unholy, and not for the ears of children. But Jesus, like other significant theologians, did not always behave with such decorum. This story may free us to be better theologians. It helps us to see that theology is not primarily or exclusively academic or clerical. It calls us to take the talk about God seriously even when it is rough rather than polished, simple rather than sophisticated.

Through their self-seeking, the disciples were making serious mistakes in theological judgment, vision and style. They were setting themselves against each other, rather than enjoying each other's company. And they were not coming near to entering the kingdom they talked about so eagerly. What is more, they were way out of line with Jesus, though they called him Lord and Master.

Before criticising their lack of understanding and mixed motives, we do well to look for the plank in our own eye. After two thousand years of Christianity, in which the churches have expanded to include around a quarter of the world's population, Christians need to be very humble about claiming to be better than these first disciples. How consistently do we seek above all God's kingdom and righteousness, as Jesus advocated in the Sermon on the Mount?[4]

The idea of kingdom as Jesus and his disciples inherited it

The kingdom of God was not, of course, an idea invented *de novo* by Jesus. He and his disciples grew up with it as part of the legacy of Israel, evidenced in the Scriptures.[5] Rooted in the historical adventures of Israel, the people of God, the idea was scarred and loaded with a long and chequered tradition. This rich and inspiring concept was not a purely reliable or authoritative inheritance. All tradition is ambiguous, and like language itself, carries various types of baggage. What we find in a tradition depends in part on where we are coming from and what we are looking for.[6] Its ambiguity compels us to ask what "the kingdom of God" means; finding an answer involves us in exploration and experiment. It is not a merely intellectual exercise. We live in whole-life, social traditions, which both help and hinder us. We learn what the concept is through action and failure, discovery and disappointment.

But we must take one further step. Being ambiguous, tradition is not always a simple good. It cannot be trusted without question, but needs to be tested. It can be a temptation to evil. Hence the admonition: "Prove all things: hold fast to that which is good".[7]

In itself, the word "kingdom" is a temptation. Jesus knew this when he met Satan in desert. The story of the origins of the kingdom in Israel, as told in 1 Samuel 8–12, uncover kingdom as a deceiving seduction. The people wanted a king to "be like the other nations" without thinking what it meant for their relation to God and for their quality of life. God demurred, for the wish for a king was an implicit rejection of God and His reign and authority. The kingdom they asked for, he warned them, would not work out comfortably: its costs would be heavy on ordinary people in everyday life and the compensation inadequate. Earthly kings are bossy; they tax, conscript, punish, and build cults around their own glory.

Yet neither God nor the people abandoned the project of kingdom. The people got *their* kingdom, with its moments of glory and defeat, without being abandoned by God. The idea of the kingdom of God lived on: rejected in one form (the Judges ending with Samuel) it was open to being re-formed and tried out through the history of earthly kings. The reality of the kingdom of God, interacting with earthly kingdoms, is mobile and varied. As it moves on, it is garlanded with triumphs and disasters. God is faithful to his covenant even when the people are unable to be faithful; God wills to realise his true kingdom, in, through and beyond its being rejected or misinterpreted by the people.

God's true kingdom is contested in the world, denied, obscured and blocked; but since God does not give it up as a project, it is bound to take unpredictable and unusual forms to squeeze past the defences of the world. In much of Israel's history, as in the world in general, God does not appear as a securely enthroned king of obvious, conspicuous power.[8] God is often in the world as one who is looking for his kingdom, who goes in disguise into the enemy's camp and relies on the loyal little people, the seven thousand who have not bowed the knee to Baal.[9]

The Scriptures tell how God, for centuries, exercised his kingly rule partly by taking up the alien enterprise his people had embarked on, of having a king like other nations. If that was their purpose, it did not quite succeed, for it had only small moments, like the time of Solomon, when it prospered as a kingdom. It played out the games, common to all kingdoms, of dominion and political creation, war and trickery, glory and disgrace, but it was chosen and cherished as the (unlikely and unmerited) next place where God the true king would reveal his own kingdom. God blessed David, as God's chosen king on earth, the symbol, servant and reminder of the great king over all.[10]

The concept of the kingdom of God is a visionary hope and invitation. The rule of God over all things ("where God has his way"; "where things are done as he would want them to be done"; "on earth as in heaven"; "where people relate as mutually understood and respected beings just as in the Trinity") cannot dispense with visionary patience. When God as king is represented on earth by human kings or other kinds of rulers in Jerusalem or anywhere else, what is achieved on earth is not the kingdom of God. The people put their hope in God and so look for blessing on and through the earthly king while they have one. They want kings who will do justice: "Give the king your justice, O God ... May he judge your people with righteousness".[11] But the kings do not always do what is right: the actual kingdom disappoints.

When some earthly kingdom is destroyed, the prophets say God has judged fairly for it did not deserve to survive. But at the same time, they keep alive the idea of a kingdom truly worthy of God, and pray for it to come. The coming kingdom needs to be better than a repeat of what happened in the past: the revealing surprise of a different kind of kingdom which is well-founded and will not disappoint. Looked for here is a kingdom beyond the ambiguities of earthly kingdoms.

In the history of God, who rescued his people from Egypt with a mighty hand, destroying the armies of Pharoah, there are again and again manifestations which sometimes have a close likeness to earthly kingdoms and sometimes conflict with them. Thus the question of what the kingdom of God is like, and what is the norm and hope for all kingdom and rule, develops and becomes more pressing and complicated. The question about the true kingdom of God was opened up at the beginning of the kingship in Israel. Then, in subsequent history, the question was variously ducked, sharpened, experimentally answered, tested or rephrased. The failure of the kingdoms in Israel and Judah did not wholly discredit the idea of kingdom in the faith of the Jews: some hoped for the Messiah,

God's anointed one, to bring a kingdom of transcending goodness and sure Shalom; some tamed the dreams of faith, to live within the limits of pragmatic calculating political compromises.

In Israel, the prayer "Your kingdom come" survived long after the project of an independent earthly kingdom in Jerusalem had been discredited and largely destroyed. The memory of that kingdom, evident in stone and story,[12] continued to inspire and shape imaginative expectation. The disciples' last question to the risen Lord before he ascends is (in Luke's telling): "Will you at this time restore the kingdom to Israel?"[13]

Any concept of God's way and rule which we can hold in our minds is radically challenged by the reality of *God's* kingdom. Yet our concepts of God's kingdom are derived from and influenced by kingdoms in human experience and history. Derivation means there is both similarity and difference between God's kingdom and earthly kingdoms. There can be cooperation or conflict between them. But there is not simple identity.

To speak of the kingdom of God is therefore to use a term which evokes questions – and a quest. What is this kingdom like? How can it be found? Where and in what ways does it show itself as the reality of kingdom?

The story of the kingdom of God in the Bible discloses itself through attempts to clarify its nature, place and meaning and to help people to relate truly to God in an earthly life largely shaped by the claims, gifts, pretensions and evils of earthly kingdoms. Sometimes and to some degree, the kingdoms of earth may even be what their proponents claim for them: images on earth of the heavenly kingdom and forms of human society in which the reality of living under God can be realised.

Those who live in a failed state know the value of a working if imperfect kingdom. Thus the earthly kingdom may sign the heavenly, even though the similarity of the two is limited. The earthly kingdom is only a seeming and, at best, a partial occasional approximation to the kingdom of God. As a sign, it must be prophetically sifted since, by itself, it does not *reliably* serve the kingdom of God. Earthly kingdoms cannot offer themselves as grand substitutes for the heavenly kingdom.[14] Besides being signs of hope for something better, they are also constant temptations to human beings to "put their trust in princes":[15] kingdoms seduce us with their promise, oppress us with their shortfall. How are we to live well, sanely, with the wild oscillations of kingdoms?

The idea of *kingdom* is itself a powerful temptation to make serious mistakes about the human calling. Values are exploited and distorted in it. Glory eliminates humility, force excludes gentleness, and rank divides community. When all this is given theological sanction and extension, it gets worse. The biblical narrative and prophetic witness is testimony to the dangers and ambiguities of kingdom. So clarification is necessary. The biblical clarifications of the kingdom are not presented in works of political philosophy, but rather in calls to the people to live in ways[16] which go beyond and even against common experience and expectations.

The writings of the prophets: Jeremiah, Isaiah and Ezekiel: at different times and in different social and civic contexts, are all overshadowed and enthused by visions of this coming, new, true kingdom of God. Jeremiah sees it as a place where Torah is warmly embraced, covenant written on the heart; Ezekiel as having a well-ordered holy precinct where God's holiness re-orders and enlivens every part of society; Isaiah as a royal homecoming where a new reign represents unalloyed holistic good news. They wrestle with particular terms and concepts, both in Israel and neighbouring kingdoms, when imagining how this new kingdom will come in practice and what it will be like in daily life.[17]

Jesus and the kingdom of heaven

Jesus stood in the prophetic tradition. He inherited the promise of the kingdom of God in the confusions of history. It was not a known and agreed quantity but something to be sought and argued about. The idea of the kingdom was thus contested and mobile and signs of its presence were always provisional and ambiguous. So the kingdom puts people to the test, searching out what they really want and what they have it in them to want. And where there is test, there can be turning, or conversion.

Jesus proclaimed the kingdom of God at a time when the kingdom in Israel had been destroyed and subjugated to Rome. What survived under Herod was thoroughly unconvincing as the kingdom of God. God's kingdom could not take one of the available earthly forms. Jesus lifted no finger to attempt to realise an earthly kingdom to beat all others. In the temptations as described in Matthew's Gospel[18] he deliberately resisted the invitation to rule all the kingdoms of the world in the way the devil would have him do. And yet, the kingdom of God as he proclaimed it was not detached from the earthly reality of the life of the people and the world. It did not exist in some ethereal, idealistic, metaphysical realm, or simply within individual human consciousness.[19] Jesus taught and modelled the kingdom in such a way that it made a difference to the way life is lived, to priorities, relationships and institutions.

The coming kingdom of God as Jesus proclaimed and signed it[20] had a specific character. Its strangeness is evident in basic statements like: "Blessed are you poor, for yours is the kingdom of heaven".[21] Jesus proclaimed the promise of the kingdom, anticipated its imminent arrival in eating and drinking with tax-collectors and sinners, and by healings and exorcisms. The kingdom of God that Jesus revealed has no base in or claim to earthly territory, political or military power or formal social programme. It is typified by a small group of friends on the road, owning nothing between them, and with no specific agenda other than listening to and following their servant leader, and in sharing good news with those whom they meet along the way. In God's way of doing things, where God has his way, there is no concern to impress or oppress, or to incorporate the glory of God in buildings made with hands.[22]

Jesus chose to sign the kingdom of God truthfully in fragmentary ways, rather than to build a people or kingdom of power out of line with the truth of God. He said the kingdom did not come by observation, imposing itself on the obtuse and rebellious with regalia and visible power. Rather its reception requires people who are seeking, watching, longing, and discerning.[23] The kingdom of God is the encouraging reward for those who take the world seriously enough to have encountered its limits, without giving way to mere disgust. The goodness of the limited world rather awakens desire for the fullness of Shalom, seeking the kingdom of God and his righteousness.

God is the king of this kingdom: Jesus built nothing by pragmatic partnership with the kingdoms of earth, yet he did not seek to depose and replace them. What happens to them is for God to decide: to him belong the times and the seasons. Jesus as his Son, the Son of Man, has his own work to do. He signs the kingdom of God by seeking it in obedience, risky faith and service. He goes the way of the kingdom of God in the world. So he replied to "that fox Herod", who was out to kill him, that he would not be deterred: "I will drive out demons. I will heal people today and tomorrow. And on the third day I will reach my goal."[24] Jesus did not envision the kingdom of God as the divinely-enabled perfecting of the known traditional political model of kingdom. It is sharply distinguished from them: "If my kingdom were of this world, my servants would fight".[25]

Although the prophetic vision of Jesus is radically critical of earthly kingdom, it is not in practice idealistically anarchic. Jesus accepts the realities of earthly kingdoms without identifying with them or letting them seem close to God's kingdom. He significantly resists any linking of the kingdom of God in himself with any kingdom on earth: he will not be a king.[26] On the other hand he does not refuse or eschew the language of kingdom: he is not looking for the kind of clarification that denies any link between earthly and heavenly kingdoms. Jesus did not try to dissuade his disciples from seeking something that could be called kingdom, but he wanted them to see it in the form it takes when it is God's.

"Kingdom" as a word and concept is useful theologically, because it points to God's engagement with world in creation, law and redemption, and stops the privatising or spiritualising of God.

The language of the kingdom does not merely facilitate, but actually provokes critical interaction between God and the *missio Dei*, on one side, and states, institutions, and the secular organization of peoples, on the other. They are different but not indifferent to each other. There is tension rather than separation between them. Jesus and the gospel live in that tension, not above it.

Discernment

By proclaiming and promising the kingdom, Jesus was inviting people to make decisions of discernment about what form and spirit the kingdom will take. As the kingdom of God begins to announce and make itself known, it brings judgment, challenge and change. We are to prepare for it by repentance. This is not just turning towards the coming kingdom as an external event, but something that enters deep into ourselves. It asks of us, "Who are you?" and "What are you waiting for?"[27] Are we waiting for the kingdom *of God*? Or, given who we are and what we are like, do we have to confess we are waiting for something else, looking for and ready to welcome an alternative or substitute? Are we like tunnellers, digging away, but on a line which will never meet up with those diggers coming from the other side of the mountain? Is our human seeking going to meet the divine promise? The coming of the kingdom of God reveals what is in us, because it shows whether we are ready for it or whether we will be offended and put off by it. What do you really want? What have you the taste for?

Before the kingdom of God is seen coming with power, and while we are yet in the dark, answers are already being ventured to these questions. When Moses had gone up into the mountain, becoming invisible with the invisible God, the people could not tolerate the waiting in emptiness. Led by Aaron the priest, they had it in them to make a golden calf and to celebrate it as the gods who brought them out of slavery.[28]

We too may be kept waiting for the kingdom of God to come. In the delay (in the "meantime"[29]), we express ourselves by imagining the kingdom, experimentally anticipating it, sketching and dreaming its nature and contours. But because we do not know the mystery hidden from us, our dreaming may be off course. All our endeavour builds up for the disappointment of judgment: we thought we were on course, saying "Lord, Lord", but it turns out we were never known, never received, for we failed to recognise the King when he came in his own way.[30] When he shows himself, the revelation will surprise us, discovering our mistake and ignorance. Our sin, our straying, our wasting, have all been in the ignorance. Was the ignorance avoidable? With Jesus, the time of ignorance passes, for the light shines to dispel it.

How is the kingdom of God perceived? It is not merely that we do not see clearly what is heavenly. That is, it is not merely that the eyes of our heart are dim, and the light in us is no more than darkness. Our problem lies partly in what we see of the goodness of the kingdom on earth. The kingdom in the history of Israel was a good gift of God, even though it was also a rejection of God, for God in forgiving patience and solidarity gave it to the people and accompanied them in its history.[31] The kingdom given on earth brings the gift of plausible and hopeful social order, space for living, even space for sinners to live under the forbearance of God.

The ambiguity of the earthly kingdom does not make it wholly and finally evil: it can be an invitation to life as well as a temptation to sin. Ambiguity is to be lived through with discernment and decision. The goodness that we have so far seen in the idea and the history of kingdom gives us opportunity and material for making mistakes. Even what is good is capable of misleading us; at least it does not guarantee that we will avoid getting the wrong end of the stick. The good we see is not necessarily able to overcome our tendency to misdirect ourselves. And then the mistaken view we hold loops back on the original good and reshapes its material to confirm us in our mistake, to cover up our error. For us, as for the first disciples, the *idea* of the kingdom of God (which is not the same as the kingdom of God) is cloaked and carried in a complex tradition.

Tradition is a process where truth and error, imaginations on target and off, intermingle and are carried and transmitted through generations by users.

The disciples and the kingdom of heaven

The disciples had responded to Jesus when he proclaimed the approach of the kingdom of God: they had left all to follow him. They were not those who had no interest in God's kingdom, nor so rich that they could live without caring about it. They were human in Aristotle's sense: they were neither gods nor beasts who could live and seek true full realisation of their being outside some sort of city.[32] They were not those who were so crushed by poverty and pain and contempt that they could not believe there might be a kingdom for them. Their experience of life, hard and hopeful, made them seek it. They were ready to pray as Jesus taught them: your kingdom come. Nor were they like those who looked for God's kingdom but could not see it in Jesus.

They were with Jesus: not the sort of persons who are ignorant and indifferent to Jesus and to his witness to the coming kingdom of God. They were not atheists, confident that since there was no God, and thus nothing higher to answer to, they were free to do whatever they pleased. They were not fools in the sense that they were prepared to live their own lives regardless of God or the realities of earthly politics.[33] Their response to Jesus as they went with him on the first steps of the way involved talk about God and his kingdom. They were the sort of people who were interested in the kingdom of God, indeed believing in it and eager for it. They were not hyper-spiritual people thinking that God, being Spirit, was above having a kingdom. They wanted God to come and make a saving difference.

Yet, though they had travelled so far along the way with Jesus, not all was well with the disciples. They followed Jesus because they hoped for the kingdom of God he proclaimed. But what they expected as kingdom did not match the offer of God in Jesus. What was wrong? It was not that they were devoid of faith and hope, so that they gave up on God. Rather, they had *enough faith and hope in God to mistake God.* Indeed their greatest mistake was rooted in confusion: they trusted God to bring the kingdom of their imagining. They believed God had a kingdom: they did not try to purge God from all power and involvement in the world. But they misunderstood what the believed and hoped-for kingdom of God was like.[34]

The disciples were tunnelling off line. The mistake the disciples were making about the kingdom of God was rooted in part in the theological tradition(s) in which they stood, and also in their anxieties and ambitions: that is, in the sort of people they were.

The inherited ideas of the kingdom of God evoked in them misleading dreams of greatness. The errors came from two sources.

One was the content of the dream: the idea of the kingdom itself, in the various exemplars and experiments. Kingdom is a hierarchical ordering of society where there is one at the top, the great one, the king, who has authority and glory. Then there are those who are in his favour, close to him, raised by his power to a high place. The king holds the kingdom together by judicious patronage or silly favouritism. He exploits his subjects' ambition for greatness by offering them a great place under him. He asks his servants and subjects to forego being the greatest individual of all, but softens the disappointment by giving them a share in some social or imperial greatness. The ruler relies on the majority of little people accepting their station in life, content to go on being little people, thus ruling out greatness for themselves and not disturbing the order of society. He is however threatened by rivals: those who want greatness for themselves by themselves, not by his grace and within his order.

Kingdoms thus depend on glorifying greatness and stimulating the ambition for it, and on disciplining the quest for it and even suppressing rivals. Kingdoms are often unstable and riven with strife because it is hard to manage the problems caused by mobilising greatness as a motive and a measure. Kingdom and the idea of greatness are hardly to be separated – that Jesus could envisage this distinction is akin to his comical yet serious insistence that the camel must go through the eye of the needle.

This kind of kingdom was as commonplace in the disciples' world as in ours – the rulers and the great men, whom Jesus referred to, manipulated others in this way. Republicanism has done little to change it for us. Kings may depart, but the rich, the celebrities, the powerful, the media people, the elected rulers, all establish and protect their positions and glorify status in principle. They see to it that such a social order is made to seem natural, inevitable and safe. Education may be a route to freedom, but it can equally be an instrument to fit people into the hierarchical order, equipping them to find their place in the competitive social game.

The second source of the mistake comes, not from the subject matter of the dream, but from what is made of the subject matter by the dreaming of it. We put ourselves into dreams, often without knowing what we are doing. So the dream of greatness evoked by the inherited and public manifestations of kingdom exacerbates people's uncertainty about themselves and their self-concern. Ambition and anxiety drive them: they wonder where they are in the existing or emerging kingdom. Hopes inflate and deflate when the kingdom is inevitably seen as the arena and prize of competition.

These two drivers, ambition and anxiety, make people susceptible to the blandishments and pressures of greatness. If we cannot be at the top of the pole, we can get a bit nearer to those at the top and thus feel that life is significant. The fellowship of disciples afforded no insulation from the drives of ambition and anxiety. They clung to Jesus, wanting to possess him for the sake of what they would get out of him. So the mother of James and John, the sons of Zebedee, pushed their claim to the highest thrones in the kingdom.[35] They expected, impatiently, a kingdom that would satisfy their dreams, rooted in personal and national self-interestedness. They looked for a kingdom that would confirm their highest view of themselves.

Indeed, they may have thought they were already on track to achieve their ambition. They were members of the inner circle of the disciples, questing for the kingdom of God, as they envisioned it. Sadly, they were turning discipleship of Jesus into a precious isolated sect rather than into a light for the whole world, shining through service and giving signs of hope. Were they overly self-assured or desperately insecure? Or both?

The disciples seemed to have expected a special reward for giving up everything to follow Jesus. They had no sooner responded to the true call of Jesus than their dreaming distorted it. For all their closeness to Jesus, they were in greater danger than the poor ignorant people around them, like the gentiles and tax-collectors, who knew they were not close to the kingdom. The danger lay in their belief that they were on the right track and were very nearly in the kingdom of God. They were, in their self-understanding, like the righteous who had no need of repentance. In this assurance, they could easily resist learning the truth of the kingdom of God, and unlearning their mistakes. They could become arrogant as those who were its privileged heirs and incipient possessors.

These were the men Jesus had around him. Jesus had called them together by his proclamation of the good news of the approach of the kingdom of God. He chose them to be with him and to send them out to preach. Is the news of the kingdom of God safe in their hands?

Greatness, competition and the kingdom of heaven

For the disciples, like all human beings, the idea of kingdom implies greatness. Kingdom realises and makes greatness available. If a kingdom does not bring rewards, it falls to someone else, just as a failing business gets taken over. Greatness is comparative: it becomes apparent through being different from littleness, meanness, and what is negligible. Great is big, noble, and perhaps most important of all, conspicuous and noticed. Greatness takes various forms, according to context, fashion and opportunity: sometimes it means authority or power, the ability to make others do what we want; or wealth, freedom from dependence on anything outside one's own resources; or celebrity, being encircled by flatterers who inflate the ego.

The quest for greatness often traps us into making comparisons with others to our own advantage. It thus tends to limit genuine self-knowledge: armoured by apparent superiority to others, we deny that we in reality are poor, weak, blind, and naked.[36] We go to God to praise ourselves and thank him that we are not like other people, certainly not like the publican overcome by shame.[37] We see all too clearly the speck in our brother's eye, while quite ignoring the beam in our own.[38] It thus prevents an honest and open relation with others. It encourages competitiveness: others are not companions on the way, sharers of the common loaf, but threats and limitations. For some to be great, others must be little; for some to be honoured, others must be despised. It is a zero-sum game. This is how the human situation is often perceived.

If it is seen in this perspective, the kingdom of God, the highest of all kingdoms, becomes the place of ultimate competition for ultimate and surpassing greatness. Instead of judging and transforming the secular concept of "kingdom", the qualifier, "of God", merely raises the stakes. Such a kingdom of God will not liberate us from life as competition. The kingdom of God in this case validates the principle of the kingdoms of this world, and actually intensifies the competition. That is why religiously-sourced wars can be amongst the most fiercely fought. But if our quests for greatness infect our view of the kingdom of God, we implicitly deny that it is the kingdom of God.

Even if we reach the door of the kingdom of God that Jesus announced and embodied, we will find it closed to us. We are then likely to revenge ourselves upon it, by calling it in question. There is a fundamental spiritual conflict here. It is not a battle of our religious world-view and organisations against other religious and secular powers and ideologies, which is inevitably pharisaic in the bad sense. It is a conflict of our sinning humanity against God who is denied and blotted out by sin. This is the battle where we find ourselves opposing God, no matter how pious we are. And thanks to the mercy of God, it is a battle that always, in God's way and time, we human beings lose: God will have us in derision.[39]

The glory of the kingdom of God is beyond comparison with the kingdoms of the earth. Often in the Bible it is argued that their glory is a mere bauble ("man's empty praise"[40]). The argument goes a certain way to warn us off the quest for glory – but it is not enough to free us. Eager for the highest, most spiritual, glory, those who seek the kingdom of God may share one spirit with those who compete for earthly prizes. Whether we are material or spiritual in our ambition, we may be brought to wonder in despair whether anything is sufficient to free us from this "body of death".[41]

The act of comparing the kingdoms of this world, our human ways of running things, with the kingdom of God, can tend to sanctify competition, so that even God gets imprisoned. Then we no longer confess "God is love" but acclaim God as supreme competitor. We are invited to be partisan for God in the last and necessary competition. We choose God because he is and will be the victor. In this competition, God is proclaimed the winner by his earthly champions. Faith expresses itself in the language of war, which, even when it is spiritual warfare, traps us into the competition for relative greatness, and hardens us in the desperate sense of both being in the right against wrong, of defending the threatened good against its despisers and of being aggrieved martyrs who make an as yet unrewarded sacrifice and will at the end rejoice over their enemies.

The language of war in religion is very dangerous, even when there is a consistent acceptance that the weapons of our warfare are not fleshly or material.[42] In this language, it is impossible to see beyond the rightness and necessity of the competition for greatness. Whatever its limited usefulness, such language is a dangerous temptation. It invites us to come over to the winning side, bringing all our competitive, glory-seeking anxiety and ambition into the service of God. This may be an effective motive for recruit- ing people into some kinds of religion. But its outcome is what we see in the first disciples: it goes beyond distorting the kingdom of God to denying it under cover of holy war. It makes it impossible to see or understand what the kingdom of God is like. It does nothing to free us from the futile competition for greatness.

So, however worthy it may seem, it is not enough to choose to make God our king in preference to all other candidates. We are not on the right path, let alone at the point of arrival, until we truly choose God's kingdom in God's way, spirit and practice. Truly choosing God's kingdom is not achieved or signed by contrasting it with all other kingdoms and ways, and then rejecting and denouncing them, in order to proclaim an uncompromising alle- giance to God. We may say "No" to the kingdoms of the world, sin- cerely reacting against their present visible embodiment while living in their essential spirit and dynamic. A true relation with God is not defined by negation of the world, but grows from its own roots in the knowledge and love of God. We do not come to God simply by rebounding from the world, as though, when we reject the world, there is only God left. When we reject and flee the world in one form, seeking an alternative in God, or in being reli- gious, we may do no more than pursue the world in another form.

To enter the kingdom of God cannot be done by rejection of the world (which in truth is ultimately under the rule of God and in the hands of his holy love). It cannot be achieved by hate of, or weari- ness with, the world, whatever limited justification for such reac- tions to the world there may be. There are detectors on the door into the kingdom of God which sound the alarm at all such nega- tive baggage. The kingdom of God is found where there is positive love for it: where it is seen for what it is and loved and desired for the sake of God revealed in Jesus.[43]

The disciples told Jesus that they had left all to follow him.[44] They had given up the world in one form. Yet they ask: what will we get? If this were an innocent question, it might be good: it would monitor their progress. It would show them precisely where they are in following Jesus, in an unfinished pilgrimage. They still do not know what they will get or what is really on offer. They have not yet come home to God and his perfect rest. So they persevere in hope and humility. In the gospel story, however, this question was not asked in innocence. The asking was driven by anxiety, ambition and competitiveness, tinged with grievance at investing so much for so little in return. The consideration of the return on this investment cloaks the deeper, and for us contemporary question, "Is it really worth following Jesus at all?" There is the awful dawning anxiety that they might have backed the wrong horse for nearly three years. "We see the wicked prosper, the great ones of the world enjoying life in palaces: is there a commensurate greatness for us?"

John the Baptist in prison was another who asked about his investment: "Are you the one who is to come, or should we look for another?"[45] John had called on people to repent because the kingdom of God was coming. They had to prepare to be ready for the fire of judgment. Later, John was disappointed when he saw that Jesus was not bringing that kind of social revolution in such a public kingly form. What hope did Jesus really offer?

Jesus did not answer John in his own terms, but invited him to change his mind. Jesus offered no more than a repeat of what had already stirred John's doubts about him: works of healing and mercy, a welcome for poor and ordinary people. He asked John to ponder these good deeds, even though these healings of the deaf, blind, and lame are not the marks of a conventional kingdom working through organised coercion, law and political persuasion. They were not achieved by the mighty and did not serve to glorify kings. They were the ministry of a precarious individual, called by God, and without the support of the machinery and prestigious institutions of earthly kingdoms.

Jesus offers John illumination and comfort, but only if John himself comes under a judgment which is outside the bounds of what he can imagine and proclaim. Good things are going on: can John see them as the kingdom of God coming near? He can only do this if he revises the view of the kingdom he has worked with hitherto. Jesus does not minimise the cost to John – he makes him an offer which might confirm John in his doubts, driving him to give up hoping in Jesus altogether. If he does that, Jesus implies he will lose the blessing: "Blessed is the one who is not offended at me."[46] The blessing does not make itself easy. The blessing itself brings us to the brink of giving it up, like the rich young ruler who went away sorrowful.[47] It makes being offended plausible. It does not seem to measure up to what the erring world needs, especially the world of powerful kingdoms and sinning people.

So to go on thinking that Jesus is the One who is to come "in the name of the Lord" requires a revision of our idea of the kingdom of God. And this involves something more than some minor, seemingly cosmetic changes of emphasis: it is a radical turning, deep in the heart, values and action. Jesus offers a strange hope, which will seem no hope at all to John unless he can change his expectation and his values. That is a big demand: Jesus is really asking John to change what he has been and what he has become through his own notable ministry and witness.

The child and the kingdom of heaven

Jesus argued with his disciples along the same lines as in his response to John. In face of their conception of the kingdom of God, he places a child. His act is a positive signing of the kingdom of God, just as the healings shown to John were. But it is also an argumentative act, questioning the disciples' view, and bringing them to a point where they must decide to "turn and become like the children" or be offended at Jesus and never get into the kingdom of God. Jesus could not afford to let anyone think they might enter the kingdom of God without seeing its nature truly and giving informed consent to it.

Jesus responds to the disciples' views of the kingdom in at least two ways.

Firstly, he questions and unsettles the disciples. He argues with them to get their tunnelling on the right line. He is concerned that they should enter the kingdom of God. He talks to them to question any confidence they might have that, merely because they are disciples who follow him, their families and work left behind, they will get into the kingdom of God. Becoming his disciples brings them into a relationship and a history where the kingdom of God is not already given, but becomes the testing possibility before them.

Secondly, he speaks and acts to give a clearer picture of the kingdom of God, even though the mystery of it cannot be eliminated ahead of its full appearance. In this setting particularly, he spurs them to dream and experiment in openness towards a kingdom where competition for greatness is excluded.

Jesus placed a child in the midst, as a substantial, revelatory clue to the kingdom of God. He would not let the disciples forbid the children to come to him, for "of such (beings) is the kingdom of God."[48] If the kingdom of God involved a competition to be the greatest the child would be excluded, out of the running. The disciples argued amongst themselves who should be the greatest. In such a race children did not need to be considered, for they had no chance. Strictly speaking they could not even be thought of as "also-rans".

As they studied each other over time, the disciples saw plausible threatening competitors. In the competition for greatness, each could make a plausible case: they are all in the inner circle of the Lord's choice, all on the short short-list. Peter might hope to be greater than John in the kingdom of God, but John was big enough to warn Peter it would be a close-run contest. The near equality between disciples could make the competition more intense and fearful. The closer the contest, the harder to keep it clean. Peter might be pipped at the post, tricked in some way, as Esau had been by his wily brother Jacob. When he looked at John, he might say, "Unlucky me, I have Esau's problem: John has this fearsomely ambitious mother behind him." So Peter feels vulnerable in the competition and is spurred to being even more competitive. But when Peter or any of them saw a child, there was no threat: it was reassuringly self-evident that a child could not in any way beat him in the competition for greatness. He did not need to take the child into account.

Like people in the Hobbesian state of nature,[49] the near equality of the disciples means each is vulnerable to every other. Since all have a chance of winning, all can compete and each can feel aggrieved if they are worsted. Each looks over his shoulder at the other disciples. The competition breeds anxiety, annoyance, bad-mouthing and falling out. But competitive people need have no fear of the little child. Since he cannot hurt their chances, they can be kind, patronising and dismissive to him. The child represents a world of values – the kingdom of God – which is incompatible with any world to which the competitive quest for misconceived great-ness is intrinsic. The child is a completely unexpected intrusion into the disciples' worldview. And for this reason the child is avail-able to say something to the disciples which has not been heard in all their discussions on the way.

They were embarrassed to have to reveal what they had been arguing about. Why? Maybe because they already had some sense that it was out of place in the circle of Jesus' disciples. Whatever they knew about the kingdom of God, they had learned that Jesus resisted any praise and did not grasp at position or status. Their embarrassment might show that the truth of the kingdom of God had some foothold in their hearts. Or perhaps their embarrass-ment derived from the protective tactics of competition. They did not want to expose to Jesus and even more to themselves their raw fear of each other, arising from the fundamental dynamic in which they, as ambitious seekers of the kingdom of God, were co-habiting.

They could not trust each other; to let others see themselves as they really were would weaken them in the competition. Competi-tors keep secrets; they rely on confidentiality, for even innocent secrets might be used against them. Fearfully cautious, they could not rejoice in the success of others. Fearfully sensitive, they felt inferior, even while they fought for superiority. All this was not merely a failing of individual character. It was inherent in the structure of competitive discipleship insofar as they had learnt it within their misconception of the kingdom of God.

Jesus places a child in the midst of this situation, where almost unspoken, unspeakably embarrassing ambitions and anxieties swirl about the vision and calling of the kingdom of God. The child-sign is contradictory, searching and eloquent. It is like the word of God, sharper than any two-edged sword, judging the thoughts and intents of the heart, so that we are naked before the eyes of God.[50] The child is thus a vital clue to understanding this elusive kingdom.

The child is needed by the disciples as a clue to the way by which they might *enter* the kingdom of God. Jesus takes them right back to the beginning, where they must see themselves as out-siders who are looking for an entrance ticket. Unless the disciples change their ways of thinking and acting, they will not enter the kingdom of God. Their interest in greatness is thus not merely mis-directed: it is futile. If they follow the clue of the child, and respect the child as "the stuff of the kingdom," they will be liberated from the quest for greatness, and of its drives rooted in self-interested anxiety and ambition. They will be free to see the kingdom of God more truly and so to be faithful witnesses.

But if the child signs the kingdom of God by being out of the competition to be greatest, she tells us the kingdom is a very strange affair indeed. It does not work by the rules and dynamics we are familiar with. It is indeed hard to imagine how anything can work without competition. And yet God's is not a lackadaisical kingdom without compelling incentives and drives, so that noth-ing ever gets done there and no one cares. Somehow, in this king-dom, Shalom is realised, without money, without price, without lifting up the voice in the street, without striving.[51] Learning how that is so is what discipleship, following Jesus on his way, is about. This is the challenge of the kingdom of God: it frightens us by being so different, beautiful, apparently impractical, and yet prov-ing itself true.

This is the point made in Matthew 11:25.[52] The wise and prudent saw the good things Jesus did, but they did not respond positively. They were like children who could not agree what game to play: whether the kingdom of God was shown to them in John's asceticism, or in Jesus' feasting, they found reason to reject it.[53] Jesus told parables which call wisdom and prudence into play, and his good works provoke thought about what they mean and where they lead. There is no general attack on wisdom and prudence in Jesus. But people of an age to be recognised leaders of the community by virtue of their supposed wisdom and prudence, could misread the signs, refuse the opportunity, show themselves so obtuse about the kingdom of God that they missed it altogether.

Besides seeking to persuade them to be truly wise, Jesus upbraids them for missing the kingdom when it comes near (Matthew 11:20), but that is not the last or purest theological word. He also thanks the Father – gratitude is the heart of theology – for something else happening alongside this sad and painful blindness. Their rejection does not spell the end of the project. Wisdom is justified by her works (Matthew 11:19) or as Luke 7:35 puts it, "by her children". The signs of the kingdom of God in the works of Jesus are received by the "babes" (Matthew 11:25) and in that reception, the Father's gracious will is known and is being realised. The signs, the mighty works in the cities, bear fruit in those who come to know the Father as the Son does and by the gift of the Son.

Competition for greatness shrivels in the kingdom of God because it gets no oxygen there. Jesus stops the disciples talking about being the greatest in the kingdom of God, by rephrasing the issue: How will they enter it? The answer has been waiting for them all along in the history of God's gracious hospitality: before it is too late they need to hear it. It is enough to be in the kingdom: "I would rather be a doorkeeper in the house of the Lord, with the sparrow and the swift, than dwell in the tents of the wicked."[54] To be just inside, on the margin of this kingdom, does not put one in danger of being pushed out or deprived. That is how people normally feel when they are on the margin, because then being excluded is closer than being "well in". But it is not so in the kingdom of God. The light of God shines equally through the whole, and no one is caught in a shadow of an intervening building.[55] To be just inside is to be as much inside as one who is at the centre. Indeed true community with Christ is paradoxical: being on the margins with Jesus is to be surely enclosed in the love of God. Anxiety is unnecessary, just as ambition is pointless (so Jesus taught in the Sermon on the Mount).

NOTES

1   For the purposes of succinctness and consistency we use the term kingdom of God throughout the book, aware that in Matthew he uses the equivalent, kingdom of heaven (in order to avoid unnecessary usage of the word, God). Jesus, of course, spoke in Aramaic and the words Matthew probably translated into Greek were *malkuta dishemaya*, which mean literally "kingdom of the heavens" (Mark and Luke use "kingdom of God"). Whatever it means, Matthew makes it clear that it was at the heart of the message and ministry of both John the Baptist and the message of Jesus. In fact Matthew is the only Gospel writer to record John's message as about the kingdom of heaven. So we are encountering and dealing with something that Matthew saw as having considerable significance. "The kingdom of God is the very keynote of the faith of Jesus himself and to understand what it meant to him is arguably the primary task of any who claim to be his followers." (John V. Taylor, *Kingdom Come*, 2012, p. 16). The literature on the kingdom of God is enormous. Cf N.T. Wright, *Jesus and the Victory of God*, 1996, Part II.

2   Matthew 20:20-28 shows that Matthew knew the disciples did not always ask the question about greatness without unholy passion. Mark 9:33-37; Luke 9:46-48.

3   1 Corinthians 15:35-58

4   Matthew 5: 33. *The Cape Town Commitment*, 2011, pp. 54-56, "Christian Leaders"

5   N.T. Wright, *Jesus and the Victory of God*, 1996, p. 199ff

6   In the time of Jesus there were at least four distinct perspectives on this kingdom reflecting quite different understandings of the Jewish Scriptures: Pharisees, Essenes, Sadducees and Zealots.

7   1 Thessalonians 5:21

8   Keith J. White, "Children as Signs of the Kingdom of God: a Challenge to us all", *Now and Next*, ed. Keith J. White et al., 2011, pp. 43-44

9   1 Kings 19:18. John Bunyan, *The Holy War*, pictured the kingdom in this way: the city of Mansoul has been taken over by rebels supporting Diabolus, and a battle and siege go on to win it back to its true Lord. No doubt, Bunyan wrote out of his experience of the English Civil War with the execution of King Charles I, and the exile of his son and heir, who was in his early life, a king seeking to recover and come into his kingdom, rather than being in possession of it.

10 For example, Psalms 45–48

11 Psalm 72

12 For example, the words of Jesus in support of the crowd welcoming him into Jerusalem: "I tell you, if they keep quiet, the stones will cry out" (Luke 19:40), and also the impression the temple made on the disciples: "What massive stones! What magnificent buildings!" (Mark 13:1)

13 Acts 1:6

14 Daniel 4

15 Psalm 146:3

16 Micah 6:8

17 W. Brueggemann, *OT Theology: an Introduction*, (Nashville: Abingdon Press, 2008) 283-291.

18 Matthew 4:1-11

19 Luke 17:21 means "The kingdom is among you," not "within your inwardness."

20 We have used the word "signed" in this way as a reminder of how Jesus pointed to the coming kingdom of God, and invites us to take note of the signs of the times. See, for example, "Child as Sign of the Kingdom of Heaven", Keith J. White in *Now and Next*.

21 Matthew 5:3

22 Isaiah 66:1-2; Jeremiah 7:1-15; Acts 7:48-51; 17:24-25; 2 Corinthians 5:1; Hebrews 9:11; 11:10

23 Luke 17:20-21. Isaiah 57:15. "I live in a high and holy place, but also with him who is contrite and lowly in spirit, to revive the heart of the contrite."

24 Luke 13:32

25 Matthew 19:25-26; John 18:36

26 See for example, John 6:15

27 T.S. Eliot, *Choruses from "The Rock"*: "O my soul, be prepared for the coming of the Stranger, Be prepared for him who knows how to ask questions."

28 Exodus 32

29 Keith J. White, *In the Meantime*, reflects on forty occasions in the biblical narrative when nothing tangible seems to be happening from a human point of view, except waiting on God.

30 Matthew 7:21-23; 25:31-46

31 1 Samuel 8

32 Aristotle, *Politics II*: "Man is by nature a political animal. And he who by nature and not by mere accident is without a state, is either a bad man or above humanity." "... he who is unable to live in society, or who has no need because he is sufficient for himself, must be either a beast or a god: he is no part of a state." (Translated by Benjamin Jowett, http://www.constitution.org/ari/polit_01.htm) For Aristotle, a city, (*polis*) is not identical with kingdom, but the one gives insight into the other. The issues presented in the Bible in terms of the kingdoms of God and of the world confront us today and become more intelligible when they are considered in terms of politics, rather than of monarchy.

33 Psalm 14:1; 53:1

34 The debate about Christendom and post-Christendom is a contemporary point where issues of this sort arise, often in a simplistic form. http://www.anabaptistnetwork.com/node/609

35 Matthew 20:20-28

36 Revelation 3:17

37 Luke 18: 9-14

38 Matthew 7:1-5

39 Psalm 2:1-6

40 "Be Thou my vision, O Lord of my heart ..."

41 Romans 7:24
42 2 Corinthians 10:2-6
43 K. Barth, *The Christian Life*, 1981, p. 210
44 Matthew 19:27: "Peter answered [Jesus]: 'We have left everything to follow you! What then will there be for us?'"
45 Matthew 11:2-6
46 Matthew 11:6
47 Matthew 19:22
48 Matthew 19:14
49 Thomas Hobbes, *Leviathan*, (1651) is a seminal classic of modern political theory. Its account of state and church begins with what Hobbes called the state of nature, where people live without government. Because they are roughly equal, they are all vulnerable to each other. In the state of nature, each person has a right to anything they could get hold of. The world is open to each, so the competition is nothing less than "a war of all against all." Not surprisingly, human life turns out to be "solitary, poor, nasty, brutish, and short."
50 Hebrews 4:12-13
51 Isaiah 55:1; 42:1-4
52 K. Barth, *The Christian Life*, 1981, pp. 80-82
53 Matthew 11:16-19
54 Psalm 84:3,10
55 Revelation 21:22–22:5

Chapter Three

Temptation

*"Jesus was led by the Spirit into the desert
to be tempted by the devil."*
MATTHEW 4:1

About Jesus who placed the child

W E HAVE SEEN how kingdom, even the kingdom of God, excites and organises ambition and anxiety in competitive engagement. We find to our shame that we ourselves are susceptible to the blandishment and corruption of "kingdom" in its many social forms, whether republican, corporate or familial. Discerning the difference between God's kingdom and others is not easy. Desiring the kingdom of God with our whole being is testing. Holding on for God's true kingdom to come threatens to wear down faith and hope. It is not surprising the disciples were failing. And neither should it come as a surprise that we fail with them.

Jesus would not and could not fulfil his mission without disciples. His calling was not to be a lone hero. The good news of the all-embracing kingdom of God could not be told or realised if he did not have them to send into the world to the end of the age, generously sharing a corporately-earthed witness to it.[1] But the disciples could only follow his way if they "turned" and "became as the children." This was asking a lot: they needed help if they were to enter the kingdom of God. Jesus acted to make clear what he was about: he placed a child in the midst of them and talked about what he was doing. He did not simply talk about the child – he did not offer the slightest fragment of what might be called a "theology of childhood." He alerted them to the move they had to make: "turn".

What the kingdom of God is like is not spelt out in descriptive or analytical words: rather, for those with eyes to see, it is revealed in the whole event which is essentially mobile. Placing a child in the midst is the first step on the way; but it comes to nothing if there is no movement. On one side, there is a specific and demanding two-part invitation: to become like the children, and to receive a child like the one Jesus placed in the midst. On the other, there are those who are pressingly invited, but have difficulty in responding to an invitation whose inbuilt conditions are not obviously attractive or feasible. Who wants to become like the children? Who can?

We have already argued that this text asks us to think about an ordinary child who is nonetheless special by virtue of having been *placed by Jesus*. If it is Jesus who gives the child in this situation a definite meaning, signing the way to the kingdom of God, we are led to attend to Jesus, as the Gospels do, asking questions like, Who is this man? Why does he do these things? Where does he come from and where is he going? When Jesus leads us into mystery and pain, can we just let him go without suffering loss, or do we say, "To whom else shall we go? You have the words of eternal life".[2] The disciples found they could not let Jesus go, because he did not let them go. People still find themselves in this situation, gripped by Jesus. Sometimes it is just a small word, look, act or story of Jesus that will not let us go.

So now we ask what this story shows us about Jesus. How do we see Jesus in it? It may be that Jesus in this story does not have a good fit with the understandings of Jesus we bring to it. Just as the disciples came to the incident with their own conceptions of the kingdom of God, so we may come with presuppositions about Jesus.

Jesus: in control or seeking?

Do we come to this story, for example, with the assumption that Jesus is the Lord and Master: in complete control of what is going on? Does our unreconstructed notion of kingdom infect and disfigure our understanding of His kingship and nature? Do we even refrain from asking the question which Mark and John, perhaps more than Matthew, show was repeatedly provoked by Jesus: What sort of man is this? Where does he get this authority, this wisdom and this capacity to do strange things?

We may accept what Jesus did without such questions because we do not wish to speculate beyond the texts as we have them. Or we may curb curiosity out of respect for the Teacher who is known to come from God (John 3:2). We generalise Mary's instruction: "Whatever he tells you, just do it."[3] So when Jesus places a child in the midst we think about what the child might mean or signify, but we pay less attention to questions like: Where did Jesus get the idea of putting a child in the midst, as a telling action in this crisis? Did Jesus see the child would be a useful dialectic and didactic tool in the work he saw he had to do with the disciples? Was Jesus the skilled training manager controlling the disciples as they moved by stages from ignorance to understanding of the kingdom of God? (That is unlikely: there is no evidence that Jesus was like the modern Sunday school expert producing age-related progressively stepped learning programmes.)

Did Jesus possess a clear, steady hold on the idea of the kingdom of God, so that his mind was stocked with an adequate understanding of its own, which he could then give out in accessible sound-bite packets, or signs? Is it shocking to ask such a question? If we answer, "Perhaps not", then we are faced afresh with the question, "Who is Jesus?" Is it possible that, like the disciples and many others, he also is a searcher for the kingdom of God? Is it conceivable that he could be both a searcher for the kingdom of God, and also Lord, Master and Teacher? Being a good teacher does not mean being quite unlike one's pupils; indeed it involves being where they are so as to hold their place open for them.[4] So we may explore the possibility that Jesus was genuinely close to the people he was calling and working with, because he taught as an on-going Learner. This parallels his being Lord because he was a servant. He made the kingdom of God come so near that it was essentially present, because he was so persistently seeking it and waiting in readiness for its coming.

If Jesus was a seeker on a journey of discovery, a learner-teacher, his act of placing the child can be seen as an experimental try-on. We might imagine he said to himself, "I will get them to focus on a child, because it might help the penny to drop for them." This is admittedly speculative, but not silly. And there is more to it, if we surmise that Jesus had confidence that the child would have meaning for the disciples in this situation, because the child had such meaning for him. Now the child might have such meaning for him because he was not only a searcher for the kingdom of God, one who waited for God to come, but also one who needed for himself to sort out and resist the temptations inherent in the idea and project of the kingdom. Jesus gave the disciples the child in order to help them when they were falling to the temptation of a false idea of the kingdom of God. Did the child help him in a similar temptation?

For some, not surprisingly, this suggestion would be to go too far. "He was tempted in all points as we are," but because he came through "without sin", he is different; he was not tempted to breaking point and he did not, and could not, go wrong about central issues like the kingdom of God.[5] We know Jesus had deep struggles, "learned obedience through what he suffered" and "in the days of his flesh, offered up prayers and supplications, with loud cries and tears, to him who was able to save him from death" but "was heard for his godly fear."[6] These significant hints from Hebrews give a strong steer, but it is possible to take from them a picture of Jesus as the overcomer, who has passed into the heavens and is safely removed from temptation. He no longer seeks, because he has arrived.

In any case, even if the learning, seeking Jesus is seen in Hebrews, that concept is rarely carried over into our reading of the Gospel stories. There, the power and authority of Jesus, rooted in his knowledge of and assurance with the Father, tend to shape the way Jesus is viewed. So Jesus appears to be very different from the disciples and from us. Guided by this difference, faith takes Jesus as Lord, one with the Father, a solid ground for assured belief and theological statement. All this curbs any speculation about how Jesus might be a seeker for the kingdom of God, an explorer vulnerable to deepest temptations.

Jesus, seeker for the kingdom of God

Nevertheless, let us pursue this speculation, to see where it might take us.

During the period of his ministry Jesus did not merely teach about the kingdom of God: he lived the whole of his personal and social life in relation to God his Father, whose kingdom it is. He represented the kingdom of God in his own way of being. He did not merely outline ideas of the kingdom of God, but revealed it obliquely yet sharply in the shaping of his own life. The kingdom of God becomes visible as presence in Jesus; but Jesus also helps and requires us to respect and trust the Rule of God as that which is still coming, still on its way, hidden in the waiting. Jesus leads us by himself engaging, as a pilgrim, in a whole-life quest for the kingdom of God. When Jesus told others to seek the kingdom of God, this did not imply (as is commonly supposed) that he had already found it and was fully realising it. It means rather that he knew and respected it as that which was imminent and was there for the seeking. And so he gave himself to a specific seeking, watching, experimenting. The kingdom of God was present in Jesus only in the sense that it was coming very near; it is a call, an invitation, a task: life to be ventured.

The kingdom of God came close in Jesus and called for decision. Being present in signs means it was cloaked in mystery. A sign is a reality which gives us something weighty now, but in a form that tells us to wait for more. Jesus did not take the "waiting out of wanting"; the waiting is both necessitated and sustained by the light of the kingdom of God as it comes near. The kingdom of God is present in Jesus because he saw, made, valued and risked responding to signs. He had faith in what was signed, so that signs were in him the reality of God and his kingdom. The kingdom of God is presently limited, not because the sign implies deficiency, but because it is promise, the first instalment.[7] Sign is promise, both already here and not yet. Jesus, like us, walked by faith, not by sight. Faith makes seeking a fundamental mode of being. Disciples and followers of Jesus are *in via*, on the way, within God's way of doing things.

Jesus' witness to the kingdom of God was one with his whole way of being himself as the Son of the Father in heaven. He did not merely preach welcomingly to the outcasts that the kingdom was open to them, but he found identity with them as those who could do nothing but *seek* God and his kingdom. Jesus himself looked forward to being received in the feast of the kingdom of God (Luke 22:14-17). But like everyone else, he had to wait on God's time, because no one knows the hour of the coming of the Son of Man, not even the Son (Matthew 24:36). The waiting time is not empty, but filled with watching and readiness (Matthew 24:42-44).

Jesus taught with the humility of one who himself was seeking to enter the kingdom of God. He sought it because he was called; and in obedience to that calling, he invited others with the authority God gave to him. Jesus is the called seeker and the seeking caller. He was entering the kingdom of God by serving God the King in the most fitting way, witnessing to the kingdom and inviting people to share in anticipatory signs of the kingdom as they were enacted in and around him. The invitation combined surprising announcements and persuasive argument, to help people see the coming kingdom of God truly and to turn towards it.

To see Jesus in this way is not to question the oneness of Jesus the Son with the Father in heaven. Rather, it shows us a little more of the inner constitution of their fundamental oneness, and what it opens up for those who follow Jesus. How do Father and Son share the particular history we see in the life of Jesus? How then does God's way of doing things involve human being in abundant life? Often what God does is pictured as direct, instantaneous and irresistible action – "He spake and it was" – but in all God's dealings with human beings, and centrally, in Jesus, God's saving gift comes to us in the form of a human quest, shaped, enabled and accompanied by God. Every new day, we receive the gift which keeps us searching, on the verge of finding, but not there yet. Blessed or burdened with whatever past we have, we nevertheless stand afresh at the beginning, seeking, thanks to the promise of God. To be seeking the kingdom of God is not the same as being a lost and abandoned wanderer. Seeking is finding just as finding is seeking.

In order to be faithful and open to the call of the kingdom, Jesus had to make, and persevere in, life-shaping choices and precarious venture. In his ministry on earth Jesus himself refused to be made a king, or lord, which would have imprisoned him in the glorious but compromising categories of the present world.[8] The freedom of the kingdom of God requires unkingly ways of living. The baby placed in a manger became the servant, obedient unto death. Raised up by God, he is given a name above every name: it is forever and only the name of the Son who humbly lived a fully open human life, not trading on his equality with God (Philippians 2:5-11). God's kingdom is signed now by the exalted Christ, who forever is what he was in his earthly living and dying.[9]

The resurrection of Jesus from the dead and his exaltation to the right hand of the Father should not lead us to think that the kingdom of God has arrived and is now an established static reality, with a visible glory beyond all competition. It is neither like that in the world at large, nor in its most pure representations in some corner of the Church or outside it. Resurrection does not cause the kingdom of God to lose its adventist character, that is, its "being present in coming". God's raising of Jesus in the power of undying life confirms the way of Jesus on earth as life in readiness for the kingdom of God, offered to all people in the preaching of the good news. The Holy Spirit, who witnesses to Jesus, as the first instalment of the realisation of the promise of God, is the Kingdom-Seeker, moving in and with the church and the world.[10] A church that thinks it has got past the seeking stage is a church without Jesus and without the Holy Spirit. Between resurrection and *parousia*, we wait, watch, work, suffer, pray for the kingdom's coming. We make and see and respond to signs. We do not think we have arrived, for we are walking with Jesus the seeker – no other way is given to us.[11]

Jesus told his disciples: "If anyone will be my disciple (learning from me, and sharing in my service), let him deny himself, take up his cross and follow me."[12] Jesus lived the very same pattern that he gave his disciples. When he was raised from the dead, he came again to his disciples who had failed him, not to discard them because they had deserted him, nor to comfort them as though no serious wrong had been done, but to give them the opportunity to start with him all over again, on the path he had in himself made the Way. They were offered life in following Jesus, for he had come calling them again. He gives them what he is and has become as the one who has lived this particular life: not merely the crucified one, but the Son who lived a whole life with the Father in a way which did not shun the cross.

Temptation

We are called by Jesus to seek the kingdom of God with him in a confused and confusing world, which is both around us and within us. As we have seen, the confusion is present in the word "kingdom" and in the ambitions and anxieties it stimulates. The kingdom of God is obscured from our sight. Even as it comes near to us in Jesus, it does not become unmistakeably clear in any flash of light. That is why signs are to be welcomed. Signs not only make present what must be waited for, but they light the path amid the encircling gloom. Yet signs have limits; they do not make everything immediately clear. They stimulate and guide searching, but they are vulnerable to being misunderstood and lost in the dark. Searching therefore requires discrimination, not so much to guard against error but to see the good.

The real kingdom of God – the kingdom that is truly God's because it is true to God – has to be distinguished from false and misleading notions. Seeking it involves sorting through ambiguity. Its proclamation always requires discernment in both messenger and hearer. That the kingdom requires discernment is another way of saying it is the site and substance of serious temptation. False ideas of the kingdom of God are often cloaked in plausibility, like wolves in sheep's clothing.

It was so for Jesus too: indeed, it is primarily true for him. Already we have suggested that Jesus himself was seeking the kingdom of God, opening up the path as a pioneer. To be a seeker of the kingdom of God in this complex, confusing (and as Christians say, fallen) world involves internal as well as external struggle.

Jesus was called in his baptism to be the beloved Son, living with and for God in the light of the imminence of God's kingdom.[13] Within that affirmative calling Jesus was led (or driven) by the Spirit into the wilderness to be tempted. One sort of temptation occurs when a decent moral person, who knows and respects the law, is somehow enticed to break it. The temptation of Jesus was different because the question was not whether he would keep a known and accepted law. His calling was to something more specific than keeping a law which defines particular duties and offences. He was tested on his faithfulness to his calling as the Son of the Father. Being faithful turned on discernment of what the calling was.

What practical interpretation was Jesus to give to his being the Son of the Father? What would he aim at in working out his calling? More than a detached intellectual analysis of options was required. Being able to discern the way of God in the realities of life is not to be separated from being willing to see it. "Could discern" uncovers "would discern". Ability and desire grow or atrophy together. So what Jesus did in the temptation was not merely to clarify an idea of what his calling involved but to take the first steps in following it under pressure.

He was hungry after forty days: Satan invited the Son of God to command the stones into bread. Jesus refused: human beings must "live by every word that God speaks." He was put on a pinnacle of the temple, at a dangerous height, and invited to throw himself down, trusting the angels who had been given the responsibility to look after him. Jesus said: "You shall not tempt the Lord your God." Then Satan took him even higher, to view the whole world from the top of a high mountain and offered him all its kingdoms with their glory – at a price: "Fall down and worship me." So the fundamental and ultimate choice was uncovered. Jesus made it: "Begone, Satan, for it is written, 'You shall worship the Lord your God and him only shall you serve.' "[14]

Imagination

The story of the temptation of Jesus can easily be narrated reductively. It is sometimes read as a battle in which the assaults of an external, alien and evil power are beaten back by a strong hero. As the anointed Son of God, God's values were written on the heart of Jesus so that he held his course without wavering. Neither his morale nor his judgment were shaken. This is to picture the temptation as though it were an enticement of a good, upright person to stray from the known right path. Temptation comes from evil (represented here by Satan) which seeks to destroy goodness by making evil attractive or expedient, tricking it out with "the sights that dazzle, the tempting sounds." The good person overcomes temptation by being negatively protective of already existing virtue and by keeping on the known right path.

In contrast to such readings, it is often recognised that the story is an account of Jesus' struggle for discernment. Being called raised testing issues. The vocation did not give the security of a clear external rule to be observed. What truth or value could there be in his Sonship if it were not the whole action of his heart and mind and will? Only as he fulfilled the great commandment could he be the Son.[15] Preserving existing virtue or reputation is not enough when God calls to the venture of Sonship in the search for the kingdom of God.

The concept of temptation as an attack on a morally well-groomed person, who has no vocation beyond protecting his rectitude, does not explain many important issues about living which human beings face. It does not get near seeing what is involved in the temptation of Jesus, or that of the Christian disciple. Those to whom it is given to know the mystery of the kingdom of God, as described in Matthew 13:11, are called to something positively transcendent. Being good by avoiding known evil is too limited. They are called to discover and enter into creative living which goes beyond what they already understand and seem to be comfortably fitted fit for. What they take to be clear standards or plain rules, grounded in a socially accepted order, is not enough. They are called to what they have not yet reached.[16]

To be called in this way is more than being asked to turn from evil. That was not how it was with Jesus.[17] The good are called to go beyond themselves, to move from the known and possessed into the unknown and not yet attained. They must venture the kind of action which imagines possibilities, discerns options and discovers identity. God's calling of human being involves the whole person – or community – in an unfinished pilgrimage.[18]

As a pilgrimage its meaning lies partly hidden in the unreached goal; but the meaning is imparted on the way, not so much in packets of knowledge which progressively add up to the full clear picture, but as momentary disconnected glimpses which spark hope and further experimental sketches of what is coming. Such a pilgrimage is composed of imaginations conceived and risked in experimentation. Discernment is integral to such living, not to detect the "wiles of the devil" but to test all the imaginations and hold fast the good as it is found. What does being called as the Son beloved of the Father bestow and require? Is it all known in advance at the time of calling? Is the Son commissioned and given a plan, a timetable with benchmarks along the way? If the kingdom of God were in the hands of a modern planner it would be organised in that way, but it was not so for Jesus.

Did Jesus come to be baptised knowing it would be the occasion of his being acknowledged from heaven as the beloved Son? Or was something surprising given him there, which he then had to come to terms with? Called the Son, he needed to find out what that meant and how to live it. This is why the testing in the desert was the necessary next part of the process: he had to discover and learn. What was not yet fully understood could not be lived as though its definition was already known. The divine voice from heaven did not exempt Jesus from the task of living in an experimental human way. To know a calling is not to be assured of a settled or mastered practice.

Jesus had to find out what his calling involved. He was learning through the things he suffered, as Hebrews tells us. To the end of his days, he would be taking one new step after another, risking a free and total response to God, walking by faith into the unknown. Always lurking was the temptation not to persevere in this human response to God's call. There was always the danger that one part of the prayer of Gethsemane, "Let this cup pass from me," might overwhelm and block the praying of the second part, "Nevertheless, not my will, but thine be done." When the answer was heard – "this cup is for you to drink" – it deepened, rather than disposed of, the temptation.

For temptation is pressure to evade the calling. The call can be so demanding that opting out seems the best thing to do. The pressure, as seen in Gethsemane, can be persuasive because a deadly threat looms out of the night: at the end of the Son's way of seeking God and his kingdom, will it be discovered that there is no God there for us? Following the call leads into temptation which can shake a person to the core.[19] Effort seems futile if the outcome is empty, courage, wisdom and suffering unavailing. This prospect was already imaginable in the bleak loneliness and hunger of the desert and then again in Gethsemane. Yet Jesus discerned a way of living in the face of this final dark possibility.

It was not a way of assured safety, with success guaranteed in advance. Before he built the tower he counted the cost, open to its demands. He would live by the word of God, not from an independent, self-possessed or privileged identity. If he was the Son of God, his identity was not an impregnable strength in itself, though it could be free, personal and responsible. Jesus saw what this implied. He would not tempt the Lord by taking his protection for granted, let alone taking advantage of it, as though his value to God had to be actualised in self-preservation or worldly success.

There is no trace of a prosperity gospel in Jesus. He was to worship God and serve him alone, "giving and not counting the cost." Called to live in the world for its redemption, Jesus could not avoid being engaged in enterprises that might seem to involve trying to "gain the world". Jesus and those who follow him are always at risk in their mission: they want power to save the world; they cannot bear to leave the world in the hands of the evil one. Jesus wept over Jerusalem: God desires that all be saved: the globe needs transformation. So disciples properly ask: Why should the Devil have all the best weaponry or methodology, any more than he should have all the best tunes? Too easily, these good, practical concerns lead disciples to build their religious empires, their worried dogmatic fundamentalisms, and their projects of global transformation using tools best left in the Devil's shed.

Jesus did not resist the temptation inherent in mission by giving up the world in principle; that would be to deny that the world is what God loves, owns and reconciles to himself by his redeeming of it in Christ. Jesus did not decide he was called to an individual self-saving asceticism, "content to let the world go by, to know no gain nor loss," living within the pietistic confines of a personal Sonship with the Father's blessing and love. Jesus was called to proclaim, represent and to share the earthly anticipation of the kingdom of God. He taught us to pray: "Your kingdom come; Your will be done on earth as it is in heaven." Had he resigned the world, the story of his temptation tells us, it would have gone to Satan who was asking for it with the boldness of a usurper thinking he had a right to it. Jesus was faithful to the kingdom of God even when Satan came in the guise of a mission strategist; nor did he give up on a kingdom which is truly God's in its universality and reality, quite different from any private comforting religiousness.

Reading the temptation in this way suggests that it was a struggle through which Jesus clarified for himself what was not so clear to him before. Satan aimed at the destruction of the creature: Jesus reached out to serve in the project of God the creator. Satan does not value what is, nor does he want to see it sustained. Jesus did not answer Satan merely by holding on to and protecting what is, but rather lived in all that is towards what is not yet. He accepts his being as the Son of God by responding to the call towards what has to be discovered through living. So the subject of temptation is not only an assessment of what is, but a discerning openness towards the future. That is, discerning takes the risk of envisioning, hoping and aiming at a particular future even while respecting its being unknown and unknowable until the day of its coming. We need to venture pictures in order to live towards what is not to be captured in pictures. To hear the call involves some provisional but serious ideas about God's future, about what the kingdom of God might be like, when it comes. Imagination is therefore indispensable in being faithful to the call of God.[20] The temptations of Jesus were intrinsic to life as a venture of risky and costly imagination.

In imagination there is a kind of knowing to which not-knowing is intrinsic. Our pictures of the future are unreliable, for they are extrapolations from experience in, and knowledge of, the present world. They will be surpassed by what God reveals in the End, when we shall, not for the first time, be taken by surprise.[21] To envision the future, so that it shapes action, and yet to act within the limits of knowledge, is characteristically human. Often, however, we do not live in this human way: we swing between claiming assurance about the envisioned future, to living as though vision is empty foolish fantasising. At election time, bold promises are made by people protesting their competence to govern; sometime later, we fall into chastened cynicism about politics and politicians.

We need to learn how to imagine wisely and boldly, to be engaged without being hubristic, for God in Christ gives us no escape from being oriented to the future even though the future is hidden to us. So we live all the time as tempted and tested beings – and not surprisingly, often straying. We need to be discerning without being driven by our fears into opting out. The first step in opting out is to refuse to imagine hope. We are called to watch and be alert, but this alertness is not primarily being on guard against signs of trouble, but rather being ready to go along with the kingdom of God wherever its coming is signed.

Choosing the way of God rather than Satan is not a response to a future known with sufficient detailed certainty to make planning feasible. It is imaginative faithfulness to a preference for one way over another in a world where discretion is indispensably called for. The preference for the coming kingdom of God differs from the mere assertion of self and opinion in a relativistic wilderness. The preference can never be insulated from the suspicion that there is nothing but the wilderness which is where it has to be made. It has to be imagined and ventured beyond what can be seen and counted as visible evidence.[22] To be called is more than being given a clear command. The call dignifies by giving responsibility for doing something original and creative, making something out of a little bit of entrusted, but unknown, space. Command, in its strict sense, takes away freedom, while calling necessarily requires and risks it. The call of God evokes the play of imagination as well as guiding it. Imagination is susceptible to temptation: so discernment is the indispensable companion of imagination.

Imagination: faithfulness to calling, not fantasising unreality

The question of the reality of what is imagined is an important one. Too often, Christians are no different from others in discounting what is imagined as unreal, untrustworthy and impracticable. Yet discipleship without imagination collapses into moralism. The call to divine Sonship and service in the kingdom of God is only heard by an act of transcending imagination. Temptation is a conflict of imaginations.

In C.S. Lewis' *The Silver Chair*,[23] the Queen of the Underworld argues that the Prince, Puddleglum, and the children, Jill and Scrub, should accommodate to her world because she has made it so palpable, so undeniably real. Puddleglum struggles with the Queen by arguing for a different world where the air is fresh and the sun is shining. In the underworld, with little hope of escape, his testimony is forlorn, lacking evident support. Yet, although he cannot prove his point, he holds on to what he knows from his past. He is beaten back to the last ditch, where he can only insist that even if his vision and values are no more than a dream, the dream is far better than the reality the Queen commands and wants him to fit into.

By his weak stubborn witness, the reality he knows but cannot prove is present to empower resistance and hope. What can be dismissed as empty imagination turns out to have reality. The Queen will not and cannot take the risk that Puddleglum's witness is true. He points to beauty and goodness outside her benighted imagination, which is concentrated in a monstrous work of darkness. More than a difference of opinion, a radical conflict opens between them, but only because the gloomy Puddleglum persists with his precarious imagination. The call of God is not followed through to liberation and reality without the testing, suffering, venture of imagination. The revealing call of the transcendent God stirs imagination, which opens our settled littleness towards God's renewing of all things.

The temptation of Jesus and his childlikeness

We are concerned in this chapter with Jesus. Who is he who placed a child in the midst of an argument about the kingdom of God? We have considered his call as the beloved Son of the Father which made him a seeker as well as proclaimer of the kingdom of God. Seeking is an imaginative activity and with it comes temptation because there are conflicting imaginations of the kingdom of God.

The question now arises as to how the temptation of Jesus, the seeker of the kingdom of God, relates to the child who is a sign for seekers?

Two connections are possible. The first by a short circuit would find a likeness between the child and Jesus as seen in his temptation; the second way brings child and Jesus together in the struggle to save the disciples from themselves. The first way does not need Matthew 18; the second derives from it.

The short circuit: child has a lifetime to live

What direct link can there be between the temptation of Jesus and the child? No child appears in that story. Jesus was tempted as an adult alone. Because of its subject and manner, a child could not be tempted with his temptation. A child in the wilderness forty days is unlikely to survive at all, let alone have the ability to sort through basic choices about how to live an adult life. An adult is dependent (independence is largely a pretentious illusion), but a child's dependence is of a different order. A child needs appropriate care and protection; he is not allowed to wander into the desert. Jesus was strong enough to be driven into the wilderness, lonely, hungry. He was not an abused, neglected child, but a grown human being. Nor was he a child who does not yet know how to make decisions about living and who must therefore be watched and guided all day long by parents, or by health and safety policing.

The temptation of Jesus was not child's play. Jesus the grown man did not remodel himself as a young child in order to be the Son of God arguing with Satan. He did not return to live within the

specific limitations, dependence and weaknesses that are characteristic of the child. It is popular in some Christian discourse to
make a virtue of littleness and weakness as though that harmonises with the gospel of the cross. This is more romance than
reality. We do not find the likeness of Jesus and child in these
terms. Instead, just as Jesus struggled through temptation to discern and follow his calling to life, so the child has his being in making sense of life and finding his own way in it. Jesus is not to be
linked to the child by returning the adult Jesus to the weakness of
the child, but by seeing the child as engaged in the venture of life
as it becomes visible in the life of Jesus.

From the beginning of life, before we have language to articu-
late it, questions confront human being and are being answered
somehow. James Loder puts these questions into words: "What is a
lifetime?" "Why do I live it?"[24] There may be other ways to formu-
late the question. We might add, for example: "How am I to live it?"
Before a child can hear verbalised questions, she is necessarily finding some way through the stages of living, developing a working
vision of self, others and the world. Being a child is an act of experimental, embodied and cumulative imagination on the part of the
child to make some order and direction in what would otherwise
be a confusion of random occurrences.

Working at these questions engages the person who is in the
making through his own engagement. The work cannot be out-
sourced. There is much that is given to the person from the love of
others; and much that money can buy, but being and becoming a
person has to be one's own work.

Parents, educators or state can to a degree take over this work
of imagination, (under the guise, no doubt, of stimulating it in the
child) thereby robbing the child of her childhood. Oppressive governments and cultures aim to do this. The contribution of adults to
the growth of the child is not to be denied: a child who has no
adults who talk and play with him will not grow. But what adults
give is only a supplementary service to what the child can and
must do in himself. Sometimes, the adult contribution stunts or

destroys children because it takes away the space they need for imagining and building themselves in the totality of their living. This space is both mental and physical. Children in less child friendly ages may have had more space than they are allowed today. Jesus got lost at the age of twelve, and he seems to have had detached children in his audiences, like the boy with five loaves and two small fishes. Few children live in a space where the best balance between being looked after and being left alone is achieved; part of the task of life for most children is to discover ways of compensating for too much control or too little care and coming out of it without crippling damage.[25]

The young child may dream of becoming a doctor, or an airline pilot, or a celebrity. It depends what visions and role-models the child is given. But as the child grows the vision becomes more specific and individual, until the child recognises it as his personal life calling. Identity, expectation and commitment then come together in a unique way.

Sad is the child who is not allowed to dream of what she will be; or whose future is prescribed, without freedom, safe from the necessary adventure into the unknown. Sad too is the child who is too lazy or scared to risk following a dream into the unknown. The disincentives besetting a child are not to be underestimated. The unknown is not a mere blank to the child; it may be the dark, less-frequented corner of the house, a no-go area where there are strange sounds, maybe signals of ghosts. Sad is the child who gets no practice, no advice, and no wisdom about how to "navigate"[26] in life, hearing and responding to a call composed of vision and the unknown.

To avoid all these different sadnesses, the child has to work at living, day by day, slowly, growing the personal self through boredom and shocks. The child grows not just through achieving simple manageable operations, but in a genuine personal complex precarious existence. Schooling mostly confines itself to what is practicable, which is why much learning and growing has to take place outside it.

Now we can see the child has a pattern of being like Jesus, in being simultaneously called and beset by temptation. To be a child, theologically expressed, is to be called and affirmed by God the Father, yet driven by the Spirit into the wilderness day by day, birthday by birthday, there to sort out what the calling means. The calling of God needs to be heard, discerned and then held to. God's calling of the child, the growing person, is closely related to the growth of the person, with specific identity. God's calling does not assign persons to "callings", putting them into boxes, "tinker, tailor, soldier, spy," where they don a uniform and lose themselves in the group. God's calling evokes distinctive identity. That is also why God's call is not a restrictive, dominating command, but rather an invitation drawing us into responsive freedom, where God is found as the space for growing. Too often, God is falsely presented as the ultimate restriction on freedom. In truth, God calls all his children out into the wilderness as liberation for life.[27]

Thus the primary life task of the child, to hear and follow the call, discerning and holding on to it against plausible misinterpretations, has the pattern we see in Jesus in his calling and temptation. In both, we see human being finding the path of life, within the frame of the Fatherhood of God, which is revealed in moments of calling and has to be followed in days of testing. If the child at root has a life shaped like Jesus', then conversely, we may say the adult Jesus was childly, not in weak dependence, but in exploration and testing, obedience and faithfulness.

The longer way: Jesus in temptation with the disciples and the child

Satan in other guises

The temptation of Jesus, told at length in Matthew and Luke, is a significant episode at the beginning of his ministry and integral to it. It is about his life in the world as the servant of God. In the desert, a final victory was not achieved; rather, fundamental issues which run through the whole of his living were sharply focused.

The devil left him after forty days,[28] but the temptation came again to Jesus in other ways. It was brought by the people he lived with. Why should that surprise us? Since the world is full of the sort of people we are, the devil can, for much of the time, sit back like a mafia godfather, enjoying the good life on some Costa del Crime, and leave it to his minions to make trouble for the kingdom of God in the world.

Temptation through the friends of Jesus

Temptation came from Satan – *c'est son métier*. It also came through the enemies of Jesus: that is not surprising. According to Luke 13:31, the Pharisees, some of whom were open to Jesus and may have cared for his well-being while others were hostile, tried to frighten Jesus by reporting that Herod intended to kill him. Jesus was not deterred and gave them a message for "that fox": "I cast out demons and perform cures today and tomorrow, and the third day, I finish my course. Nevertheless I must go on my way today and tomorrow and the day following; for it cannot be that a prophet should perish away from Jerusalem." This story, with its distinctive Lukan features, reminds us there were social pressures tempting Jesus to abandon his calling. But when enemies stir fear of what might happen, the temptation is one of the easiest to resist, because it comes advertising its hostility and provokes stubborn, proud, even reckless defiance.

More serious for Jesus was the temptation that came from friends within the apparent shared commitment to the one mission and the service of the kingdom of God. Jesus chose twelve to be his disciples – and "one of you is a devil," he said according to one dark report.[29] When it came to him through his disciples Jesus had to face the temptation again.

When Jesus asked the disciples who they thought he was, Simon confessed, "You are the Christ, the Son of the living God." He spoke because, as Jesus said, it was given to him by "my Father in heaven."[30] Jesus said elsewhere that it was the Father's good pleasure that what was hidden from the wise and learned was revealed to babes."[31] Only as a little one, receptive of the Father's revelation, can Simon see and confess Jesus as God's anointed one. Only so is Simon named Peter, which has something to do with the rock on which the church is built. Only so is he entrusted with keys to open or close the kingdom of heaven in the world.

Thus, we might say, by their confession of faith, the followers of Jesus arrive at the point Jesus had reached at his baptism. There, the voice from heaven acclaimed him as the beloved Son. Here Peter acclaims: "You are the Christ, the Son of the living God." So what was said from heaven is now said on earth. But merely saying it is not enough, even though it seems, for all the world, to be clear: a truth once glimpsed that can never be forgotten. The question arises in both cases: how to live out this revelation in the world? What next? What substance in human being does the word of God have? After the baptism, Jesus withdrew for forty days. After Peter's confession, Jesus charges his disciples to tell no one he is the Christ, and then withdraws with three of them to the moun-tain. In both cases there are issues that have to be sorted out in seclusion. This seclusion is not to privatise or individualise faith, but to see it more clearly, to accept it more entirely, even to be open to its distinctive worldliness. What had the disciples let them-selves in for by confessing Jesus as God's anointed?

Within this community of the faith confessed by Peter, Jesus explained to them for the first time the nature of his calling and the kingdom of God: he began to teach his disciples he must go to Jerusalem, suffer and be killed and the third day be raised. Then Peter, to whom the confession of faith had been given by God, took him and began to rebuke him, saying, "God forbid, Lord! This shall never happen to you."[32] Peter was being consistent with the uncon-verted ignorance he carried within his confession of faith. He was calling Jesus to act on what he imagined and wanted the Christ to be: a Christ fit for a kingdom constructed around the quest for greatness. He still had some way to go as a disciple.

Jesus did not react to Peter as though he had made a little mis-take to be put right with gentle remedial teaching. He turned fiercely upon him: "Get behind me, Satan! You are a *skandalon* to me for you are not on the side of God but of men." What Peter said touched Jesus personally. It tempted him with another way of being the Son of God. The desert encounter with Satan came again to him, from his friend. Instead of finding strength in the companionship of the disciples, he became freshly aware of his vulnerability. The basic human desire for security (health, safety and the leisure to enjoy life with friends), was plausible and attractive. It is generally to be affirmed as a good. Here Peter makes it specific to Jesus, thereby redefining his call and mission, and threatening the integrity of his relation with the Father.

Jesus discerns a stumbling-block being put in his path. To scandalise a little one who believes in Jesus, causing them to trip up, is terrible beyond imagining, according to Matthew 18:6. In this story, we see Jesus is one with them in their vulnerability. Both have a life to live in a world where offences arise. By this temptation, Jesus was placed before the fundamental Either-Or, for or against God and his will and way. So he did not see the situation as a teaching opportunity, but as a clash between contrary imaginations. At this moment, Jesus for himself had to make afresh the decision for God in a hard place where it would be easier to take another path.

Jesus' words to Peter are an astounding outburst, for it means that being a disciple, knowing who Jesus is, confessing Him and being designated as the rock on which the church is built, does not prevent one from tempting Jesus Christ as Satan did, and doing it all under cover of being his friend, a partner in his mission, concerned for his best interests, and serving for the glory of his kingdom.

If disciples could be the vehicle of temptation in this way, perhaps in the innocence of their uninstructed enthusiasm for Jesus and the kingdom of God, it is not surprising that they should themselves be vulnerable to such temptation, and less able to resist it than Jesus. In fact they showed by their actions and words, again and again, that they were falling into it. Their search for greatness answered to deep hungers within themselves. It matched their drives and anxieties. The kingdom of God provoked desires which prevented them entering it. They had to "turn" if they were to have any share in it. Greatness was represented for them by "kingdom", with its competitive ordering of the difference between great and little, powerful and weak, glorified and despised.

Jesus resisted the temptation to misread the kingdom of God in this way. Such a temptation was like a missile targeted at the heart of his calling and mission. Under its assault, he had to hear again the call and affirmation of the Father and choose God rather than man. Doing this brought him into painful conflict with hostile power. It tested his capacity to discern true from false and to choose to be faithful. We can imagine that its deceptive good sense was unsettling.

When people are beset by such feelings in situations where they must take momentous decisions about serious matters, they may become intensely sensitive to loneliness. Being left without companion or support deepens the temptation. Jesus suffered in the desert alone. But he called disciples "to be with him and to be sent out to preach." He wanted not just to train them, but to have companions on his way. In Gethsemane, he asked them to watch and pray with him – was that just for their own sake? Jesus welcomed the support of friends. He appreciated being anointed by the woman, in preparation for his death.[33] So when he told the disciples the Christ was going to be killed, it was hard to find himself deserted and left alone, even by Peter who had said, "You are the Christ." Not that Peter had yet denied him and walked away, but in his imagination of the kingdom of God, he was deserting Jesus.[34]

When the disciples pursued greatness in the kingdom of God, Jesus found himself on his own again. He placed a child in the midst, to show them what the kingdom of God was like; but also, we can guess now, because he wanted some kingdom-of-God-company in the place where his little incipient community of the kingdom of God was falling apart around him. The child, the sort of human being of which the kingdom of God consists,[35] was more than a teaching aid in the hands of Jesus; the child was a friendly strength for him in the struggle of temptation, an abiding reminder of his calling. When the devil left him, at the end of the desert temptation, "behold, the angels came and ministered to him." When the disciples were inadvertently but painfully becoming a stumbling block to him, Jesus placed a child in the midst who, without saying a word, partnered his witness to the kingdom of God.

The disciples were not reflecting back the sign of the kingdom of God to Jesus, showing what it was like and how to enter it. When the disciples left him alone, when they did not comfort him in his troubles or strengthen his discernment and commitment to the way he had to go, he found help in the child. He could have gone on alone, but that would suggest the quest for the kingdom of God was a lonely task for very special people. Jesus did not give up the principle and hope of a shared quest for the kingdom of God, of a community which was faithful to it, demonstrating and sharing it as an open possibility for all. If the disciples would not, at least in that moment, work with him in community, he would find another way. He found a child, who stood in as a representative and companion on the way to the kingdom of God.

Through the presence of the child, we may suppose Jesus found more than emotional refuge from the loneliness caused by the hardness of the disciples. As the disciples brought Jesus back into fundamental temptation, the child strengthened him as an unspeaking witness against the false kingdom. Placing the child was another way of pursuing his work. What he found in the child was a way of signing the kingdom of God, of reaffirming his vision and commitment to its character, and of pressing the argument upon the disciples. Placing the child was not choosing the child against, or instead of, the disciples, but of carrying on the argument with them. And since Jesus wanted them to make a communal witness to the kingdom of God, (so that it is more than a refined individual spiritual quest) he had to carry on the argument with them in a social communal way. He could not simply say: "Be like me, as an individual model." It was rather, "Join in the community. I begin making this community with a child."

NOTES

1 Matthew 28:18-20
2 John 6:68
3 John 2:5
4 Dorothee Sölle, *Christ the Representative*, 1965, pp. 115-116. Sölle's book, as a whole, is of extraordinary importance for our work, not least in distinguishing substitution and representation and showing how the distinction is significant in theology and in practice.
5 Hebrews 4:15
6 Hebrews 5:7-8
7 Ephesians 1:14; 2 Corinthians 1:22, the Spirit as *arrabon*, the first instalment
8 This is explicit in John 6:15; 18:36
9 Philippians 2:5-11; Hebrews 4:14-15; 1 John 4:2; Revelation 5:6; George F. Macleod, *Only One Way Left*, 1956, p. 145: "There is a Man crowned in heaven ... a Lamb as it had been slain." This striking sentence is a major theme of this remarkable, sadly forgotten book.
10 Ephesians 1:13-14
11 Philippians 3:8-16
12 Matthew 16:24-25
13 Matthew 3:17; 4:17
14 Matthew 4:1-11
15 Matthew 22:34-40
16 Philippians 3:7-16; Hebrews 11
17 Matthew 4:13-25
18 D. Bonhoeffer, *The Call to Discipleship*, 1959, chapter 6; *Letters and Papers from Prison*, letter of 21 July 1944; *Ethics*, 1955, section on "History and Good".
19 Romeo Dallaire led an inadequately supported UN Force in Rwanda before and during the genocide in 1994. In *Shake Hands with the Devil: The Failure of Humanity in Rwanda*, 2004, he tells a devastating story of how being faithful to a good call may break a strong person.
20 Haddon Willmer, " 'Vertical' and 'Horizontal' in Paul's Theology of Reconciliation in the Letter to the Romans" in *Transformation*, vol 24, nos 3 and 4, 2007, p. 159
21 Gerard W. Hughes, *God of Surprises*, 1985
22 Hebrews 11:1ff: all these people of faith "endured as seeing him who is invisible" (v.27)
23 C.S. Lewis, *The Silver Chair*, 1953, Chapter 12. The Queen denies all their talk of the sun and a lion (Aslan) as a mere dream: "Put away these childish tricks. I have work for you in the real world. There is no Narnia, no Overworld, no sky, no sun, no Aslan." Puddleglum stamps out her bewitching fire and defies her with an argument for what, in the Underworld, he cannot prove.

"One word. All you've been saying is quite right, I shouldn't wonder. I'm a chap who always liked to know the worst and then put the best face I can on it. So I won't deny any of what you said. But there's one thing more to be said, even so. Suppose we have only dreamed, or made up, all those things – trees and grass and sun and moon and stars and Aslan himself. Suppose we have. Then all I can say is that, in that case, the made-up things seem a good deal more important than the real ones. Suppose this black pit of a kingdom of yours is the only world. Well, it strikes me as a pretty poor one. And that's the funny thing, when you think of it. We're just babies making up a game, if you're right. But four babies playing a game can make a play-world which licks your real world hollow. That's why I'm going to stand by the play-world. I'm on

Aslan's side even if there isn't any Aslan to lead it. I'm going to live as like a Narnian as I can even if there isn't any Narnia. So, thanking you kindly for our supper, if these two gentlemen and the young lady are ready, we're leaving your court at once and setting out in the dark to spend our lives looking for Overland. Not that our lives will be very long, I should think; but that's small loss if the world's as dull a place as you say."

24 James E Loder, *The Logic of the Spirit*, 1998. In March 2012 CTM convened a conference in Princeton on the work of Loder and the papers delivered there are being prepared for publication.

25 This issue is wonderfully explored, not without Romantic extravaganze, in Jay Griffiths, *Kith: The Riddle of the Childscape*, 2013

26 The word "navigate" came up in the Cape Town Child Theology consultation and has not been developed since in any Child Theology discussions. In our view it merits further attention as a metaphor for understanding both child and kingdom of God.

27 Galatians 5:1

28 Matthew 4:11

29 John 6:70; 13:2

30 Matthew 16:17

31 Matthew 11:25-26

32 Matthew 16:22-23

33 Matthew 26:6-13

34 On this view, the child was doing for Jesus what Jesus said the disciples had done, according to Luke 22:28: they had "remained" – stayed all the way – with Jesus in his trials. But strangely, Luke places this positive remark in his account of the Last Supper, alongside a report of the disciples disputing about who was the greatest. Jesus then rebuked them, by reminding them that the kingdom to which they were appointed as disciples of Jesus was quite unlike the kingdoms of the world. With them, the greatest should be as the youngest who serves (Luke 22:24-30). So, in Luke's telling, the disciples continue with him in his trials, even though they are not living in his way and spirit. Jesus longs to have this meal with them before he suffers – he wants company, and behaves as though it is there for him (Luke 22:14-23). And yet at the same time, he bluntly warns Peter that before dawn he will deny three times that he knows Jesus, notwithstanding his protests that he was ready to die with Jesus (Luke 22:31-34).

35 Matthew 19:14

Chapter Four

Disciple

*"... unless you turn and become like little children,
you will never enter the kingdom of heaven ..."*
MATTHEW 18:3

*"He who does not take up his cross and follow me
is not worthy of me"*
MATTHEW 10:38

JESUS IS THE SON seeking the kingdom of God. He has his own way to find, even while he is opening it for others. So Jesus chose the disciples to be with him, to be his partners in his mission, and to share a range of experiences and encounters with him, day by day on their journeying together. Notable among these experiences were the Transfiguration (for Peter, James and John), and for the eleven, Gethsemane. And when he was moved to place a child amongst them, this out of step and competitive group stands over against him. As he heads towards Jerusalem to drink the cup of destiny, the chosen twelve are on a different tack. Is it illicit fancy to imagine that, confronted with these disciples, Jesus felt isolated, and even deserted, as he was to be at the end?

Was his feeling at this moment akin to his reaction to their failure to heal the epileptic boy: "O faithless and perverse generation, how long am I to be with you? How long am I to bear with you? Bring him here to me." (Matthew 17:17)? Here is more than impatience and a rebuke for faithlessness: there is disappointment and loneliness. Jesus has chosen twelve disciples to walk with him on the road. When he finds out what they are arguing about, he senses how alone and weak he is; how little has he been heard, heeded or understood. He looks for friends to walk the same road and to have the same mind and finds none (Psalm 142:4). Who is there for him? Not the disciples, it seems.

When he puts a child in the midst, (a little child: just a child?) Jesus acts as much more than a teacher or a good communicator who has found a neat visual way to make his point. The act of putting a child in their midst is richly textured and full of potential meaning. Jesus himself is at this point in the journey, the Calvary road, a lonely seeker for the kingdom of God, looking for friends in the quest. All he can find is a child, who is quite possibly drifting about open-eyed and without pressure, with no plan – it is too early to settle on a career. Jesus takes him, not only as a useful lever in the argument with the disciples, but as good company in his quest. Jesus will not be alone. He will be strengthened in his disappointment and impatience by receiving for himself a sign of the kingdom of God. Just as he gave John the Baptist signs to encourage him, so Jesus draws some affirmation or comfort, however implicit and fleeting, from the child.[1]

The inner content of Jesus' placing the child in the midst – that is, what Jesus thought about it and what led him to do it – is not made explicit in the telling of this incident. It may be shown to us elsewhere, for example, in Matthew 11:25-30. Even if these are not the actual words of Jesus, they tell us what the Evangelist thought was in his mind. Jesus upbraids the cities which were not persuaded to repent by the signs done amongst them and have therefore chosen to operate independently of the rule of the kingdom of God: he was disappointed, impatient, threatening – and rejected. It is in that situation that Jesus rejoices in the Spirit saying: "I thank thee, Father of heaven and earth, that thou hast hidden these things from the wise and understanding and revealed them to babes."[2] Thus Jesus repeats his rebuttal of Satan's offer of all the kingdoms of the world; he accepts that the cities are not going to be his kingdom; in fact only the little ones[3] see and respond to what is on offer. Jesus is glad about that.

His disappointment is overcome by recognising that this is God's gracious will. So Jesus finds rest for his soul (Matthew 11:28-29) and on that basis has it to offer to those who are weary and heavy laden. What wearies these people? It might be the same experience of life in the world that Jesus had. In the world, signs and offers of the good are turned down; the outcome of much of urban life and powerful organisations is frustration. In this dark occluded world, intolerable destruction fills the horizon of the future. But not quite. There is a little, precarious chink, opening towards life, to be seen by those who are themselves humble and ready to receive and be friends with the little ones. Jesus thanks the Father[4] for that opening, and steps forward through it. He calls others into the same path, offering himself as the guide, because he goes that way for himself: "Take my yoke upon you and learn from me."

Thus Jesus' placing the child in the midst is to be read as much more than a communicative device to get a point over to the disciples who need it. It reveals something about what went into the choice Jesus himself made for the kingdom of God, in the course of a fruitful ministry beset by frustration and friendlessness. Jesus did not tell the disciples to become as the children, as though that was the medicine they needed, while he lived and thought of himself as the Lord and Master who was above it all. The story in Matthew 18 thus has christological importance; it is a clue to the Gospel as a whole, and not a mere minor incident within it. Through it new light is thrown on the very nature and calling of God in Christ.

The challenge of the loneliness of Jesus today

Christians see themselves as disciples of Jesus, and assume Jesus and his disciples are one in the fellowship of the kingdom of God. Admittedly, Christians accept they are disciples in training, and have much to learn: sometimes they are slow to learn, sometimes even seriously wrong. But the basic relation, as it is pictured, is of an agreed and mostly harmonious working community of Jesus and his partners. Our self-image as church is that we are the company of the friends of Jesus. The twelve were the prototype or seed of the church, which is "Us Today".

So we resist any suggestion that Jesus was left lonely and friendless by disciples who were not with him in spirit and practice. Each year in Holy Week, we remember that they betrayed, denied or forsook him at the last, but the movement of the Christian year enables us to downplay that as an aberration in an extreme situation. We meditate on it deeply for a couple of days, but then revert to a template or dominant image, which derives from a generally rosy reading of the Galilee ministry, and of the love and excitement with which they left all to be his disciples when Jesus first called them. Even if we do not work very closely with Jesus, we are confident that he loves us unconditionally, as we like to say.

We, the friends of Jesus, are the church in the world today where obviously, oppressively, many around us are not at all friends of Jesus. The external negative pressure intensifies the sense that "we" insiders are the friends of Jesus. And so we do not begin to read the gospel story with antennae for the loneliness of Jesus *in the company of his disciples*, who symbolise the church of which we are a part.[5] Our failure to take this point from reading the Gospels derives from and feeds back into our inability to think that we today may be leaving Jesus to his loneliness.

Consider a not uncommon sort of church. It keeps going and even grows by being a friendly community. So it cannot risk imagining that it might be failing in the core friendship which makes church: the relation with Jesus. Its identity is rooted in the assumption that Christians are those who are *with Jesus*.[6] Such a church can confess fallibility, mistakes, imperfection without disturbing the underlying assurance of being with Jesus, who embraces us in forgiving faithfulness.[7] Being so befriended by God in Christ can blunt sensitivity to the ways in which we leave Jesus to his loneliness amongst us.[8]

The crux for disciples

The disciples found it difficult to keep in step with Jesus, on the road and in spirit. So the gap opened and widened. In the Gospel, the loneliness of Jesus becomes most acute when he makes clear that he is going to the cross and that is the path he opens up for those who follow him. "If anyone would be my disciple, let him deny himself and take up his cross and follow me." (Matthew 10:38-39; 16:24). At this point they resist, object, drag their feet, and even try to take control of Jesus and keep him from an end so unworthy and dark that they can see no goodness or hope in it.

The call to discipleship is often interpreted as an abrupt, peremptory summons: Jesus calls us saying, "Follow me," and those he calls immediately leave all and go after him.[9] There is a "take it or leave it" choice. The uncompromising starkness of the call is not to be softened. Yet there is another side: Jesus loved to the end the disciples he had chosen and did not want to lose any. The gospel narratives suggest that Jesus was engaged in a persistent, versatile and inventive process of persuasion. So when the disciples showed they were evading the call to follow Jesus in cross-bearing, he found other ways to help them understand and respond. Thus Jesus followed the method of the owner of the vineyard, in one of his parables: a succession of slaves goes to the farmers to collect the fruit at harvest time and are killed or treated badly. Finally the owner sends his son, saying, "This will turn them round, they will be shamed into reverencing my son."[10] As we know, the tactic did not succeed, but what is significant, here as elsewhere, is love's intentional commitment to a process of persuasion in presenting the call of the kingdom of God.[11]

Besides saying baldly, "Take up your cross daily," Jesus placed a child in the midst of the disciples who were evading the cross by seeking greatness. By her mere presence, the child silently restates the call to discipleship. When the child and the call are taken together, gentle, strong persuasion bears on those who, understandably, hesitate to entertain the invitation to "come and die."[12]

The link between cross and child that we are suggesting is not made explicit in the Gospels, and it is therefore easily missed. As far as we have been able to determine, it has rarely been made by commentators. But it is arguably artificial and unimaginative to hold them apart and to stop them informing each other. The Gospels give us a picture of running conversation between Jesus and his disciples, in which the call to discipleship, predictions of his passion, and the placing of the child all occur. Did the hearers keep them in separate compartments in their mind? Or did they get a feel for the spirit of Jesus as his various words and actions jostled in their thinking? It seems reasonable to let them come together in our hearing and in our following.[13]

Some restatement of the call to discipleship is needed

A restatement, reframing, reiteration of the call to discipleship was needed because the disciples were not following what they had already heard. Did they understand it? Was it too paradoxical for them, with its talk of losing life to save it? Or just too frightening? How could the joy of the kingdom of God come through or be represented by a shameful and cruel death? What possible relationship is there between glory and a dying seed? Even an ordinary death, let alone a humiliating one, is the end of conscious earthly living, and dashes hope and self-esteem. So the disciples persisted in what made sense to them, according to the ordinary wisdom of the world: they sought greatness in a plausible kingdom, where it is normal practice for the subjects to exclaim, "May the King live forever!" A dying king is not much use.

Both the helpful teacher and the effective salesman know that when their message is not understood, simply repeating it in a louder, more threatening, voice will not help. It is likely to frighten people out of their wits, and then there will be no chance of their getting the point. It may well provoke resistance. Inventive restatement is needed. Varying the presentation does not necessarily mean altering the message; rather it can serve to make the same message more accessible and intelligible. It aims to overcome obstacles to its acceptance, freeing the hearer from the fear that freezes and leaves him like a rabbit caught in headlights. It puts the hard truth in a different light without changing it, so that instead of being faced with a blocked road ending in death, a narrow way leading to life is seen to be open. It encourages, so that people can go along with the challenge rather than being put down by it. So we may discover that the child in the midst has this positive meaning: as God's gift of, and commitment to, life in its fullness, the child witnesses to the full meaning of the cross when it is borne by God in God's hands, as it was with Jesus, whose hard dying is swallowed up in victory.[14]

But can the call to take up the cross be reiterated by putting a child in the midst? Is "child" in this context a faithful dynamic equivalent of "cross", or is the message being changed into something different? If it loses its authentic bite and value, the outcome is not a reinforcement of the original invitation but the emergence of a comfortable alternative. The challenge of the cross is softened to appease the resistant disciple. It becomes "cheap grace"[15] permitting complacency, asking for no sacrifice or commitment. The disciple may then celebrate his success in negotiating himself out of austerity, but that is a sign of his poor understanding of his calling.

Let us read the text on the assumption that when Jesus placed a child in the midst of the disciples he was not signalling a change of course and being inconsistent with himself. He was not modifying and downgrading the terms of discipleship which include cross-bearing. Jesus wanted disciples who would "stay with him in his troubles and so to enter the kingdom appointed for them" (as Luke puts it, 22:28-30). As Jesus wept over Jerusalem,[16] so he struggled for the life of his disciples, leading them through all their hesitation and resistance into finding life by losing it for his sake. He prayed their faith would not fail.[17] The child for Jesus could not mean there was a way into the kingdom of God without the cross. If that were so, Jesus would have been finally defeated by the obduracy of the disciples, like a trader who has had to reduce his price drastically in order to make any kind of sale.[18]

It is implausible to think that, for Jesus, cross and child symbolised two different ways of faith. It could be that the first disciples saw both as equally unattractive and unreasonable. We would do well to consider the possibility that we, as disciples now, find it temptingly convenient to choose between cross and child. Christians have often shown themselves able to read the gospel and then do something different from it without doubting their conformity to Christ. There may be a few Christians who follow Jesus perfectly in spirit and truth, but most Christians fall into one of two different sorts. One listens to the gospel and then makes a compromise with "reality" without being troubled in spirit. The other listens to the gospel, accommodates the practicalities of living, and is continually disturbed by the gap between call and response, faith and practice.

Is child-centred Christianity cross-centred Christianity?

It is good to let the child be placed in the midst, to seek to enter the kingdom by becoming as the children, and to share the gospel with children in accessible ways. Yet care is needed lest this missional cultural accommodation builds a Christianity without a cross for disciples to take up. The growing size and dynamism of child-oriented mission means that it is more than a marginal compartment of Christian practice, with little or no power to define or shape Christianity as a whole.

The point we are making here is unusual. In most Christian thinking and practice, the child placed in the midst is not seen as a restatement or reiteration of Jesus' call to discipleship in the way of the cross. So the question of whether the child offers an escape from the cross does not arise. Rather, the child speaks directly out of her own natural presence and "intrinsic" value. Her human meaning, as it is universally accessible to Christians and non-

Christians alike, does not include the cross. Child, as we know and care for her in practice, is not seen in the context of the gospel's story of Jesus.

So, in much contemporary Christianity, the way is open for the child to become the focus of forms of thought and practice which cushion or occlude Jesus' call to follow him. The cross has always been foolishness to some Christians and a stumbling block to other Christians, as well as to non-Christians,[19] so it is not surprising that we produce varieties of Christianity without the cross. Some of them are beautiful, some powerful. They seem to fit more happily with the peaceful world we want to make, free for religious co-existence, and not dehumanised by a fanatic readiness for death.

Secular guardians of the child do not object to the Jesus who welcomes little children and blesses them, but they want to protect children from the crucified Jesus, who frightens even grown men by asking them to come and die. Many Christians recognise the caring precautionary wisdom in this discrimination. They are rightly aware that any cult of suffering is dangerous; it is inconsistent with the whole way of God in Christ and encourages indifference and abuse. So they too may be attracted to the child as the symbolic inspiration of an alternative to cross-bearing discipleship.

As individuals, as well as members of organisations, which are often impressive and sometimes mighty, Christians engaged for and with children do well to ask themselves whether the gospel as they profess it, explicitly and implicitly, is a true restatement and reiteration of the call of Jesus, or whether it constitutes an alternative to it. When the churches are urged to give a greater priority to children, are they being invited to a fuller and more faithful following of Jesus as the Lord incarnate, crucified and risen? Or are they looking for Christian activity to be more concentrated on and defined by children in themselves? Does the "child in the midst" remind the church in general that salvation is in Christ? Or does Christ recede into being part of the background furniture of the church, which is more than ever busy for children, often in ways shaped by secular practice, which for all its virtues tends to exclude the cross?

It is worth pondering whether Christian history shows that child-centred alternatives to the cross have been more powerful than faithful reiteration of it. One way of testing the hypothesis might be to enquire whether giving more emphasis to the Christian life as cross-bearing lessens the significance given to the child. Does concentrating on the cross, the centre of the gospel, tend to marginalise the child as a sign of the kingdom of God? Put another way: where the child is seen as sign and substance of the kingdom of God, does Christianity become impatient with the cross? At least on a superficial view, affirming life in the child and aiming at the fullest development of his potential would seem to sit uncomfortably with the call to deny self.

In contemporary Christianity much operative theology,[20] religion and vision can be seen to revolve round creation, incarnation, resurrection, family, personalism, well-being, development and human fulfilment, without being questioned by any serious *theologia crucis*. We have theologies of abundance and prosperity and quests for inclusive humanistic, even hedonistic, spirituality. In our modern risk-averse culture we think the cross is unsuitable for children. Who wants to be broken, despised, rejected, acquainted with grief? Who wants to worship a crucified God? It is good to care for children, to affirm them and their rights; to be glad when their faces light up like the shining of the image of God; even to find ourselves in them, as they teach us to become the eternal child it is said we are called to be and become.[21] It is good to respect the child as mystery within the mystery, especially since the child is not the sort of mystery that takes us out of this world, but rather a being who involves us in active, sensitive, hopeful humanity. The question that emerges from all this is powerful: immersed in life with the child, what does it mean to us to be crucified with Christ, baptised into his death?

Even if valuing the child does not exclude the cross, it may nevertheless serve to soften the cross. Many forms of Christian piety help us to forget that the cross was an instrument of torture, punishment and hateful rejection. Building plausible alternatives to the cross and its way has been a major dynamic in the growth of historic Christianity, in its various forms. Where the cross has not been denied, it has been quarantined as the special glorious privilege of saints and martyrs. Sometimes soft Christianity provokes rigorist reaction. The call to discipleship is stridently restated in protest and struggle against easy popular alternatives. One Jesus is promoted, turned against another Jesus. The gentle Jesus, who loved and welcomed children to his arms because he knew they belonged to the kingdom of God is made to seem incompatible with the Christ who died in apocalyptic struggle and pain.

Wanting the kind of kingdom where children play in the streets, a kingdom of joy, freedom and peace is not wrong.[22] It could be argued that their desire for a kingdom of God where they might enjoy power and glory, plenty and ease, without the cross, showed the disciples were healthy in mind. When Jesus persisted in offering them the cross, they were tempted to wish for a kingdom without him or to despair. Today, disciples may choose some progressive secularity, even a Brave New World. It is more easy to stay with Jesus when he says, "Become like a child, belong to the kingdom of God simply as a child," for that seems painless, or at least less painful. And more importantly, it is life-affirming, not focused by a death because the child is life here and now in natural and promising form. Here is a good earthiness, not disrupted by apocalyptic conflict and eschatological irrevocability. Both the child and cross are on earth, earthy, but in very different ways. One can be gladly received as a good gift, the other strains faith and gratitude to breaking point.

Child and the call to discipleship

The child and the cross are plainly different, which is why the question whether they are alternatives is not to be evaded or blurred. Yet the argument of this book rests upon our accepting that when

Jesus placed a child in the midst he was not offering the disciples an alternative course or an easy reduction of terms. Rather he was renewing a costly call to discipleship, to follow him along the path he was taking.

So we come to the question: How does the child in the midst re-state the call to discipleship, given the obvious differences between them? The key elements of the answer to this question are given us in Matthew's text and will be discussed in the remaining chapters of this book: "Humble yourself as this child" has some likeness to denying self (Chapter Five). "Receiving a child in my name" involves a practical, costly following, in which Jesus and child are found together (Chapter Six). In all this the cross is not denied but is taken up in true everyday translations. Receiving a child is the action in which adults become, as nearly as they can, like the children, not only in the freshness of life but also in precarious vulnerability in relation to God and the world (Chapter Seven).

The child who has this meaning is placed by Jesus. Jesus who places the child gives this meaning. This meaning is more than a mere idea, a way of looking at things or a teaching. It was wrought out in flesh and blood by Jesus, and in the risenness of Christ it continues to be embodied action. The meaning is in what Jesus does. By placing a child in their midst, Jesus did something decisive and authoritative to the disciples. It is Jesus who thus brings child and cross together and stops the disciples fashioning a convenient alternative instead of a saving but costly reiteration. Jesus still places the child in our midst and invites us with the child to receive him, the Sent One and the One who sent him.[23]

NOTES

1 Luke 22:43-44: in Gethsemane, when Jesus prayed with blood dropping to the ground, an angel from heaven appeared giving him strength. In other contexts, a child might do that for him.
2 Luke 10:21
3 In our view, the term "little ones" includes children and many others who are marginalised in and by their social contexts.
4 The words of Jesus are unique at this point as he enthuses with the cry, "Yes, Father!" (nai, o Pater).

5 Compare the idea of the "lonely crowd" in which the emotional distance is magnified by the physical proximity.

6 The Pauline images reinforce this oneness and unity: e.g. 1 Corinthians 3; 12

7 Luke 22:31-32

8 The loneliness of Jesus is noticed in some Christian devotion. Samuel Crossman's *My song is love unknown* tells the whole story of Jesus as a sad, moving and transforming journey in loneliness.

9 This is the tone, and the intended meaning, of the way Bonhoeffer talks about discipleship, at the beginning of his book, *Discipleship*, 2001, p. 57: "How is this direct relation between call and obedience possible? It is quite offensive to natural reason. Reason is impelled to reject the abruptness of the response. It seeks something to mediate it; seeks an explanation." And, "This encounter gives witness to Jesus' unconditional, immediate and inexplicable authority."

10 Matthew 21:37

11 Francis Thompson's poem, *The Hound of Heaven*, is a profound and illuminating reflection on the divine persuasion of the resistant person. William Harmon (ed.) *The Top 500 Poems*, 1992, p. 848 comments that the "canine pursuer" of this poem shocked some readers who "were more accustomed to Cecil Frances Alexander's holy "Child so dear and gentle" who "leads his children on/to the place where he is gone".

12 D. Bonhoeffer, *The Cost of Discipleship*, 1959, p. 79: "When Christ calls a man, he bids him come and die". This is R.H. Fuller's translation of the original, "Jeder Ruf Christi fuehrt in den Tod", literally, "Every call of Christ leads into death." D. Bonhoeffer, *Discipleship*, 2001, p. 87, note 11.

13 Christ's predictions of his passion and the placing of the child in the midst of the disciples are not conflated in the Gospels, but they are close to each other.

	Matthew	Mark	Luke
First prediction	16:13-33	8:31	9:18-22
Second prediction	17:22-23	9:31	9:44
The child in the midst	18:1-5	9:33-37	9:46-48
Third prediction	20:17-19	10:32-34	18:31-33

14 Isaiah 25:8; 1 Corinthians 15:54

15 D. Bonhoeffer, *The Cost of Discipleship*, chapter 1

16 Luke 13:34-35; 19:41-44

17 Luke 22:31-32

18 Compare the encounter of Jesus with the Grand Inquisitor, in Dostoevsky's *The Brothers Karamazov*.

19 1 Corinthians 1:18-30 correlates the preaching of Christ crucified with God's choosing the foolish, weak, low and despised in the world. Adding child to this list would not be alien to his meaning, though it lay beyond Paul's imagination, perhaps.

20 By operative theology, we mean the theology which is implicit in what we do, as individuals and communities. Thus operative theology may be at variance with the theology that is professed. We may not know what our operative theology is, but it is the rationale that inheres in our actual practice and has power through that practice. It is unsatisfactory to make a profession of faith unless it is in harmony with practice. Professed theology needs to be a really operative theology. Bonhoeffer criticises people when they hide behind the "teaching of the Church" (or, as others do, behind what "the Bible says") while ducking the question, What do we really believe? F.D. Maurice uncovered the operative theology of many of his contemporaries when he said they were "practical atheists" although they were members of churches. His explanation

of this prophetic discovery was very simple. God, said Maurice, is the Father of all and Christ is the Head of the Human Race. That means we are all children in the one family. But in early nineteenth century capitalist England (not a quite unusual time or place), all people were not treated as brothers and sisters in God's one family. So there was a practical or operative denial of God as Father. Sometimes, operative theologies can be better and closer to God and the goodness of God than our professed theologies. It is a mercy that people are often better than what they say, better than their religion might lead them to be if it had its way. But operative theology contradicted by professed theology is in a weak position; it is likely to get confused and atrophy unless it is partnered with explicit confessing and exploratory theology. We can never rest complacently with an assumption that our operative theology is like a cultural substratum giving us a good foundation for living even though it is not brought to expression, where it can be both tested and influential. And we certainly cannot make excuses, for whatever operative theology we are living, by developing more beautiful professed theologies that make no difference in practice.

21 Karl Rahner, "Ideas for a Theology of Childhood," *Theological Investigations*, Volume 8, 1971

22 Isaiah 11:6-9; 65:17-25; Zechariah 8:5

23 Luke 9:46-48

Chapter Five

Humble

*"Whoever humbles himself like this child is
the greatest in the kingdom of heaven."*

MATTHEW 18:4

W E HAVE SUGGESTED that the child placed by Jesus in the
midst reiterates the call to discipleship. The claim on disciples is not weakened by talk of receiving a child rather
than taking up the cross. Yet the two are as different as life and
death, hope and despair, joy and sadness, affirmation and aban-
donment. Is there any perceptible and practical meaning of child
so that reiteration is achieved?

Matthew offers us three ways in which the child might be a reiteration:

▪ First, only Matthew reports Jesus as saying: "Unless you turn[1]
and *become as the children*, you will not enter the kingdom of
heaven."

▪ Secondly, Jesus continues: "Whoever *humbles himself as this child*
will be the greatest in the kingdom of heaven". Sayings like this
appear in a variety of contexts in all three synoptic gospels.[2]
Some state the basic principle of the "upside-down kingdom:"[3]

"Whoever humbles himself will be exalted." Others give challenging examples: "if you would be great, or the first, be the servant and slave of all." Luke 22:26 says that the greatest must be
as the younger (*neoteros*) but with the emphasis on one who
serves, being inferior in rank, rather than being simply a child.
Uniquely Matthew inserts the remark about humility in the
story of the child placed amongst the disputing disciples.

▪ Thirdly, Jesus says: "Whoever receives one child such as this in
my name, receives me." (Matthew 18:5). Reception is the only
explanation of the significance of the child which is offered by
Mark (9:37) and Luke (9:48) whereas for Matthew, it is one of
three.[4]

We will look at each of Matthew's ways,[5] allowing our reading of
one to affect our reading of others. In the end, they all serve to illumine the same mystery of the kingdom of God. So their meaning
only comes to light as they are woven together and an overall pattern emerges.

Unless you turn

Turning is an important concept in the Bible's portrayal of the relation of God and people. They are called and owned by God and yet
they turn away from God, disown him and forsake his way. They
abandon God for idols and they do wrong in their social life. Unless
they turn, there is no relation with God and no well-being. Turning
to God involves a change of conduct and a change of mind
(*metanoia*). The scope of the change is set out in the great commandment: Love the Lord your God with all your heart and mind
and soul and strength, and, Love your neighbour as yourself.[6] Social,
moral and spiritual change is bound up in the Bible with turning to
the Lord – and hoping he will turn to us (James 4:8). This turning is
a personal movement to face someone, moving towards them,
rather than turning one's back to them. The physical metaphor
illumines the human relation with God (Jeremiah 2:27; 32:33).

The call to turn is a repeated note in the life of the people of God. God sends prophets to them: one after another. It is not a call made and answered once for all. It needs to be heard day after day. So turning becomes more than an incident in life, a "happy day which fixed my choice;" it indicates the daily spiritual, personal and moral mode of life with God.[7] One who is living in fellowship with God is one who does not pretend he has no sin, but confesses it and "keeps short accounts with God," in the words of the old saying.[8]

"Turn" in Matthew 18:3 has more in it than a call to the disciples to change their view of themselves and their behaviour. It would not be inappropriate to see it as urging them to turn *to God, their heavenly Father*, and so to become as "the children", that is, his children, who are to be like him (Matthew 5:48; 6:9). The call to turn in this text is like the traditional Old Testament call, a call to turn or return to God who turns towards us. Since the God to whom we turn is revealed as Father, turning to God means, in some way, becoming as the children. The adult disciples are called to be his children and are taught to pray, "Our Father". But, because Jesus placed a child in the midst, these adult children of the Father are not to interpret their being his children as though earthly children (which they are no longer) have nothing to do with their spiritual relation with God. Rather, children of the heavenly Father are to understand themselves with the help of the child in the midst.

What does a genuine turn to God consist of? This is a crucial practical question, since different courses of action are counted by different people as turning to God. Fasting that is a religious cover for fighting and quarrelling is unaccceptable, for the fast God chooses is to let the oppressed go free and to share bread with the hungry (Isaiah 58:1-14). Jesus asked the same sort of question.[9] In Matthew 18, becoming as the children is the most striking characterisation of the change. Although this might seem to define the turning that is called for, it is not obvious that it has a clear and practicable meaning. The words are frequently abstracted from the whole text so that speculative interpretations can be ventured by adults whose delight, amazement and concern for children is mixed with nostalgic fantasy. But instead of taking this phrase out of its setting, we look for the help of the whole story to find its meaning. Help is found in two ways. First, it is safe to assume that "whoever humbles himself as this child" (Matthew 18:4) will find that this is a key constituent of "becoming as the children." That is why this chapter is about humility. Secondly, we will find in the next chapter how receiving a child helps us to become as the children (Matthew 18:5).

Humble yourself as this child

Jesus placed a child in the midst to call his ambitious disciples to humility. What is the meaning of this call for us and why it is so difficult? How do child and humility go together? Why is the child not a sign of humility for us in our culture? Certainly the child is not an illustration of our common ideas of humility. Does the child in the midst really reinterpret and reinforce the call to humility?

1. Humility in Christian history

A commitment to humility is rooted deeply in the Bible and the gospel of Jesus Christ. Humility is the appropriate response to God. Whatever is going on when there is peace between God and the human creature, humility is its mode. To rise up against God, in any way, to be haughty or vainglorious, is not merely unfitting, it is disastrous, for it puts the creature at odds with reality. Humility is essentially realistic.[10] The proper attitude of those who are God-fearing is contrition and lowliness of spirit.[11]

Humility is not easy. It is no straightforward or natural thing for people to humble themselves under the mighty hand of God as biblical and Christian history shows. The call to humility is not discerned by everyone. It is feared and resisted by many. It is misrepresented by its advocates, whenever they corruptly preach it to others so as to gain power and status for themselves. And yet in the history of Christianity, humility has been seen to be essential to the realisation of true human being. It has been modelled by some saints: unforgettably, for example, by St Francis of Assisi, as well as by the "humble poor" who believe but often have no memorial.

In the context of Christendom humility was seen not only as a private virtue of saintly individuals, but as a value to be embodied in the order of society. Humility was at the heart of life as envisioned in the City of God and the whole company of heaven and earth with and under God. Society was subject to the command and calling of God; its norm was heaven, not what could be pragmatically achieved on earth. There was thus a perennial struggle between humility and the state of the world. Despite the lack of humility in practice, humility was respected as the ideal for all human beings as creatures of God, living in God's one world and answering in the end to God's comprehensive judgment achieved in the full revelation of the glory of God.

In early modern Europe, in an epochal change, humility was dethroned. This was not a change in human nature – in practice human beings have always exhibited various degrees and combinations of humility and arrogance. It was a change in the valuation, social endorsement and institutionalising of humility. Machiavelli can be taken as a mark of the change, though he only had a small part in making it. He saw how his society in 15th and 16th century Florence operated, told princes how to make it work efficiently for them in their quest for power, and made a virtue of political success. He was not afraid to pay the price for such success, which included marginalising humility as monkish, characteristic of the professedly unworldly devotees of a religion oriented on heaven.

This sort of religion was irrelevant or dangerous to the practical earthly quests represented by the prince and his necessary concentration on the "political kingdom". That kingdom could not afford to risk humility: the prince knows being feared is more important than being loved. So he does not shy from ruling by force and fraud, and is aware constantly that signs of weakness will be exploited by his enemies.

Humility, by contrast, implies giving space to others, becoming vulnerable, and living by faith. It does not seem to make for success in battle, in diplomacy or in the market. Social climbers of any sort or rank, the prince highest of all, have to eschew humility. Thus the political enterprise sets its own norms and is its own goal. It is confident in itself, not yielding to the judgment of anything beyond itself. It broke with the unitary universal moral order which in medieval times was centred on the Christian God and made a virtue of humility. Instead it pursued its own goodness free of any obligation to answer to alien and impracticable ethics.[12]

The West has long since given up humility as an ideal value. What purports to be humility often disgusts us, as Dickens meant it to be when he gave us Uriah Heep.[13] Nietzsche rejected humility because it subverts the proper dominance of the strong and healthy and hands a devious victory to the weak and mean. It is absent from school mottoes and mission statements.

Humility discarded by Christians

Christianity in the past inculcated humility as a key virtue: in our relation to God, to others, and in the art of good living.[14] But now even Christians neglect or reject humility. Contemporary Christians, like others, are suspicious of humility as a value. It is commonly confused with low self-esteem and lack of confidence, which Christian counsellors, along with their secular colleagues, aim to counter. What place has humility in personal healing and renewal?[15] Some forms of Christian worship and teaching impress on people that they are precious, wonderful, beautiful, "intrinsically valuable" and important to God. It is possible that all this is compatible with true humility but how that might be is not explored or explained. Liberation and feminist theologies have a standing suspicion of humility because it serves blatant and subtle forms of oppression which should never be condoned, but rather unmasked, resisted and eliminated.

Christianity tends to assimilate to culture. No one can escape being encultured. Pride, bravado, and not selling oneself short are all inherent in much contemporary cultural enterprise. The refusal of humility has deeper roots in human nature. Piety is no reliable defence against pride, as the Pharisee at prayer reminds us (Luke 18:9-14). Preachers may urge humility and yet be caught out by their pleasure in their own performance.[16] Consequently, we do not give informed consent to humility: it has no beauty that we should desire it (Isaiah 53:2). Even when humility is not definitely rejected, little is made of it, because we are not sure what humility is. It is useless to defend or advocate what flips from one form to another.

Humility and cross

Humility is lowly: the word probably shares a root with the Latin, *humus*, which means "near the ground". To all who are not lowly, humility threatens a coming down. It means loss of position, or a destruction of pride, or both together. Humility may therefore be feared and resisted. It is seen as loss, and it is not clear what the value of accepting the put-down would be. Humility is close to humiliation, which makes the instinct to resist humility seem right and healthy.

Humility may be an event, but it can also denote an ongoing condition in which lowliness and loss are to be accepted with contentment or possibly masochistic pleasure or broken acquiescence, apathy and despair. Humility is more than the abdication of ambition; at its extreme it resigns from life.

The deep embarrassment of Christianity about humility is disclosed here. Central to Christianity is the death of Jesus: the cross. He humbled himself to the cross. This is interpreted as the ultimate in human humbling: the humbling of self under the judgment and will of God. It is the way taken by God as Trinity, realising and revealing God's will, character and glory in humility. The preaching of Christ crucified was a stumbling block to Jews and folly to the Greeks (1 Corinthians 1:22). The shame of the cross has to be endured and overcome by despising the shame (Hebrews 12:2), by actively refusing to be ashamed (Romans 1:16) and by glorying in the cross (Galatians 6:14; Philippians 1:20; 2 Corinthians 11:30; 12:9).

Christianity radicalises humility. Dying becomes the symbol and the realisation of ultimate humility, letting go of all claim and expectation. Humility can thus be seen as a threat to life. What can justify it? Humility and suffering have sometimes been glorified, as though they were blessed and happy in themselves.[17] To accept the loss of wealth and health, of beauty and friendship, of life and future, have all been seen as godly virtue at its most heroic, daring and uncompromising. The cross has often been assimilated to this kind of humility. The intensification of humility, when it is conjoined with the death of the cross, provokes radical criticism: can it avoid being inhuman and unhealthy in secular terms, and a sinful denial of God and the grace of life when seen theologically? In practice, while it may be accepted out of respect for what is sacred, this kind of humility is likely to breed smouldering resentment.

Humility is not a natural characteristic of human beings, whether we see them through an evolutionary anthropology, or in a Christian perspective of creation, fall and redemption. Trying to be humble is a strain which does not improve human being. As a virtue, is it worth its costs? So the discarding of humility is not to be dismissed as nothing but an act of sinful pride. In some cases, humility is given up in order to find healthy, happy and even prosperous, ways of being human.

In the light of the humility of God in Christ, Christians, would-be disciples of Jesus, accept the invitation to humility. That is what they are pursuing, but not as though the objections to it are trivial. They believe that the invitation has a good meaning though it may be hard to discern it amongst so many confused and bad examples. They have to seek that meaning in company with the child in the midst. Finding it opens the way into the kingdom of God, into life not death.

2. Child and humility

Because humility has largely been discarded as a virtue or style of being in action and spirit in our culture and history, we can see the difficulty of following Jesus when he says, "Humble yourself". He puts the child in the midst to help: "Humble yourself as *this child*." But might not the child compound our difficulty?

Whatever the child meant in the time of Jesus, children today are not models of humility and cannot be for social reasons

When we look at how the child is understood in post-Romantic and modern scientifically-based childcare cultures, we do not hear the gospel's call to humble ourselves. We do not see, or want to see, the child as humble. The child as such and children in general do not universally and naturally point to humility as a healthy option.

The logic of the pastoral polemic of the gospel story presents the child in the midst as an embodied criticism of the ambition for greatness. This is not because the child is naturally humble, in her own person. The small child cannot be a model of any virtue, for virtue requires self-control, responsibility and disciplined self-aware aspiration.[18] Only as we grow up does the call to virtue become conceivable, and as the example of the disciples reminds us, it may be a long time before it makes enough sense for us to choose it. Virtue is adult practice to which children can only come to, step by step, along the path of their growing up.

It was not on the basis of her own chosen, responsible, spiritual practice that the child in the midst was a challenge to the disciples' lack of humility. How then does the child lead us to humility? It is not a matter of the particular character of the child. Rather, the child placed by Jesus represents humility because the social construction of the child at that time made her low in social status. The child in this story signifies humility only because and as Jesus said so, and Jesus could say so convincingly for two reasons. First, Jesus with the Father went the way of exemplary humility, as servant and sufferer (Matthew Matthew 16:21; 20:25-28) and his embracing of children was part of that humility.[19] The child signs humility because the child is with Jesus as his deliberate, counter-intuitive way of signing the kingdom of God. Secondly, the child serves to sign humility because in the culture which Jesus shared with his disciples it was accepted as normal that the child was lowly, a servant, near the margins.[20]

▨ Humility, poverty, low status and esteem

Social and economic realities shaped the idea of humility in the tradition of Israel, as reflected in Scripture. The poor are lowly, primarily because they are relatively weak, not because they cultivate the virtue of humility as a personal characteristic. They are *under* those who are powerful, rich and lordly. The humble are servants, not masters; the young, not the old. The Magnificat is premised on this view of the world (Luke 1:46-55). It is by virtue of this tradition that the child was available to Jesus as a sign of humility.

When we compare what Jesus did and said with what we think about children, we are likely to be shocked and even alienated. It is difficult, even impossible, to learn humility from the child in modern, western, enlightened culture. The child, as we desire him, is not humble by nature or nurture. The child envisioned in our care and aspiration is not expected to be lowly or meek. The shy child is likely to be seen as needing remedial help lest she fall even further below her potential and has problems in relationships. We no longer recognise meekness as a kind of strength and beauty; so we see nothing in shyness but a lack. Desiring the best for our children means wanting them to make the most of themselves. We do not want them to sell themselves short. We want children who are adventurous, socially as well as physically. We know the value of cheekiness: the precocious child is to be counted as promising rather than irritating or ill-mannered; those caring for him must give him space.[21] There may be some humility to be found in this intergenerational situation but it is not in the child: elders are called to practise a kind of humility and self-restraint so as to avoid any put-down of the child.[22]

The characteristics of a healthy child, in much contemporary understanding, do not include humility, either as personal modesty or as social submission. Children are naturally small at the beginning, but we like the fact that their littleness contains an assertive, even aggressive, power of life, which is like a mighty seed that will grow into a great tree. The resilience of the child is a valued capacity giving hope even when they are disadvantaged; it can be drawn upon when children are in trouble; it is to be nurtured, encouraged and supported. Resilience resists being put down; it bounces back; it does not humbly accept its lot.

We admire Oliver in the workhouse.[23] The lot fell on him to be the spokesman for all his comrades when they had decided they would not go on being hungry: "Please, Sir, I want some more." "Please, Sir ..." might sound humble, but it could not obscure the "I want some more." Oliver's polite frailty was not enough to dissuade the beadle and the fat feasting ignorant governors from sensing subversion. They missed in Oliver the grateful humility and ungrumbling subordination which they thought was their due, the tribute from the lower orders on which their status and pride rested. We do not reject Dickens when he would have us rejoice at the spirit, the solidarity, the hungry protest of Oliver in his refusing to demonstrate the humility expected of him. Oliver, we think, was not asking for charity, but properly claiming his rights.

Many parents are charmed by little children, because some of them sometimes are simultaneously manageable, amusing and precocious. Yet the same parents may be wearied in later years by teenagers who, in growing to the stature of adults, have ceased to be manageable or amusing. But, whatever the trouble, no parent really wants the nearly adult child to be as dependent and suggestible as the infant. Spiritual teachers may quote St. Thérèse of Lisieux,[24] to make a virtue of being dependent and vulnerable, but practical people like parents, educators, intelligent employers and governments cannot afford to encourage that kind of personality. They expect children to develop into helpful partners, capable of independent and innovative initiative, sharing in the hard work of making and keeping human life human in the world.[25] Indeed "preparation for independence" is one of the contemporary slogans of professionals engaged with children.

So, even when it seems too near to a gambler's optimism for comfort, parents stay with teenagers, holding on in the hope that, in time, a reliable, capable adult will emerge. Then all the refined or gross revolt of teenage, the wild or discreet transgressions, the trivial or grave insults to parental dignity and expectations, can be seen in retrospect as growing pains, costly investments that paid off. A good man or woman has been developed through experimenting with anxiety and ambition, assertion and aggression. How can the growth of this sort of person, along a path like this, be explained in terms of humility? It does not seem to be a key word here. It does not describe the way a normal child develops or the way we want the child to be.

It is evident that the child in our culture is not the child as Jesus, and the society of his day, saw her. If Jesus came to do his work today and tried to publish his message to the world through the medium of our culture, he could not take a child and put him in the midst as an obvious pointer to the kingdom of God along the way of the Crucified. At several points our sensibilities and convictions would be offended. The child as we perceive him could not stand alongside a prophet with this message.

This is not to say that no trace of humility can be found in the child today, but it is neither obvious nor socially affirmed. It is not part of popular conceptions of the child. Reflection after the event, using sophisticated but not therefore invalid ideas of humility may discover it to have been there in the child as she grows. Seeing oneself truthfully, being realistic in action, cool and willing to learn from experience, are valuable elements in a practised humility. But they are not what we unreflectively think of as humility and they are not prominent in our view of children.

Jesus did not audition and test children, to find one who displayed humility as a personal quality or virtue that could provide an example to the disciples. A nameless, unexplained child served his purpose, precisely because the representation of humility Jesus was working with, in this argument, was socially ascribed. The child, regardless of personal qualities, was generally of low status in society and so could be the focus for a serious positive discussion of humility.

When Christians seek humility, as they still do, little reference is made to the child. This is only partly because the child today is not a strong sign of humility. In Christian tradition generally, humility has long been taught without the child in the midst. Christians looking to Jesus Christ see radical unstinting humility being modelled.[26] In that great light, what need is there of the little star of the child? Humility is generated in a devotion focused on God, revering his incomparability and holiness: the Lord is in his holy temple, let all the earth keep silence before him.[27]

Stalling

There are weighty objections to humility and large-scale abstentions from its practice, amongst Christians as much as others. If we summarise where we have got to in trying to expound this text, it seems as if our argument has stalled.

There is widespread aversion to humility as a personal quality, style of spirit and behaviour. It is judged more dangerous than useful in practical affairs. Any recommendation of humility is suspected as being a device of the powerful to hold on to what they have and to keep those who want a share down and out. Humility as social lowliness is escaped by those who can and is resented by the subordinated weak who cannot. People react against suffering and limitation, refusing the acquiescence which sometimes counts as humility. Their sense of worth, dignity and right grounds the resistance to it. We are inspired by visions of living in societies which work without humility.

Christians share this aversion to humility. They have largely left behind spiritual disciplines oriented by humility. They are impressed, even bewildered, by the social and moral objections to humility. Yet they still confess Jesus as Lord. They still respect the witness of Scripture. They still pray for God's Name to be hallowed and his kingdom to come, and for themselves to be fit to be received into it. And they still sometimes read Matthew 18:1-5. There they are confronted by a child who, whatever her personal character, is carrying in herself a limited social reality of humility and may thus be proposed as a sign of the humility, the opposite of that ambition for greatness which is an obstacle on the way into the kingdom of God.

We have seen, however, that the child in the old story does not immediately help us in the search for a positive understanding of humility, for our child today is not the same. Rather if the child were to be seen as an example of this saving humility, there would be objections to an apparent endorsement of the oppressive social conditioning of the child. We do not want children humble in character or status.

Jesus put a child forward to urge the disciples to humble themselves. This was a possible persuasive tactic because the child had a low status in society;[28] he knew the disciples saw children as lowly, beneath them, and certainly not serious competitors in the race[29] to be the greatest. So they would be shocked to be asked to become like the children. The invitation to a radical new-shaping of self would be an extreme comedown for them. Thus Jesus could reiterate the call to take up the cross by placing a child in the midst.

Our hesitation about instrumentalising the child provokes questions about Jesus who placed her in the midst. Does Jesus collude with an oppressive social cultural situation by using a child to make a point? Does he exploit its unfairness or inhumanity for his own purpose? If so, was Jesus enclosed uncritically within this culture? In view of these problems, shall we abandon Jesus or at least the Jesus of this story? Many do. Many abandon Jesus altogether, paying no attention to him and being resolutely non- or anti-christian. Others, including Christians, hold to Jesus selectively. All Christians, conservative as much as liberal, are equipped with Nelson's telescope in their knapsack when they read the Bible and work out how they will follow Jesus.[30]

But, however selective they may be, Christians do not want to abandon Jesus altogether. In their bewildering experiences of Jesus, they look for what is good and glad and trustworthy in him.[31] They seek hopefully because they believe the kingdom of God is to be found along his way. This selective faith may seem to be shaky. It will be judged by many Christians, as well as militant anti-christians, to be inadequate, because it is often assumed that faith is absolute certainty, and so shaky faith is no faith at all. But it is more realistic and helpful to live in the spirit of the man who cried, "Lord, I believe, help my unbelief" (Mark 9:24) than to abandon the venture of following Jesus because we do it so imperfectly.

While there is much about Jesus which makes people give up on him, Jesus himself provides grounds for going on with him. When many were leaving Jesus, some disciples stayed with him, because, as they said, they had come to believe he had the words of eternal life, even though they often did not understand what he was saying (John 6:68-71). Sometimes they stayed grimly: "Let us go that we may die with him." (John 11:16). In the moment when abandoning Jesus seems the rational, even necessary, option, it is possible to hesitate and take a second look. That is what we will do now. We have read Jesus, the child and humility in one way which seems to have run into the sand. Can there be another reading? Can the stalled motor be restarted?

A second look at humility

We take a second look by distinguishing four kinds of humility, which are crudely labelled as **put-down**, **come-down**, **look-forward** and **look-up**. What we do now is to explore two of these combinations, before focusing on look-up.

1. Humility: put-down and come-down
We have already met these two kinds of humility. Come-down humility is what the ambitious disciples are called to. Their path is decided for them and opened up by the Lord. They follow him as

the Master. If they are in conflict with him, they may find themselves put down as the Lord humbles the proud. But essentially the disciples' difficult and costly coming down is a voluntary self-giving venture. At its heart, there is willing acceptance and free obedience. Only so can humility be an authentic act of the whole person in the meaningful personal relation of Lord and disciple. It is the way of entering, discovering and making a really human way of being. Jesus in Gethsemane is a paradigm of this voluntary humility: he gave his life rather than having it taken from him.[32] He came down and was not merely put down. Similarly, the disciples could not be brought to humility by mere compulsion. Even the humility that can be achieved by training is limited, even flawed. Disciples can only come to humility if, in their wholeness, they come down, giving themselves as free people endowed with will and insight.

Come-down humility is thus quite different from the second kind of humility: put-down humility. Put-down is prevalent in human affairs, from the family to the biggest of organisations, including church. The world could not work without it: it is an implicate of power. Sometimes it is intolerable, sometimes not. Relatively benign put-down humility is found in fair and humane social order. People put themselves under it and accept the powers requiring subordination because it can be seen that it may roughly serve human purposes. Here put-down humility is qualified by look-forward humility, which we discuss later. There are also malign forms of put-down humility, which ought rather to be called humiliation. They lack all respect for the humanity of the subordinated. The put-down is not modified by offering any hopeful forward look.

There are pedagogies of control that utilise and justify humiliation of some sort. Machiavelli was wise to the dangers of humiliation as a technique of rule, but did not shy away from it: he advised the Prince to ensure that humiliation, when used, was drastic, disempowering the humiliated so they could not retaliate. Humiliating practices and attitudes are deep-rooted in human being.

Sometimes they are claimed to be practically necessary, sometimes emotionally satisfying. Nothing, however, justifies humiliation: it is an affront to the dignity of being. It fails to see and respect the image of God, wherever God places it.

Humiliation does not deepen humility, but rather shows that humility is not understood or respected by the humiliator. It is the extreme result of working on two fallacious assumptions. The first is that humility is expected of others, not ourselves. The second is that humility can be imposed, by putting people down. But being put down can be no more than *ersatz* humility, having the appearance but not the reality of it. Inviting those who are humiliated to rejoice in their enforced humility rightly gives humility a bad name.

Come-down humility and put-down humiliation are incompatible with each other, but in human living they are often entangled and confused together. Like the good seed and the tares, they are not to be separated until harvest comes. Some of the objections to humility discussed earlier arise because voluntary self-giving gets lost and discredited under the humiliating power of oppression and depression. So, hard as it may be, the two need, ever and again, to be distinguished from each other. A conceptual distinction is not enough: it is a matter of action and how we live. Even in the present mixed up, confusing world, we are called to practise true come-down humility, even under the humiliating powers that shape the way of the world. Jesus lights the way for us, because he lived come-down humility all along the way, even to the cross, which in the hands of the Romans was the instrument of extreme humiliating put-down. The cross was transformed by God in Christ as it was suffered by Jesus and interpreted by the Spirit in the church. Only in this "history of salvation" has the cross been redeemed, taken out of the hands of the humiliating princes of this world (1 Corinthians 2:7). It is by the grace of God that the story of Christ crucified can be told as the story of a come-down humility that was persistently true to itself against all pressure, so that the light of come-down humility shone and shines still in the prevailing darkness of put down humiliation.

We live still in the confused mixture of put-down humiliation and come-down humility. Faced with the call to come down, on one hand, and the reasonable fear of humiliation on the other, we need light to see the choice before us and encouragement in making it. Help awaits us in the whole gospel: Jesus said, "Humble yourselves as this child." "As this child" does not excuse us from coming down, but it affirms and clarifies it and so rescues it from humiliation. The child leads us into humility that looks forward and looks up.

2. Humility: look-forward and look-up

Look-forward and look-up are ways of reframing come-down humility so that it is not stymied by objections and abstentions. This is achieved partly by giving a clearer view of how, in faith, come-down humility is separated from put-down humiliation and so comes to its authentic fullness. They inform humility with the wholeness of the gospel.

This reframing reveals humility more as narrative than as a state or condition. The oppressed one is pushed down into the pit. The meek self-giver comes down voluntarily. Both stories run into humility as a lowly state or quality of existence. But is that the end of the story? Eeyore gets stuck in gloom, but others around him in Pooh Corner are resilient and hopeful.[33] A forward look implies movement between now and next, today and tomorrow. Temporal imagination is called into play. Still pictures abstracted from a movie have truth, but they do not tell a story that gives understanding of action. Humility needs to be seen as narrative.

A seed falls into the ground and, dying, bears much fruit.[34] Thus in one sentence Jesus tells the story of humility. The humility of the little one who falls and dies is revealed in the whole story of a coming down which goes as deep as death but does not end there. It disappears only to reappear surprisingly in plentiful new life. The coming down is thus not directed towards a bleak final put down. Taken in its entirety, the story has a flow requiring us to look forward. It encourages hope.

Put-down can be endured, the shame despised (Hebrews 12:2) if it is set within the context of hope. Put-down implies some hostile or indifferent oppressor. Hope resists being put down and meets the oppression with defiance, because what is seen in hope is that the oppressors' hold is not definitive. Hoping, looking forward, even in its weakness, already shows and probes the gaps in the prison wall. Even under the put-down, look-forward humility enables come-down humility to be a fighting resistance, a voluntary engagement against the oppressor even in the situation shaped by the oppressor. Humility as a partnership of coming down and looking forward redefines the realm of the oppressor from within, for it contests his power and right to define and hold it.[35] He is not now the only actor in it. There is Another in the field, who may indeed be put upon, but is not simply or finally put down.[36]

Look-forward humility is fragile. Hope as the resistance of love to a world misshapen by humiliating powers does not have the certainty which is the boast of powerful planning and management.[37] Put-down humility and even come-down humility properly generate the desire to escape to freedom. As we have seen, it is natural and right for people to say: If this coming down is all there is to humility, I do not want it. Why should I acquiesce in loss, humiliation, in falling to rise no more?[38] Hence the longing for a simple reversal in which the mighty are put down from their thrones and the humble and meek are exalted (Luke 1:52). Desire may go further: the oppressed may be tempted to look for more than being free from oppression; the momentum of conflict may carry them forward to strive for the freedom to be oppressors, wreaking vengeance upon their enemies. Sometimes what counts as liberation is gaining the power and right to return evil for evil. Thus, looking forward in this way can involve calculations and validate preferences which eliminate come-down humility. Because put-down humiliation is rightly unacceptable to any who suffer it, there is a temptation to protect our own freedom and domination by aiming at power to put others down, or to be indifferent to the humiliations of others, discounting it as mere collateral damage in what must be done. This is the fragility of look-forward hope when it is put to the test of practice in a world where so-called realism tells dog to eat dog.

3. Look-up humility

The fragility of looking forward as a form of humility leads to the question of how it can be protected from corruption and collapse. In the life given to us in Christ, hopeful freedom is kept humble because it is continually shaped from its source, in the story of God in Christ, who "though he was rich yet for our sakes became poor."[39] Faith roots us in his coming down and being put down without seeking to avenge himself. Such faith, as we have already said, is indispensable and central in Christian faith and life. But once again we need to be aware of the dangers. We have already noticed that there are ways of glorying in the cross in and by itself which cast a twisted shadow over the image of God in human life.

A common problem of Christian living comes into view here. We walk unsteadily between ambitious triumphalism and the cult of suffering and death. We flip between grasping at freedom with the exalted Christ and running from life to die with Christ, culturally, emotionally, or even occasionally physically. Any sort of flip-flopping is spiritually wearying and confusing. Yet it cannot be escaped by denying one side or the other. We need to find a truthful way of living and being where the forms of humility come together rather than compete.[40]

For this to happen look-forward humility needs to be rooted in and partnered by look-up humility. Look-up humility is also what makes come-down humility different from put-down humility. It is the matrix of humility in the Bible and in the Christian narrative of God in Christ.

Isaiah 57:15 is one text that stands for many on this theme. The high and lofty One inhabits eternity. His name is holy. It is right to hallow God's name, and pray for God to hallow it. Our Father in heaven is to be looked up to.

Looking up implies humility, for the one who looks up is lower. This of itself does not provide an escape from the objectionable sort of humility we have noticed before. If the one above is an oppressor, looking up merely reinforces the put-down. Nebuchadnezzar gave all peoples in his empire a great statue to look up to, to bring them to a public acknowledgement of their subjugation to the great leader, under threat of the fiery furnace if they refused.[41] So the key question is: what is there to look up to and what kind of humility does it bring us into? Is there any thing or any one to look up to so that humility without humiliation is realised?

In the biblical witness, we are given God as the Father of our Lord Jesus Christ with the Holy Spirit to look to and to look up to. God is seen and known in his own story of coming down, to dwell with those who are of a contrite and humble spirit.

Isaiah 57 integrates looking up to the high and holy One with the forward movement and vision given by God. It starts with the world locked in its evil so that it has only death to look forward to. The righteous man perishes and will be glad to get out of the world to be at peace, (Isaiah 57:1-2). Thus the world is left to the sons of the sorceress and goes on its disastrous way without learning anything from weary journeys, even down to Sheol (Isaiah 57:10). No thought is given to God and for his part, God holds his peace, not intervening. So men think they will get away with it, but the wind will carry them off (Isaiah 57:3-13).

Then, a switch to hope: there is a future prospect in this darkness, so that looking forward is possible. It is given to the meek, who, taking refuge in God, will possess the land and inherit "my holy mountain". They will, we might say, enter the kingdom of God. The spirit of those who turn to the Lord with a contrite and humble spirit is revived as they are forgiven, given peace and blessed with healing and the shining of God's face turned towards them (Isaiah 57:16-19).

The humble look up to the high and lofty One who also dwells with them and so they are "revived", given new life. Looking forward is one with their looking up. Humility is full of hope beyond all humiliation. Looking up to God makes for a freedom to come down in true humility, without fear of being put down: it is a relation of trust and freedom and joy.

Such enhanced and unshadowed humility is the gift of God and the response to the gift.

Looking up to whatever is good, great, holy, or beautiful engenders humility without put-down. The humble are drawn up to enjoy the good. The good tends to induce humility: secular examples are not uncommon. At his inauguration on 20 January 2009, President Barack Obama said: "My fellow citizens: I stand here today humbled by the task before us, grateful for the trust you have bestowed, mindful of the sacrifices borne by our ancestors."

If the good is perceived as a lofty perfection or scornful superiority, it does not have this result. But true goodness is generous, outgoing and welcoming. It exists in sharing enjoyment. The blessing of the Lord makes rich, and he adds no sorrow to it (Proverbs 10:22). Isaiah's High One dwells with the humble. The dwelling of God with people in creation is a running thread through the biblical story. So responsive humility is elation, wonder and astonishment: it is the laughter that greets the Lord's turning again the captivity of Zion (Psalm 126:1). The goodness of God takes us out of ourselves by revealing what is beyond our doing, our possessing and our imagining. Our pretensions of grandeur are shamed, shown up as tawdry. Such shaming is a firm put-down, but its source, mode of working and goal are not demeaning or humiliating. The put-down is framed by the evident good will and generosity which evokes wonder and hope.

Another element in look-up humility is free and joyous gratitude: "The Lord has done great things for us, whereof we are glad."[42] In such gratitude dependence is accepted without a sense of being humiliated. Charity is often resented by the beneficiary, because it is administered condescendingly or managerially from above. Gratitude always implies a difference between giver and receiver, initiator and respondent but if that difference is magnified and exploited in the process of giving, gratitude is strangled at birth. It is sometimes argued that being a receiver is necessarily humiliating. A gift creates obligation, a morally binding indebtedness, which cannot easily be dissolved by the giver's insistence that is a free gift. Even between equals, it is hard to receive a gift without feeling a challenge to one's dignity and freedom. But it would be a bleak world if giving and receiving were incompatible with freedom and dignity. Wherever giving and receiving is a shared joy, a different world is being built, sign by sign.[43]

We are speaking here of everyday human living. For example, young people are sometimes irked by living within the home which institutionalises their dependence on parental giving. Not until they have worked their way through a break with it can they come to an easier acceptance of life as a gift received from parents, a gift to enjoy and be grateful for without any element of put-down. Parents vary in their capacity to make this transition easy for their children; nothing can save the child from the hard work of finding the way.

Where there is free community, humility ceases to be the tribute the lowly make to the great. It becomes the common spirit in which all share together, the common wisdom, respect and hope by which the community negotiates the trials and temptations of life.

Humility is intrinsic to the faith which responds to grace with amazement and gratitude. Romans 5:1-5 shows how "the free gift of eternal life through Christ Jesus our Lord" (Romans 6:23) forms human beings in humility. First they are put in the right or "justified" through Christ against all powers that would put them down. They are brought into peace with God. Standing in grace, they rejoice in the hope of the glory of God. All this describes a complex but unified condition of a person, or the community of faith. They stand as the beneficiaries of the gift of God; and in that condition they are free to be joyful and hopeful in accepting what is given and in being what they are made. Humility as looking up and looking forward is integral to their being.

Within this matrix, real life rolls out, involving suffering and producing patience. Patient endurance produces tried experience and hope which does not disappoint because God's love is poured into hearts through the gift of the Holy Spirit. So pressures which threaten and crush do not achieve put down; the humility of trust, gratitude, joy and hope is sustained by living in the gift of God. The apparently linear sequence in this text becomes a circle as the end joins the beginning: the Holy Spirit in the heart is a transforming gift, lifting people so they stand rejoicing before God, confirming the justification that makes peace with God. If, as is being suggested, we take this as a description of humility, it is evident that it is without humiliation. It anticipates Romans 8:31-39 in affirming that not one of the great negative powers can or will succeed in putting down those who are in Christ, who through the Holy Spirit look up to God, crying "Abba, Father" through all the sufferings of the present time (Romans 8:14-30).

Humility is intrinsic to the constitution of this human being "in Christ". It is primarily the humility of free joyful gratitude, although in its life-process there is suffering which, left to itself, makes for humiliation and disappointment, being let down and ashamed. It is upheld by the love of God and the Holy Spirit.

Alive in Christ, we respond to the humility of God's coming down by active participation in it. To humble ourselves under God is not humiliating because it is being lifted up to share in the way and spirit and life of God. Humility is given within the fellowship of the Father and the Son.

The child again: look-forward

Just as the child placed by Jesus in the midst reiterates the call to discipleship, coming down to follow in the way of the cross, so the child placed by Jesus in the midst is a sign of new creation, chiming with the raising of the Son of Man. Humility as represented by the child is not humiliation. The child signs humility, without knowingly practising humility as a virtue. The signing of humility is achieved because a child is both little and new. This

littleness is a vulnerability and exposes the child to risks of manifold humiliation. But it is also the littleness of the seed which,
without pretending to be what it is not, without pride and boasting,
has the power of life and the future within it. And because it is little, it looks up. Humility as seen in the child is hopeful.[44]

No matter how we idealise and celebrate the child's existence, to
become like the children involves a coming down for the healthy
adult. It would mean a loss of autonomy, control of one's own life,
the freedom to plan, the assurance of having that mastery by
which desires and action are correlated intelligibly, significant
chosen goals are realised and responsibility taken.

But to be humble like the children must not be confined merely
to a process of stooping, or coming down into loss. Being like the
children also means being free for life in all its forward-looking
promise. It is to be borne along by the given power of growth, even
if it is imperceptibly slow and frustrating. The child's phrase,
"When I am grown up ...," may be dream or determination: either
way it nurtures expectation.

The child, however small, and however low its status, is thus living hope incarnate. The child is a process of hope, awakening hope.
Karl Barth's friend, Eduard Thurneysen, put it like this:[45]

> "Jesus places children before us. He uses them as a parable in
> order to say something decisive to us. Children are people
> who still stand at the beginning of life. ... For them ... every-
> thing is filled with possibility and promise; life is an open
> book filled with unwritten pages ... .
>
> "For us (grown-ups) it is too late for almost everything.
> We do not have an undeveloped life before us. On the con-
> trary, we have run ourselves fast into ruts or run our lives
> into an impasse ... we have become fossilised in our vocation,
> our work ... we work as in a treadmill. ... We are faithful in
> our married life, but we simply drag it along as though it
> were a burden. ... Still more important, our faults, our fail-
> ings, our sins ... today we scarcely resist at all. But we groan

and suffer. Is not this the really burdensome feature about growing older, that we are forced to see, in so many ways, that going back again is no longer possible?

"But listen! 'Unless you turn and become as little children.' What does that mean? ... There is such a thing as a new beginning ...

"[With Jesus] there is this possibility of a new beginning in a life that has already grown old. We have really said everything that can be said about Jesus when we say that ... It means to be an old scarred man, in just such a predicament ... one without hope, without possibilities, and then, of a sudden, to face this: 'Come to me all ye that labour and are heavy laden, and I will revive you!'

"Revitalisation that comes from Jesus [does not] mean that we must become actual children, childish people ... in many external and internal things we cannot go back again. But in the main thing we can go back ...

"There is a new beginning, and a new creation possible in Jesus Christ. ... Oh, let us hear the gospel tell us, 'We can!' Now, do not interpose immediately and say, 'No, I cannot; I am too old; too fossilised; nothing in my life can be made new again.' ... This new beginning about which Jesus speaks is God. ... and the movement of the kingdom of God from God towards us.

"We could ... say ... 'Forgiveness of sins is what is meant by the passage about becoming as children, though this particular word about sin, as such, is not found here.' For, what is sin? Sin means separation from God. Sin may be anything in my life which forces me away from, and shuts me off from, making this beginning ... These old walls and partitions are pierced. Jesus broke through them. I can, I may, I am free! That is what He tells me. This is the forgiveness of sins.

"We are all too strong in ourselves to become really weak before God, so that He can be strong in us in the power of his forgiveness. This is the strength of the humble and small and, as such, the beginning of the life to which Jesus calls us. 'Whosoever humbles himself as this little child, he is the greatest in the kingdom of heaven.' Therefore, 'if you do not turn and become as the children. ...'"

At the end of his life, Barth was still making this point. Discussing Matthew 11:25/Luke 10:21, he stressed that the revelation is "made exclusively to babes (that is, real little children, not metaphors for 'stupid or muddleheaded people')":

"The wholly new thing that has come in Jesus is open only to those people who are an adequate match, who are open to it, because they have nothing behind them, because they are not stopped or blocked up against it by any intellectual, moral, aesthetic, or religious *a priori* that they have brought with them, because they are empty pages. This is plainly the point of the story about the child that Jesus set in the midst of his disputing disciples ...." [46]

Humility is hope, it is the joy of "I can" which comes from God in the forgiveness of sins, which enacts God's hope for all held by sin. In that hope, God humbled himself even to the weakness and shame of the cross to redeem and renew the creation.

NOTES

1   The Greek word, *strepho*, in Matthew 18:3 is often translated "change". But the root meaning is to do with turning. *Epi-strepho* is a word for convert.

2   Matthew 20:26-27; 23:11-12; Mark 10:43-44; Luke 14:11; 18:14; 22:36.

3   D. Kraybill, *The Upside-Down Kingdom*, 1978.

4   Again, when children are brought to Jesus to be blessed, Mark (10:15) and Luke (18:17) refer to receiving the kingdom of God as a child. But in his version of that story, surprisingly perhaps, Matthew does not mention receiving (Matthew 19:13-15).

5   The first way, becoming is discussed in both Chapters 5 and 6; humbling in Chapter 5; receive in Chapter 6.

6   A selection of relevant biblical texts might include Deuteronomy 30:2,10: "Return to the LORD your God;" 30:10: "Turn to the LORD with all your heart and with all your soul." This is the opposite of the heart turning away from God to idols (Deuteronomy 30:17). Isaiah 6:9-10, quoted in Matthew 13:14-15 and John 12:40: "Make the heart of the people fat and their ears heavy and shut their eyes, lest they see with their eyes and hear with their ears, and understand with their hearts, and turn and be healed." Isaiah 45:22; 55:7: "Let the wicked

forsake his way ... and let him return to the LORD that he may have mercy on him." Joel 2:12; Acts 3:19; 2 Corinthians 3:16; 1 Thessalonians 1:9: "To turn from idols to serve the living and true God and to wait for his Son from heaven." Morris West explores *metanoia* ("repentance, a change of heart, a new direction," p. 90) in his seriously entertaining novel, *Lazarus* (1990).

7 Martin Luther, in the first of his Ninety Five Theses, said: "When our Lord and Master, Jesus Christ, said 'Repent', He called for the entire life of believers to be one of repentance."

8 1 John 1:5-9

9 Isaiah 58; Matthew 6:1-18; Mark 7:1-13; Luke 18:9-14; James 1:26-27

10 No one has made this point as succinctly as Thomas Henry Huxley: "Sit down before fact as a little child, be prepared to give up every preconceived notion, follow humbly wherever and to whatever abysses nature leads, or you shall learn nothing." There is no need to read into these words a contrast between natural science and faith. Charles Finney made a similar point in his paper, "The Child-like Spirit an Essential Condition of Entering Heaven," (http://www.gospeltruth.net/1852OE/520526_child_like_spirit.htm):

> "By (humility) I mean, not a sense of sin, but a willingness to be known and appreciated according to truth. The little child is in this sense humble. He feels no repugnance to being known as he is. He has not once thought of trying to conceal his real character. He is ignorant of almost every thing, and he seems very cheerfully to assume that such is the fact. Hence, he asks questions of every body and under any and all circumstances, never anxious lest he should expose his ignorance. Indeed he expects to expose it if he has it, and deems it no harm to do so. He seems to suppose that there can be no objection to being known according to the truth in his case."

11 Isaiah 57:15; Daniel 4: a story of God with Nebuchadnezzar, who through a terrible journey into the far country of losing his humanity, learned that God is "able to abase those who walk in pride" (Daniel 4:37) and then to save them.

12 Isaiah Berlin, "The Originality of Machiavelli", http://berlin.wolf.ox.ac.uk/published_works/ac/machiavelli.pdf; p. 45:

> If men practise Christian humility, they cannot also be inspired by the burning ambitions of the great classical founders of cultures and religions; if their gaze is centered upon the world beyond – if their ideas are infected by even lip-service to such an outlook – they will not be likely to give all that they have to an attempt to build a perfect city. If suffering and sacrifice and martyrdom are not always evil and inescapable necessities, but may be of supreme value in themselves, then the glorious victories over fortune, which go to the bold, the impetuous, and the young, might neither be won nor thought worth winning. If spiritual goods alone are worth striving for, then of how much value is the study of necessita – of the laws that govern nature and human lives – by the manipulation of which men might accomplish unheard-of things in the arts and the sciences and the organization of social lives?

13 Charles Dickens, *David Copperfield*

14 Frank Pakenham, Earl of Longford, *Humility*, 1969; Thomas á Kempis, *The Imitation of Christ*, http://incharacter.org/observation/humility-vice-or-virtue/

15 "Come down, O Love divine" is on the whole a vibrant, affirming, hopeful hymn with words such as: "O Comforter, draw near/within my heart appear/and kindle it, thy holy flame bestowing". But does the other side of it give us discomfort? "True lowliness of heart, which takes the humbler

part/And o'er its own shortcomings weeps with loathing."

16 A venerable Ambassador came to the dictator Mussolini to tell him about an international conference on the use of poisonous gas in war. Mussolini, looking through papers on his desk, kept the old diplomat standing before him. At last he said, "Well, Excellency, what is the most poisonous gas?" The Ambassador replied: "Incense." www.execupundit.com/2009/10/narcissistic-leader.html

17 Dorothee Sölle, *Suffering*, 1975

18 Compare Finney, note 10 above.

19 Damon So, *The Forgotten Jesus and the Trinity You Never Knew*, 2010

20 For example O.M. Bakke, *When Children Became People*, 2005, Chapter 2

21 M. Bunge, *The Child in Christian Thought*, p. 283f. Susannah Wesley's notorious first step in bringing up her remarkable children was thoroughly to "conquer the will and bring them to an obedient temper." This is not now seen as good advice by most people.

22 Francesca Simon, author of the Horrid Henry books, reports that Perfect Peter is disliked by parents, by comparison with Horrid Henry, despite the fact that the latter gives them trouble incessantly, and should make them worried about what they will suffer when, in a few years' time, he is a teenager and then a man. But it is not surprising that they prefer the honest evil of Henry to the creepy behaviour of Peter, who gets no nearer humility than Uriah Heep. This reference does not tell us anything useful about child and humility, but only about the modern parent's preference for children who are systematically unhumble.

23 Charles Dickens, *Oliver Twist*, Chapter 2

24 John Saward, *The Way of the Lamb*, 1999, chapter 1

25 Paul Lehmann made this formulation a major theme: see for example, *The Decalogue and a Human Future: The Meaning of the Commandments for Making and Keeping Human Life Human*, 1995

26 2 Corinthians 8:9; Philippians 2:1-11

27 Habakkuk 2:20

28 The low status of the child does not necessarily imply that children were not loved, cared for, enjoyed, valued for the future, held within family and culture in enriching ways.

29 An alternative metaphor used by Rowan Williams is "players in their trading game."

30 http://en.wikipedia.org/wiki/Turning_a_blind_eye

31 They apply Paul's general rule, as in Philippians 4:8-9, to shaping their view and loyalty to Jesus, as the particular central question of faith. Engaging in thinking on what is true, honourable, lovely, gracious and so on is not out of place in discipleship. Jesus knew his disciples had to think through their view of him, because by being himself he provoked the disturbing and so saving question about what manner of man they were dealing with. Jesus asked them who they thought he was.

32 John 10:17-18

33 Zolile Mbali, author of *The Churches and Racism: A Black South African Perspective*, 1987, wrote an unpublished paper for a consultation on politics and forgiveness entitled "God after the Full Stop," where the Full Stop signifies the point in the struggle against apartheid in the 1980s when it seemed it was ending in nothing but a violent hopeless stalemate. God keeps the story going after the Full Stop, or rather gets it going again.

34 John 12:24-26

35 Matthew 16:18. Here the oppressor is represented by the gates of Hades.

36 2 Corinthians 6:3-10

37 James 4:13-16, in close proximity to 4:6-10

38 Micah 7:8-10

39 2 Corinthians 8:9

40 George Herbert's poem, *The Collar*, offers profound and moving insight into this condition and the resolution he found:

> But as I rav'd and grew more fierce and wild
> At every word,
> Me thoughts I heard one calling, Child:
> And I reply'd, My Lord.

Getting the balance right – not refusing the cross but also not glorifying death – is a challenge both for practical living and spiritually and also in theological appreciation of texts like Philippians 3:2-11 and hymns like Isaac Watts, "When I survey ... My riches gains I count but loss, and pour contempt on all my pride."

41 Daniel 3:5-6,15-18,25-26

42 Psalm 126:3

43 Richard Titmuss, *The Gift Relationship: From Human Blood to Social Policy*, 1970

44 Psalm 131 harmonises with our discussion of humility and the child. "O Lord, my heart is not lifted up (not proud) ... I have calmed and quieted my soul like a (weaned) child quieted at its mother's breast ... O Israel, hope in the Lord." This psalm returns us yet again to Matthew 11:25-30.

At the memorial for Judith Bull (16 March 2013), the Revd Hilary Edgerton said:

> "King David, who wrote this psalm, had the world of the time at his feet. Military success, political power, building programmes and a growing trade in his city; good reputation for how he was wholehearted in what he did; a formidable leader with a great following.
>
> "So it pulls me up short every time I read this psalm, to see how simple and childlike it is. The greatest king Israel had known says, 'My heart is not proud. ... I have stilled and quietened my soul. ... like a weaned child.'
>
> "When you become successful, powerful, responsible, well known – it's easy to fall. Some people use their power to boost their own sense of importance at the expense of others; some crack under the strain.
>
> "Some do go on with great cost to themselves, serving other people. David says, 'My heart is not proud. ... I do not concern myself with great matters or things too wonderful to me.' He sees God and himself in the right perspective – any of his own greatness comes from God.
>
> "So now he's like a baby again, who can't work it all out, who can't do anything except lie in his mother's arms. He's weaned, he's on solid food, he can feed himself now, as it were, but there are times when it doesn't feel right and you just have to go back to the place where you are given safety again.
>
> "For me, there is no clearer, simpler picture of trust in God than that: a powerful person who cannot possibly be proud because he still has times of saying, 'It's too big for me, so I'll go back to God like a child to its mother and trust it will be alright soon.'"

45 Karl Barth and Eduard Thurneysen, *God's Search for Man*, 1935, is a collection of early sermons by the two friends. One is called "The New Beginning", on the text of Matthew 18:1-9. We are indebted to D.J. Konz for the evidence that Thurneysen was the preacher of this sermon.

46 Karl Barth, *The Christian Life*, 1981, p. 81

Chapter Six

Reception

"Whoever receives one such child in my name receives me"

MATTHEW 18:5 (ESV ANGLICISED VERSION)

"Receive the child" in the three Gospels

ALL THREE SYNOPTIC GOSPELS speak of receiving a child. Immediately after Jesus places the child amongst the disciples competing for greatness, Luke (9:46-48) says: "Whoever receives this child in my name, receives me; and whoever receives me, receives him who sent me." Only after that does he add: "The least among you is the one who is great." This remark points to humility, but without the word or the emphasis given it in Matthew.

In Mark 9:33-37, Jesus asked the disciples what they were arguing about on the way. When they were silent, Jesus said starkly, "If anyone wants to be first, let him be last and the servant of all. Then, calling a child to stand among them, he put his arms around him, and said: Whoever receives one such child in my name receives me, and whoever receives me, receives not me, but the one who sent me."

In Luke and Mark, nothing distracts from the call to make a

practical response to the child in the midst: the child is there to be received. By contrast, Matthew's order puts distance between the child and reception by first calling the disciples to turn and become "as the children", and then to humble self "as this child", in order to enter (or be great in) the kingdom of God. Mark and Luke do not mention the kingdom of God when they tell this story, though elsewhere they link child and the kingdom.[1] If this book were based on Mark or Luke, we would have come to reception much sooner. As we are following Matthew, it is only now, in Chapter Six, that it has been reached.

Reception central to the meaning of this story

Humbling self, becoming as the children and receiving a child may be treated as three distinct concepts and practices. Or they may converge, as three interrelated ways of participating with Jesus in the way of the kingdom of God. If they are interrelated, what is the pattern they make and what organises the pattern? This chapter suggests that receiving a child shapes the relation of the three, so that humbling and becoming find their meaning within the frame of reception.

Receiving the child is, as we shall see, a natural commonplace process. But as enacted and interpreted by Jesus, it is a path into the kingdom of God, the living fellowship of Father and Son.

The story as a whole is an example of an actual and seminal reception. *Jesus' placing a child* in the midst of the disciples is itself an act of receiving the child. Jesus thus does first what he tells the disciples to do: he receives the child. He takes a child bodily and places him in the midst. This act of reception reveals his mind and heart. He saw that the kingdom of God was "of such as children" and makes the child a sign of the way of the kingdom of God. In his own living he sought the kind of kingdom of God which could be signed by a child, and is even to be encountered and received in a real child. Jesus had this earthy awareness of the kingdom of God through his own life's learning with his Father in heaven.

Within the frame: humility and becoming as the children

Thinking within the overall frame of reception makes an important difference to our grasp of "becoming as the children" and "being humble like this child." These phrases might be understood as directions to engage individualistically in some sort of self-development: by contrast, receiving the child is a social act which entails turning towards an Other. The pursuit of spiritual romantic ideals can be detached from the mundane: when the child is received, there is holistic earthing.

The pursuit of humility and child-likeness without a real reception of the child tends to intensify self-concern and serves to validate it. Learning to have faith is not compatible with the desire to "make something of oneself."[2] In such a self-oriented enterprise, the child can be ostensibly honoured as a model, guide and challenge but is dishonoured by being adjusted to and absorbed in the subjectivity of another. The actual child, placed by Jesus, has her own being distinct from those who encircle her. She is not to be dissolved into an idea serving another's self-centred project. If that happened, discipleship would not include self-denial. So the person is not effectively taken out of himself or de-centred. The idealised child brings no release from self-concern and narcissism. Rather she becomes just another bit of the world which the disciple assimilates to his own interests, concerns and uses.

The truly pious disciple may take the child as an ideal model or guide for his own spiritual experience and personal development. The abuser assaults the embodied person, to satisfy some perverse taste. They are vastly different, and yet have one common characteristic: in both the child is absorbed into and adjusted to the subjectivity of someone else.[3]

Yet the child is in her own skin, which is a boundary of bodily visibility signing irreducible otherness and the capacity for relationship. The presence of the actual child invites the receiver to be open to and to respect what is beyond the self. Only as a respected other can the child change and bless the receiver. When the otherness of the child is denied and dissolved in any way, the blessing is lost and the abuse of the child begins. The freedom and integrity of real children are not respected, so they are in danger of being instrumentalised by the superior power of the adult.

We have already explored how the child in the midst signs humility, reiterating the call to following Jesus in the way of the cross. Receiving a child thus implies the hard and costly discipline of humility. Genuinely to receive a child, in the spirit and way of Jesus, is sustained hard work on earth. It strips away mere romantic feelings and dreams around child. Humility and the costly giving of self are integral to receiving a child in practice. Humility involves coming down low, to the earth, to the cross, to the denial of self. And yet humility is the door to life, not the sealed stone endorsing death. The hopefulness we have seen to be integral to humility in the gospel is intrinsic to the act of receiving the child.

Becoming as the children

In a similar way, when a child is received, "becoming as the children" ceases to be a project of false self-development. If becoming as the children is taken literally and by itself, it is both impossible and dangerous. It is impossible to return to being a child. It is foolish of the adult to try to go back on the gift of adulthood, and to change himself by taking the child as model, for that is a goal he can never attain. To refuse adulthood is disobedience to God's will indicated by the course of ordinary trajectory of human life: we cannot help growing older. To regard adulthood as a loss because it falls away from a romanticised infant intimacy with the divine makes no sense in the following of Jesus.[4] An adult may, in odd moments, show some partial likeness to a child; but for an adult to try to become as the children, within the limits of being adult, produces only a childishness which caricatures and insults real children.[5]

Children want to respect adults. They do not on the whole like to see them making fools of themselves. They resist having the kingdom of the child, their way of being, taken over, exploited and implicitly mocked by adults. But that is all that adults are capable of when they try, with all their inappropriate adult equipment, to transform themselves into children.[6] The child asks, wisely and with distaste, "What can I trust, if the adults around me have abdicated? What have I go grow up to, if the childishness I see in these people is what is in store for me?" The adult who attempts in himself to become as the children will soon be frustrated; unless he is stupid, he will see that he is not really achieving what he aims at.

We run into folly and frustration by understanding the text in this way. If we attended to it more closely, (like a child who makes out the words one by one, and misses nothing) we would be protected, not only by seeing the child placed in the midst, but by the little word "as". The text does not say: "Become a child again," or "Recover or make peace with the child you were," or "Go on to become a child," or "Be the child you are eternally."[7] These options tend to override rather than respect the "as". They are oriented towards individual self-development. They are quests that fail because they bypass receiving a child.

Becoming as the child through receiving a child

So the attempt by adults to "become as the children" leads into danger, irresponsibility and impossibility. It distorts those who attempt it. More seriously, it brings the gospel into disrepute. It does not help the growth of faith, in thought or practice. But when "becoming as the children" is understood through the practice of receiving a child in her full integrity, it is found to be viable, creative and responsible, a genuine gospel way. Why? Because the adult can then stop worrying about trying to become like a child. Instead he lets the child who is received do all the "being child" that is called for, and that frees him to blossom as a true adult in humility.

The adult who receives a child has to give warm, enabling,

secure, respectful, open space, a sustained welcome fit for the child.[8] He has to walk at the child's pace, to talk and think with the child, to feel with the child, reaching out to learn anew what the child is learning for the first time. He comes to see through the eyes of the child.[9] Thus he finds new being with and through the child. He starts at the beginning with the child and take small steps through little doors in the world's being, as it opens up to the growing awareness of the child. Keeping close but not stifling company with the child, as real reception requires, yields more than an external observation of the child getting on with her own life. The receiver may be given vivid glimpses of how the child sees this strange new world, so that there is an imaginative participation in the child's own seeing. Thinking and living with a child involves much listening and looking, much silence, standing by to let the child be. It is a kind of humility that resists the temptation to claim and possess.

Receiving the child gives a plausible if partial sense of seeing through her eyes, living through her living; but this sense comes with an intrinsic warning not to overrate one's knowledge of the other. Becoming as a child, sharing in her being in the world, is always partial, fleeting and dependent. This becoming is the kind of gift which cannot be held as a standing possession of the receiver. Childlikeness, unlike childhood, is a repeatable event but not an abiding characteristic. To come close to a child in this way is to stand on holy ground and to be aware of a beauty which is inevitably destroyed by covetousness, envy or robbery. Reception requires responsible work to manage and protect the child. That can be a powerful and insidious temptation to trespass.

Play

We come to humility through giving self to be a servant in a child's little world. Humility takes form as the courage to risk the unpredictability of life embodied in the particularity of "this child". The humility of Mary, the servant of the Lord, included her openness to the sword that would pierce her own soul (Luke 2:35).

The received child will do all the "being child" that is needed for the adult to become as the children. The child *is* child; the child in herself does not need to "become like children" to be child. No child needs to *play* at being a child, but that is all that adults in themselves can aspire to.[10] Each child does the real thing in his own way, and with his whole being. For example, should there be concern about a child who seems to be older than her years or too serious? Probably not so long as it is her way of being child, and not oppressively imposed on her. Being a child may look like play to adults, but that shows how easily adults can mislead themselves and then fossilise their errors in their language. What appears to adults as play is life to the child.

Adults looking down upon the child may call what they see, play, and even think, "Little things please little minds." Kindly maternalistic adults say the child should be given help and space "to play". But if it is given to us to glimpse what being a child is and what it is to find one's way in life as a child, we will know better than to despise their activity as "child's play". The child really is child in the serious continuity of her being, which she has to find and possess as her own growing identity and responsibility from moment to moment, with its challenges and opportunities.

It is the adult who plays, living a polyphonic life of many parts and doing so with varying degrees of conscious control and good and bad duplicity. Adults exploit their capacity for deliberate play: sometimes they enjoy it and sometimes they are disgusted by it. They look about themselves warily or star-struck, asking what game others are playing. Playing is part of the blessing and the curse of being adult. Knowing that he plays can be a saving grace in the adult, so that he does not take himself too seriously and rather finds some experimental freedom from the habituated self. The adult who will not play is sad; but it is worse to think adults do not, or ought not, play. Dignity plays itself up to pomposity, to the point of denying that it is play.

A child becomes a playing adult only through years of practice, becoming conscious of play and learning to distinguish it from work and from lethargic weariness with life. As childhood is left behind, existence becomes pluralist and activities are segmented and provisional.[11] Adults are called to become as the children. Responding to that call depends on, and evokes, the capacity to play. It is not so much that adults join in the play of the children, but that the child helps the adult in living life.

Play is important to life in the kingdom of God because it is fundamental to sociality. The player (the actor is a better example than the competitive sportsperson) finds freedom to make his own being available to playing others. Thus he gives expression to what is other than himself; explores and brings to light what lies beyond the boundaries of the known and the possessed. The actor lends his being to others. The part to be acted is received deeply into the actor; costly space is made for it.[12] In all this there is both humility (though often it is hidden behind celebrity and competitive show ing off), and also becoming as others.[13]

Reception in everyday practice

The child as a sign of the kingdom of God may become a metaphorical idea and thus spirited out of the world. But the child placed in the midst by Jesus, the child received, is earthed rather than idealised. Earthing the kingdom of God is not the fully present realisation of the kingdom of God. Heaven is not brought down to earth so that there is no longer a difference between heaven and earth. That way the kingdom of God would be dissolved into some version – perhaps a religious version – of the world, and thereby denied. The world meanwhile would remain fallen and mixed up, bereft of transcendent redeeming invitation. Earthing the kingdom of God is the substance and principle of prayerful living; it is a quest which has the pattern "as in heaven so on earth."[14]

The child does not earth the kingdom of God by realising it in his own being. Receiving the child in the name, way and spirit of

Jesus is to receive a sign that points to more than its present embodiment, and thus moves us to pray for the coming kingdom of God. But praying for the kingdom of God which is not yet fully here is not to leave the world behind and "soar to worlds unknown". Rather, when such prayer is enacted in the reception of a child, there is an earthing of what is being prayed for. The kingdom of God is "among you" by the presence of the child.[15] With all people and in all situations, earthing is the authentic way of signing and seeking the kingdom of God. It is impossible to truly seek the kingdom of God without the real planting of a seed. Whether in theology or popular religion, the kingdom of God is not to be sought by a flight to heavenly otherness.

The act of seeking and praying for the kingdom of God is essentially an act of seeking for earthings true to the kingdom of God. And that seeking has to be with our whole being. It cannot be done by mere praying in words, leaving God to do the work. God, Creator-Father, Incarnate-Son and Outgoing-Spirit, has already earthed and is constantly earthing the kingdom, but not without human being. Humanity is created and called to image and partner God. The human search for earthings of the kingdom of God involves work with earthly material. Thus we envision and experiment with actions which are eligible and legible as signs of the kingdom of God.

Some say this earthing of the kingdom of God is done in liturgy; liturgists take the things of earth: colours, sounds, textures, movement, bread and wine and water: and out of it produce earthings. The word is earthed in sacrament. That is true but limited. Liturgy easily gets trapped in the separateness of churchly practice, the preciousness of religious aestheticism, the ungodliness of making more of correct procedures performed by correct persons than the liberating love and generosity of the kingdom of God as it was earthed in the ministry of Jesus who placed a child in the midst. The child makes noise in church; and anyone who tries to model an ordinary family on a conventional liturgical basis will be deservedly frustrated. The child is a critical reminder of the heart of the matter. Liturgy may be saved from itself when the outsider is received.

Jesus points to and prioritises ordinary, untidy actions like receiving a real child. This practice is, for many, personal, intimate and life-long. For others it is occasional, more remotely professional, scientific or political. Reception is not restricted to parents and professionals working with children. People who do not have their own children cannot avoid living in society with children. The mere presence of children calls us all to share in receiving them. It takes a whole village to raise children.[16] Children at the start of life may not need more than a couple of parents or others they can bond with but the nuclear family requires a supportive social infrastructure. If children are to realise their all-round potential a pluralist, intergenerational society must receive them. Remote and occasional figures as well as close and warm ones make significant contributions. Protection from any kind of abuse is essential, but children need a fascinating many-circled context which includes people who strike awe and even a little fear in them. The trick is to get all the different people to live together as a village of complementary variety, making useful relationships with the child.[17]

Some people have no contact with children and do not want to be involved, but they still pay taxes for their care and education. Money is an indispensable instrument in receiving the child and it needs to be given with love, intelligence and unpossessive humility. The resolutely single or childless person should not begrudge paying taxes for what he may dismiss as "other people's children". He should at least remember who is working now to ensure that his pension will be there when he needs it – other people and their children. But we all need to pray he will see there is much more than a pension to be gained through taking a share in receiving a child, for he too is invited to enter the kingdom of God.

Many people find that receiving a child is given to them in the ordinary course of life and they simply go along with it. Some find reception is thrust upon them shockingly. Children are conceived and born in thousands every day and each new arrival cries out for reception. Being received is intrinsic to the reality of the child. Without it the child cannot survive, let alone thrive. Nature requires reception but cannot compel it. Nature thus puts us to the test: do we see that reception is naturally required and encouraged, and will we respond to the invitation to work with nature to give the child an adequate reception? Will we enter upon and persist in the long pilgrimage of discovering what receiving a child means and how it is to be achieved? Or will the child be neglected?

The child in herself comes into being in an event of reception which is fundamental to society and is celebrated in many cultures as a blessing. The child is conceived and carried in the womb: nature has no way of bringing children to be without this really costly reception. Women take the lead here. Receiving children is often the product of a powerful instinct, though even the maternal instinct is not universal. It is, however, common enough for receiving children to seem natural. Such an instinct registers the truth that the reception of the child is given by and encouraged in bodily nature, alongside and even prior to deliberate thought.

The physical and instinctive reception of the child is not in itself enough to realise the blossoming of humanity in child and parent. Many children are received in the womb, but somewhere along the road, through nursery to school and into adult life, reception fails and they are neglected or rejected, physically or spiritually. The child signs the natural reality of reception, so that we can see that reception fits child and parent; but it is not guaranteed by nature. Reception thus includes a demand for responsible human action, aiming to make beauty, love and abundant life out of the raw material of our earthly being.

Where contraception and abortion are available the birth of every child becomes a matter of choice. Thus the natural parent is in the same place as the adoptive parent. The woman who carries the child in her womb faces the same choice as the man who can inseminate and walk away: both are challenged by the advent of the child to choose to love faithfully. The new child brings us all into a place where grievous sin, incapacity and failure can be discovered as the naturally implicit promise of reception is not realised. Human choosing is the fragile though inescapable basis for receiving a child. Often, what begins in this weakness is strengthened by nature as multiple attachments with the child, in the family and the village, grow through practice. Life is the concurrence of choice and the given; even though it is precarious and imperfect, it carries the seeds and signs of what is perfect and sure in the coming kingdom of God.

Receiving a child and the kingdom of God

Receiving the child is the ordinary practice of many people. In its profoundly mysterious and everyday accessibility it is worthy of reflection, meditation and celebration. It reveals human worth even to those who, with some justice, are suspicious of mere words. Human reception earths and incarnates the heart of the kingdom of God. It opens our eyes to the generous reception of the welcoming God, Father, Son and Spirit. On earth we are made glad by the liberating embrace of the hospitality of God, the *koinonia* of all creation. But our enjoying God's feasts as his guests[18] is not all there is to divine reception. We are called to be active partners of God in sharing and spreading his hospitality here and now. Paul encapsulated it neatly: "Welcome one another ... as Christ has welcomed you." (Romans 15:7). A varying echo in Ephesians 4:32: "... forgiving one another, as God in Christ has forgiven you," chimes with the Lord's Prayer (Matthew 6:12-15) and the story of the unforgiving servant (Matthew 18:21-35).

Fundamental to the story in Matthew 18 is the kingdom of God. What is it like and how is it to be entered and how does it drive a transformation of our values and goals? The child in the midst is given as the clue to answering these questions. There is no explicit mention of the kingdom of God in the words, "Whoever receives one such child in my name, receives me. And whoever receives me, receives him who sent me." (Mark 9:37; Luke 9:48). But these words are not to be read as though the subject of the conversation has been changed: the politically-derived metaphor of the kingdom of God has not been abandoned in favour of a personal relationship with Jesus and the Father. Choosing one against the other may seem attractive. There is much Christian piety, as well as secular culture, which develops the personal and ignores the kingdom, just as there is political realism which excludes the personal. But receiving the child, the Sent and Sender together, and "entering the kingdom of God" are two ways of saying one thing.

So the kingdom of God is not left behind as this conversation transmutes into the idiom of reception, but it is seen from another angle, perhaps in a fuller way. This is not surprising, since the kingdom of God cannot be given one comprehensive definition. No word by itself defines the reality and many words can point towards it. We have already seen that the kingdom of God is not a holy version of any earthly kingdom; the language of kingdom, in the teaching and action of Jesus, is shaken by transcendent, trans-formative faith and hope. The kingdom of God is presented in para-bles, a variety of strange images and stories, which tell us only what it is "like" and so invite and tease us to look for it, ever and again, in unobvious ways. And that looking for it includes playing with words and ideas to explore God in our living and reflecting.

We are moved to such exploration by this text. So we ponder: can whatever the words "kingdom of God" point to also be indi-cated by "receiving a child in the name of Jesus"? What is the real-ity on which these two pointers converge? To do anything in the name of Jesus is to come into line with him and to share and serve his action in the world – that is, to seek the kingdom of God. Jesus is received when a child is received in his name. And, when Jesus is received, the One who sent him is received. Jesus and his Father are the essence of the kingdom of God. What would that kingdom be if God, Father, Son and Holy Spirit, were not there at the centre? A word lost in a void. Or an evil symbol, devoid of the holy love and saving grace and victorious life of the Trinity. So to receive the Son and the Sender is to be finding the reality of the kingdom of God. We need both images to be on the way.[19]

The kingdom of God as hospitable reception

The kingdom of God is not a state of affairs or a project separable from God (often in modern times it is treated so, when talk of serving the kingdom without confessing the King, or the kingdom, as the living rule and way of God, is turned into "kingdom values".) The fellowship with the Father and the Son is the core life of the kingdom of God (Matthew 11:25-27).

This creative, surprising, translation of the kingdom of God into receiving Jesus and the one who sent him is both helpful and dangerous. We are not left to work with what a single image and model, kingdom, gives us; its limits and temptations are countered by more than contradictions and warnings, for we are now invited to see kingdom in an utterly different key. That is helpful. But the danger is that the personal is chosen against the political, the fellowship with Son and Father without any sense of kingdom. Much contemporary religion, Christian and other, falls into this error. What may save us here is to keep close to the missiological language of the text: "Whoever receives you, receives Me and the one who sent Me." Father and Son are not named in this saying. Jesus is the one who is sent, and the receiving occurs in the actual practice of mission – in the basic and transcendent sense of *missio Dei*, which is much more than the practice of missionary societies and boards. Serving the mission of God in the world prevents us from retreating into limited personal relationships, however sensitive and profound, and makes us attend to persons, situations, goals and values far beyond ourselves.

The kingdom of God comes close in ordinary life when little ones, despised outsiders and lost sinners are received. The receiving, the welcome, is itself the event of the kingdom of God. The invitation to enter the kingdom of God and enjoy its feast is earthed by Jesus who received sinners and ate with them. The meal is significant because it does much more than satisfy hunger. It is a many-sided human encounter. The poor and excluded get the message: they enjoy eating with Jesus in the moment and it lifts hopes for more, like the messianic feast in the kingdom of God (cf. Luke 22:16). Being disregarded is the ordinary lot of little ones, so it comes as a happy surprise when they find themselves being treated differently. "When the Lord turned again the captivity of Zion, we were like those who dream: our mouth was filled with laughter ..." (Psalm 126:1-2). The welcome of Jesus is so happy a surprise that it counts for them as the welcome of God. Their being received in this way awakens them so that they receive Jesus in return. They love much, because they have been forgiven much: the interaction between Jesus' receiving and his being received is brought out in stories like the woman's anointing of Jesus.[20]

The grace of the welcome of God as the invitation to pass It on

Life in the kingdom of God is life within and because of the welcome of God. The welcome is in the "amazing grace" which saves those who cannot save themselves. The love of God takes the initiative and sets the ultimate context in which we live and imagine ourselves and the world: "Immortal love, forever full, Forever flowing free, Forever shared, forever whole, A never ebbing sea!"[21] Thus we are constantly invited to live with hope, peace, joy and generosity.

But this good news of the welcome of God is not always heard as an invitation to active living. Because it is so generous and all-sufficient, and because it is addressed to those who have come to the end of themselves, it often gets interpreted as a gift to be received with an empty hand, a benefit that works by its own virtue. In this picture, the welcome of the kingdom of God does not come to us as a kit needing to be built but as a model plane ready to fly. Indeed, grace is sometimes seen in an even more one-sided way: you need do nothing but strap yourself into the seat and the pilot will fly you to your destination. If grace is complete in itself, satisfying and self-acting, it brings the activity of living to a halt. It is encourages pictures of heaven, as in F.W. Faber's hymn:

"Father of Jesus, love's Reward!
What rapture it will be,
Prostrate before Thy throne to lie,
And gaze, and gaze on Thee!"

The significance of reception in the gospel is missed if it is understood with this one-sidedness; or if the emphasis is put on receiving benefits to supply and satisfy needs. Indeed, it may do damage, for it overly encourages people to think of themselves in terms of their needs, as though they are defined by their weakness and incapacity; or by their wishes, rights and demands. If human beings are reduced to seeing themselves as discouraged or anxious dependents, they are made to fall short of the glory of the image of God, who is the great giver and active receiver.

The welcome of God is grace coming from free, unmerited love. But as such it is God's invitation to live as those who are called to image God in the world. To follow Jesus and to be entering the kingdom of God means acting in his name and receiving others, who, being despised, have no means to buy a substitute for reception.[22] Such action is not a way of trying to be saved by works rather than faith. It rather responds with clear-sighted gratitude to the grace of God who, in Christ, calls us all to the dignity of being working partners.

To live and work in the way of Jesus is the fruit of the grace given us in him. Grace does not produce smug inactivity, but life in Christ. "It is in giving that we receive." So, Jesus did not bless his disciples with privilege, but gave them something which was real only as it was shared and given away.[23] They were not to seek a high place in the kingdom of God for themselves, but to receive a child, thus breaking through the aversion and distaste of their indifference, their haughty importance, their disdain for "women's work" and their concern for their own comfort and projects. Only so could they receive Jesus and enter the kingdom of God.[24]

Receiving as the nub of mission

Jesus chose disciples so that he could send them out to proclaim the kingdom of God (Matthew chapter 10). In this mission reception has a crucial function.

Mission is commonly seen as what missionaries and mission agencies do or offer to people. It aims to provide whatever it is judged they need: food or medicine or conversion or church planting or social transformation. The missionaries, individuals or agencies or Church, are in control, as givers. They supply what others receive. They are the already converted and saved going to those who need to be converted and saved. It is not like that in Matthew chapter 10. The messengers sign the nearness of the kingdom of God by doing what they can to help, by healing and casting out demons. But such acts of powerful supply are not the goal or nub of the mission.

The key is not what they can do as agents of power but what they are and represent. They are sent (Matthew 10:16) as "sheep in the midst of wolves." Somehow they have to be faithful to the sender (simple as doves) and yet negotiate their way amongst the wolves (wise as serpents). They do not wish to be savaged; producing heroic martyrs is not the goal of this mission; rather the aim is to go on till the Son of Man comes (Matthew 10:23). The mission is not shaped by a holy death wish. The messengers look to be received rather than rejected, and in the most homely of ways, being received into people's homes and bringing peace to their houses. If they are not received they move on. Since the messengers represent the kingdom of God, receiving them is the way of welcoming the kingdom of God.

The kingdom of God does not come imperiously demanding acceptance. The missionary is not like a billeting officer requisitioning houses: the kingdom is rather represented by messengers who can easily be refused. So to welcome and receive them requires some generosity in those who receive. And perhaps more than that: it calls for some imaginative faith and hope that will see and go for the chance that these little weak messengers represent a possibility greater than themselves.

Active reception is thus full of meaning in itself. By welcoming the bringer of the invitation, the receiver earths the kingdom of God in his home. Being received is a characteristic mark of the kingdom of God. The missionary-sheep presents those he meets with an opportunity to decide not to be wolf-like: they can give hospitality to the messenger, welcoming someone who needs shelter and food and friendship. If the opportunity is taken, then the one who receives the message participates in the kingdom of God, not as a consumer of some particular good but as an active giver. The poor missionary is given shelter in the night and so peace comes to that house. Together, the giver and receiver actualise human being according to the image of God and God's way of doing things.

The saving content of this mission is not defined sufficiently by orthodox teaching or the provision of a rightly ordered church. It is carried by the missionary who comes like Jesus, having "nowhere to lay his head." Jesus needed to be welcomed. He was and is still significantly dependent on reception. When the disciples get on with their mission, as humble sheep among wolves, rather than as people with the leisure and stupidity to contend for greatness, they are cast upon the reception they might get from others. Because they come in the name of Jesus, those who receive them receive Jesus – and with him, the One who sent him. Thus the king of the kingdom of God is received when these "little ones" are received. The messengers may, on many measures, be big, competent, impressive people; but in the mission, sent by Jesus, they humble themselves and get into positions where they are little, like children. So there is a chain of receivings. This chain is a way into the core life and reality of the kingdom of God – the fellowship of persons in communion.[25]

To be received is a natural necessity for the child. Reception is visible and easily understood when the child is in the midst. This child – like a baby left at a railway station in a handbag – asks for reception by virtue of nothing but its being there.[26] Such a child may in a true and fundamental sense be a minister and missionary of the kingdom of God. The child is so only as one who calls for reception in weakness. Children should not be abused and misled by being asked to become preachers prematurely or to fulfil some adult function. Doing that closes down the open possibility of the child by confining them to an observed and limited adult model. The church should leave such exploitation of the child's malleability to evil people like those who force children to become child soldiers. The child should not be infected by the ambition and anxiety of the platform performer before they have come to understand the questionableness of public religion.[27]

By contrast with the adult, the child serves the kingdom of God as a human being who is exempted from these games, is not liable for call-up to them, and is not equipped for them. Church work, for all its vulnerability to misrepresenting Christ and the gospel, has potential to serve the kingdom of God and is constantly called to the task by the forgiving persistence of God. But it is well when those who are called to church ministries, together with the adult church which calls them, live in the genuine ironic humility of being no more than earthen vessels.[28]

This is a spiritual discipline too little known by successful Christian leaders and preachers. If they have a sense of it in their secret hearts, they are rarely able to embody and share it in the community.[29] But the child, left to himself, is outside this game, and is rarely publicly impressive. A few children have precocious gifts in some specific areas, like music and mathematics, but most children are not like that at all; and no child has the experience, words and wisdom to lead and teach. So it is not in these ways that the child can be an active servant and representative of the kingdom of God.

Simply as placed by Jesus, a child signed the kingdom of God. Nothing was asked of him. He did not speak, teach, or work. This child was not distorted by being made to grow up prematurely. He is allowed to be a child. That means the child may come and go.

Embrace is not imprisonment. At the end of a true embrace, the arms open to release the embraced one, showing respect for his own life and identity.[30] The child is not to be used, or put to work, or flattered and built up with premature public functions. The child is received not because of his capacity or his potential, but simply as child.

In the late twentieth and early twenty-first centuries it has become common to think and speak of children as "social actors" or "social agents". And some in the church have taken this to heart: seeing children as having the potential to be agents and even leaders in world-transforming mission, they seek to mobilise them for the kingdom of God in the world. Such children are at risk of being instrumentalised. There is in our view no way that this understanding can be remotely derived from Matthew 18.

The child signs the kingdom of God by being there as a personal, embodied, present, practical invitation to others to receive her. Because the invitation is embodied in the child, reception must be led and shaped by the child. Reception needs to do justice to the child. And what is that? We remind ourselves of the child's natural foundational need to be received. For example if a child is hungry, feeding him does justice to his condition. But the child is more than hungry. The child has variegated potential which cannot be fully measured and catalogued. The child has a whole life to live: how is justice to be done to all that is hoped for, sketched and repeatedly revised, but never nailed down in the life of the growing child?

Receiving the child thus implies a commitment to do justice to a claim which is not fully known. Since the commitment is open-ended, it must be an act of faith and a promise of love, which "hopes all things."[31] Indefinability is not peculiar to the child; it is characteristic of all human beings. It is necessary to respect the mystery if justice is to be done. But the practice of reception always tends towards definition. Welcoming a child requires the provision of specific limited opportunities. When the child enters into what is offered, she is formed in one way or another. It is the right of every child to have a name.[32] A name does not define or describe its bearer, but is a way of marking and respecting the individuality of the child, in his own self-awareness and in the eyes of others. To be without a name is to be in danger rather than to be free. A child has to accept and work with a given name: the undefined mystery is carried and developed within the limits of a name. The name both enables and endangers the child's being. Reception must in practice achieve two goals in one action: enabling and not endangering. All nurture, education and care is ambiguous; trying to keep children safe, it may rob them of adventure.

This is not a theoretical dilemma; it rather helps to explain why parents often feel that whatever they do is wrong. There is no escape from the problem by dispensing with the social concept of reception on the grounds that a child belongs to himself. That is a partial truth, rightly reminding parents, predators and society at large that, in receiving the child, the temptation to possess and shape must be curbed. Anxiety and ambition make for domination so that justice is not done to the child. But seeing a child – or any person – one-sidedly as belonging only to himself also fails to do justice to his sociality, his being for and with others. For "belonging to myself" is called into question by the gospel: the kingdom of God means that all things truly belong to God, with whom alone the mystery of persons is safe.[33]

In his life on earth and in his present risenness, Jesus comes like his disciples, sheep among wolves, looking to be received in a friendly, respectful way – looking to have justice. When Jesus is represented by his disciples, they do not become great ambassadors and mighty soldiers, able to impose themselves on people by the power they have from God. Jesus does not lift them out of their vulnerability and dependence on finding reception. Rather Jesus is hidden in the weakness of his representatives. And they represent him truthfully when they share his weakness and ordinariness. When they are received, he is received – as the parable in Matthew 25 makes so clear. What human beings, including Jesus, are is largely hidden from sight. It is only discerned by an act of faith, love and hope which goes beyond appearances and which sees and affirms value where it is hard to credit.

This prophetic vision is often both hidden and realised in the act of receiving the poor, or the hungry, or the child. Those who were counted sheep in the parable did not see that they were confronted by the Son of Man, and thus were given opportunity to receive him in a fitting way. It was at the last day, when the Son of Man comes to judgment, and all is revealed, that they come to know. What they did which was good, generous and appropriate had more value and meaning than they knew at the time. By this parable, Jesus tells us what the sheep and goats in the parable did not know: that the Son of Man presents himself to us in human beings who need help and are easily overlooked and treated as unimportant. By placing a child in our midst, Jesus gave the same message. None of us will be able to say when the final judgment comes, "Lord, when did we see you and did not help you?" For we have been told that receiving a child in his name is to receive him and the One who sent him.

So we are called to be welcoming, receiving people without respect of persons (James 2:1-9). All this is rooted in the simplicities of the command to love. So Hebrews 13:1-3 puts it: "Let brotherly love continue. Do not neglect to show hospitality, for thereby some have entertained angels unawares. Remember those who are in prison, as though in prison with them; and those who are ill-treated, since you also are in the body ... ."

Thus there is a constant fluid interaction between the ordinary receptions of child, as they are practised in everyday living, out of parental instinct and social habit and apparent human necessity and, on the other side, the perception and as yet merely incipient experience of receiving Jesus and the Father in the act of receiving whoever presents themselves to us. In responding to the needs of people for basic ordinary reception we come into line with Jesus and, receiving him, we receive the one who sent him.

Reception is an event of grace and welcome to vulnerable strangers, whose coming tests our openness to the strange gift of God. Faith and the refusal of faith in God is enacted in the reception and rejection of people and the earth.

The spiritual mystery of receiving Jesus and the One who sent him is largely invisible and beyond our grasp. We glimpse it occasionally; we sense it fragmentarily; we may long for it and seek it, but are left asking the question put neatly in the ancient hymn:

> *But what to those who find? Ah this,*
> *Nor tongue nor pen can show:*
> *The love of Jesus what it is,*
> *None but his loved ones know.*[34]

We can be taken up with the quest for spiritual communion with what is hardly visible. Seeking out places where the veil between this world and the other is thin can become our life, as we strive to get free of the triviality of the world and ourselves. Mary sits at the feet of Jesus and leaves Martha to be overburdened with many things to do. We can heed – or misunderstand? – Paul's direction to "seek those things that are above, where Christ is ... setting our hearts on things above not on things on the earth. For ... your life is hid with Christ in God." (Colossians 3:1-3).

There is a kind of spiritual quest which makes the child in the midst a burden and distraction, a thing on earth which imprisons us in mundanity and holds us back from the life hidden with Christ. The first disciples did not suffer much from this spirituality, for they looked for greatness in the kingdom of God as the conquering power on earth. So they ignored the child as little and weak. But for many Christians today it is different. While our ambitions are often as self-concerned as those of the first disciples, we know the kingdom of God is spiritual and we aim to realise ourselves spiritually. Then, Jesus asks us, as he asked the disciples: "What are you worrying about? What are you after?" Respond to the kingdom of God at the point where it is earthed. Jesus, the incarnate Word, challenges our spirituality by placing a child in the midst to be received.

We are intelligent and we can see where that will lead. Or maybe we do not use our intelligence, but we soon find out.

Receiving the child keeps us busy and wears us out. We do not have time to pray. The spirit no longer soars above the world.[35] We no longer enjoy praying as an adventure of our spirit rising up to explore and enjoy God, for that depends on leisure which the child interrupts. What can be done? Here is an example of a real attempt to respond to the issue in a practical pastoral way:

> A group of Christians, men and women, talk about their prayer life. A young mother recalls how close she felt to God, and how much she put into prayer in earlier years, when she was single and ardently Christian. Now, she says, my prayer life has taken a nose-dive: "I hardly pray at all. Two young children occupy me all day and in the evening I just go to sleep." She feels bad and would like to get back to how it was, because as a Christian, she should have a good prayer life, visible and convincing to herself. With such a devotional life, she would live with the feeling that she was close to God and God to her. But, notwithstanding this loss, she believes it was right to get married and to have children. Yet she goes on bemoaning her loss as though she has never heard the words of Jesus: Whoever receives a child in my Name, receives me, and whoever receives me receives the One who sent me. This word says: You are close to God, God is close to you, though you may not feel it.
>
> If she is to see this, she needs first, the concept, the text, to enable her to name and appreciate what is being given to her in her children, and secondly, the grace and strength to go on receiving the children, day by day, which is not without parallels to the way of the cross. It certainly involves saying No to the self that built itself up in the days of single freedom. It calls for faith in the darkness when it is not obvious that God is near. Churches had not put her on to this way of looking at God and Christ, prayer and children and herself. Many others like her are left without help by the church. Her experience is so common and so overwhelming

that the words of Jesus may seem to be a promise too frail to counteract the spiritual numbing she is going through. But there may be tough grace, tough promise here.

It was a mother who raised the question and got the answer. But it is not just for mothers. Fathers may find it harder to face the question and to accept the answer but they too need it. So do all who work with children and all who have responsibility for children – which means all of us, including those who find important excuses to say children are not their business.[36]

Now, as we come to the end of what we are determined will be the final revision of this chapter, a voice asks whether the note of joy has been absent, or at least too pianissimo, from start to finish. Reception is joyous. When the wayward son came home, the Father made a feast so noisy that the working son heard it in the field. "It is fitting to make merry and be glad ... for your brother was lost and is found." "There is joy in heaven over one sinner who turns." "When a woman is in travail she has sorrow, because her hour has come; but when she is delivered of the child, she no longer remembers her anguish, for joy that a human being is born into the world. So you have sorrow now, but I will see you again and your hearts will rejoice, and no one will be able to take your joy from you." 1 John begins by celebrating the multiple receptions that make up the substance of the one fellowship of Father and Son, of proclaimer and hearers, so that "joy may be complete."[37]

NOTES

1 Mark 10:15, Luke 18:17; cf Matthew 19:13-15.
2 Bonhoeffer, Letter 21 July 1944; H.Willmer, "Otto Dibelius and Dietrich Bonhoeffer" in *Studies in Church History*, volume 15, 1978, p. 447.
3 A limited example of how this may happen, even in reading Matthew 18, is found in all the interpretations which say the child here is a metaphor for disciples who are the real little ones. Thus the text is read in a way that builds up the self-importance of the disciples and encloses them in themselves, rather than opening them out towards the kingdom of God through their receiving the child and thus coming closer to the "Man for Others".
4 William Wordsworth, *Intimations of Immortality from Recollections of Early Childhood*

5   John Saward, *The Way of the Lamb: The Spirit of Childhood and the End of the Age*, 1999

6   *Chitty Chitty Bang Bang* shows how the adult usurpation of the child is horribly corrupting for adults and nightmarishly cruel to children. Baron Bomburst, ruler of Vulgaria, has all the toys for himself and his silly court and employs the Child Catcher to clear all the children out of the way.

7   These are popular ways of finding meaning in "becoming as the children." There is something to be said for them. Making peace with the child within sometimes has therapeutic value. But, especially within our individualistic cultures, they all lack defences against becoming self-centred and being taken up with individual self-development or self-fulfilment. Again, those quests are not without value, but in themselves, they are not enough.

8   Keith J. White, *The Growth of Love*, 2008

9   Anne Richards and Peter Privett (ed.), *Through the Eyes of a Child*, 2009

10 K.J. White, *The Growth of Love*, p. 148

11 Shakespeare is not infallible holy writ, but he incites and enables thinking about being human, by giving us language, like:

> All the world's a stage,
> And all the men and women merely players:
> They have their exits and their entrances;
> And one man in his time plays many parts,
> His acts being seven ages. At first the infant,
> Mewling and puking in the nurse's arms.
> And then the whining school-boy, with his satchel
> And shining morning face, creeping like snail
> Unwillingly to school. And then the lover,
> Sighing like furnace, with a woeful ballad
> Made to his mistress' eyebrow. Then a soldier,
> Full of strange oaths and bearded like the pard,
> Jealous in honour, sudden and quick in quarrel,
> Seeking the bubble reputation
> Even in the cannon's mouth. And then the justice,
> In fair round belly with good capon lined,
> With eyes severe and beard of formal cut,
> Full of wise saws and modern instances;
> And so he plays his part. The sixth age shifts
> Into the lean and slipper'd pantaloon,
> With spectacles on nose and pouch on side,
> His youthful hose, well saved, a world too wide
> For his shrunk shank; and his big manly voice,
> Turning again toward childish treble, pipes
> And whistles in his sound. Last scene of all,
> That ends this strange eventful history,
> Is second childishness and mere oblivion,
> Sans teeth, sans eyes, sans taste, sans everything.

As You Like It, Act 2, scene 7

12 Alice Minnie Herts Heniger, *The Kingdom of the Child*, 1918

13 Admitted, the suggestion that the child lives life while the adult plays is not easy to accept, especially when it is made as crudely as it is here. It cannot be adequately explored and tested here, but it is left as a provocation. It is not to be rejected out of hand: the convention that children play and adults don't,

does not deserve its almost universal acceptance. When this alleged difference serves to explain why children naturally know the secret of good living, but adults have lost it, the problem is compounded.

14 Matthew 6:12-15; 18:18-35

15 Luke 17:21

16 Or, it is wisely said, it takes a whole local church to raise a child: http://www.christianitytoday.com/women/2013/march/it-takes-church-to-raise-child.html?utm_source=ctdirect-html&utm_medium=Newsletter&utm_term= 9465739&utm_content=161010890&utm_campaign=2013. For the original saying, an Igbo and Yoruba proverb, see http://www.afriprov.org/index.php/african-proverb-of-the-month/23-1998proverbs/137-november-1998-proverb.html

17 Keith J. White, *The Growth of Love*, chapter 10

18 The truth and beauty of George Herbert's poem, *Love bade me welcome …* is not to be denied, but its ending – "You must sit down and taste my meat: So I did sit and eat" – is not all there is to the earthing of God's reception.

19 In this book we avoid the common practice of shortening "the kingdom of God" to "the kingdom". Many who do that mean no harm; they want to pursue "kingdom values" rather than privatised self-concern and escapist pietism. But the kingdom of God is not to be distilled into "values" which can be known and pursued without finding and knowing the King. To say persistently "the kingdom of God" or "God's rule" reminds us of an essential but contested truth.

20 Matthew 26:6-13; Luke 7:36-50 is a similar story which explores the reciprocities and refusals of reception more extensively.

21 J.G. Whittier

22 While a genuine welcome, like real friendship, cannot be bought, money can purchase *ersatz* approximations, as Michael Sandel argues in *What Money Can't Buy: The Moral Limits to Markets*, 2012, pp. 93-94

23 Matthew 14:16; Mark 6:37: "You give them something to eat."

24 Matthew 25:31-45

25 Stanley James Grenz, *Theology for the Community of God*, 1994, p. 305; Damon So, *The Forgotten Jesus and the Trinity You Never Knew*, 2010

26 Oscar Wilde, *The Importance of Being Earnest*: Lady Bracknell's unwelcoming refusal to receive the poor orphan Jack Worthing who had lost his parents and was found as an abandoned baby "in a handbag!"

27 *The Cape Town Commitment*, 2011, p. 55: "We are faced with many people in leadership who have scarcely been discipled … the scale of un-Christ-like and worldly leadership in the global Church today is glaring … the answer is not just more leadership training but better discipleship training. Leaders must first be disciples of Christ himself."

28 2 Corinthians 4:5-7.

29 Paul did not like the fact that his presence was so weak; he struggled to accept that this weakness was the way in which the strength of Christ could be in him; but all the time, the churches he was called to care for made it harder to be honest, since they had an insatiable and corrupting appetite for impressive leaders. 2 Corinthians 10:10;12:9; 1 Corinthians 3:4

30 Miroslav Volf, *Exclusion and Embrace*, 1996, p. 145

31 1 Corinthians 13:7

32 *Convention on the Rights of the Child*, article 7

33 At this point, we differ from Martin E Marty, who contrasts the child's self-possessing freedom with "control" and so does not spell out any kind of "lordship"

which might share freedom, being and dignity, rather than limiting it..

34 From Bernard of Clairvaux, *Jesus the very thought of Thee.*

35 Francis Thompson, *In No Strange Land*:

THE KINGDOM OF GOD IS WITHIN YOU

O world invisible, we view thee,
    O world intangible, we touch thee,
    O world unknowable, we know thee,
    Inapprehensible, we clutch thee!

Does the fish soar to find the ocean,
    The eagle plunge to find the air –
That we ask of the stars in motion
    If they have rumor of thee there?

Not where the wheeling systems darken,
    And our benumbed conceiving soars! –
The drift of pinions, would we hearken,
    Beats at our own clay-shuttered doors.

The angels keep their ancient places –
    Turn but a stone and start a wing!
'Tis ye, 'tis your estrangèd faces,
    That miss the many-splendored thing.

But (when so sad thou canst not sadder)
    Cry – and upon thy so sore loss
Shall shine the traffic of Jacob's ladder
    Pitched betwixt Heaven and Charing Cross.

Yea, in the night, my Soul, my daughter,
    Cry – clinging to Heaven by the hems;
And lo, Christ walking on the water,
    Not of Genesareth, but Thames!

36 John Collier, *Toddling to the Kingdom*, 2009, p. 250

37 Luke 15:7,32; John 16:21,22; 1 John 1:1-5.
We may also have underplayed the transforming redeeming effect that
receiving a little one may have on the receiver. Elizabeth Hassen from Ethiopia,
during a course on Child Theology in Manila, called attention to a story about
street girls in Romania. Their hearts were hardened and bitter because of the
neglect and abuse they suffered. Then they had babies.
    "... The small children changed the girl's attitudes: now, their main
concerns were for these little ones. Every day, they dressed the babies up
so nicely and brought them to me to admire. ... Today Fatima dressed
Carol in a pretty pink dress and adorable pink hat and brought here to
me; both had wonderful smiles ... These girls, having lost trust with ill-
meaning and exploitive adults, have difficulty accepting our love.
Similarly, they have difficulty accepting God as one who loves them. Yet
they trust these helpless, defenseless babies to give and receive love. In
reality, God is melting their hearts by pouring out his love through these
infants. These little babies are teaching the girls how to love and live again,
being able to not only give but also receive love."
Sue Bates in Phyllis Kilbourn (ed.), *Shaping the Future*, 2008, p. 113

Chapter 7

Father

"See that you do not look down on one of these little ones ..."
MATTHEW 18:10

Two verses on child abuse

WELCOMING CHILDREN IS RIGHT and proper. Reception seems natural, as though it should go without saying. But in reality it often does not happen: children worldwide are rejected, neglected, abused; on a huge scale, and in myriad saddening ways, they are not respected. These negative reactions and responses to children are denounced as "unnatural" and in one sense they are; but they are unhappily common. They are rooted in human being. "Nature" is ambiguous. It is not a reliable guide to what is good. Rejecting children is a violation of the norms and ideals of humanity; but it is not outside the range of what human beings can imagine, enact and even find value in. Inhumanity is human – not demonic or bestial. Receiving children is significant partly because children are so often and so easily rejected, marginalised and despised. This is why we need to be told to receive the children: sadly it does not "go without saying". Matthew 18 takes account of this ambiguity, moving directly from the sunlight of receiving a child, and with him, receiving God in Christ, into the dark night brought on when a child is rejected.

Two verses in the passage we are studying, 6 and 10, speak about rejection. We will give most attention to the latter of these: Matthew 18:10: "See that you do not despise one of these little ones, for I tell you that in heaven their angels always behold the face of my Father who is in heaven." Within the parameters set by these words we read the better-known, oft-quoted verse 6: "Whoever causes one of these little ones who believes in me to stumble, it would be better for him to have a great millstone fastened round his neck and to be drowned in the depth of the sea".

The saying in verse six is frequently taken out of context, narrowed and misread, so that it becomes a warrant for unbounded punitive anger against those who abuse children in extreme and criminal ways.[1] Its violently coloured words are used to express the feelings (simultaneously justified, pharisaical and frustrated) of good people against such offenders. It is questionable, however, whether Jesus was targeting a group such as the now commonly demonised paedophiles. The saying is addressed, as is the whole discourse, to disciples in general. The word "whoever" calls everyone to self-examination, for there are many ways to cause a little one to stumble in the life of faith.

We take Matthew 18:10 as the overall framework of our discussion because it is not focused punitively *against* the evildoer, but rather speaks *for* the little one, by bearing strange witness to God as the defender and resource of the little one. It keeps the child in the spotlight, rather than targeting those who might offend or abuse the child. What's more, it does not stir us to moralism and social fear as verse six does. One of the risks of such fear is that in our (possibly) righteous anger against abusers, God is crowded out. God is not mentioned in this verse. By contrast, verse ten leads us to wrestle with theology where it is most needed and at the same time most questionable. It makes us think about who and where we are as human beings, and who and where God is in the struggle of life. Its plain moral message, "Do not despise one of these little ones" is embedded inextricably in theological mystery. Perhaps this text is rarely quoted because its invitation to theology is judged either unnecessary or too difficult. We admit to thinking long and hard before daring to venture into this challenging territory in the final chapter of our essay.

Jesus opposed despising little ones by placing a child in the midst

Jesus did not despise a child, a little one. To see a child as a sign of the way into the kingdom of God is the opposite of despising. The warning not to despise even one little one is implied by Jesus' action of placing a child in the midst of the disciples.

Disciples are not in a position (is anybody?) to say they do not need this warning. In their anxious competition for greatness, they left no space to consider the child. He was marginal to the point of being irrelevant, if not invisible, to them. Their mindset excluded the child, counting him as nothing.[2] Jesus therefore surprised them by placing the child in the midst and inviting them to receive him. It was a new idea to them that a child could be a sign of the kingdom of God. And since this is how the disciples thought and acted, to place a child in their midst was to put the child at risk of being despised. We know little about these disciples, but we can imagine that they would not bully or rough up a child in their midst: they were not intentional or overt abusers. It is perhaps more likely they would simply overlook or ignore her, because they were great and she was small. The professional word for this currently is "neglect" as distinct from "abuse", but the word that Jesus uses is "despise". They may not have been abusers, but they could still be despisers. As such, they could not be sure of entering the kingdom of God. The child put them to the test: were they out of touch with their master, not on his wavelength?

Matthew 18:6

Let us then read verse six as spoken to anyone who will hear Jesus with respect, rather than addressed to those child-abusers whose specific offences bring them to the notice of the necessary but limited criminal law. The text is spiritual direction to us all who, with our relative power and our restricted sensitivity, might cause little ones to stumble. Just as the child is placed in our midst to point us to the kingdom of heaven, so now we are warned, not so much about hell in a traditional guise, as about the moral and spiritual consequences of causing a little one to stumble.

"It would be better for him ...." So we are asked to imagine the unbearable: having a life which is worse than a terrible death; being alive without the tiniest thing to make life worth living. This saying is not to be reduced merely to the threat of future punishment, although that is not excluded. Its point is not to engage us in imagining a future that lies beyond our experience and knowledge. What it does is frightening enough: it calls us to face up to what is true in the present for the despiser. Those who cause others to stumble – quite concretely, for example, placing a stone in the path of a blind person[3] – may think they get away with it, because no one sees or calls them to account. But judgment is already enacted in their own being, in what they are making of themselves. By causing a little one to stumble, they have stumbled in the living of their own life, so that it would be better for them if they were dead and decisively disabled, powerless to do more harm. In causing a little one to stumble on the path of life, the perpetrators put themselves against life, out of life, even while they live.[4]

It is not easy for decent people to be open to these words, as though they speak to everyone as human beings. Rather we hear them as though they are reserved for a select group of other people. It is understandable that people shield themselves from seeing how close evil is in human life and how deep and terrible it is when it invades and destroys ordinary human beings and relations.

We shy away from the visions of humanity that might be

suggested by this text. Our preferred world is a refuge from extremes of highs and lows which disrupt our managed, manageable living.[5] We instinctively prefer the quiet and relatively untroubled idea of the "middle earth" of the Hobbits. Unsurprisingly, when Jesus told the disciples he was going to be rejected and crucified,[6] Peter protested: "God forbid! Far be it from you, Lord." Peter refuses to entertain any thought that the one he was following might lead him into shame, defeat and death. But all talk of the kingdom of God and of the way of Jesus through death and resurrection confronts us with an invitation to move into unknown and unmanageable territory. It is a stumbling block on the way that we find no easier than did Peter. In cautious self-protection, we cry out, "God forbid, Lord, far be it from us." In hearing the gospel, if nowhere else, we are shown to be essentially little ones, however big we may be in girth, purse, mind or status.

Many of us lack the courage and imagination to face life outside the project of modern technological management and individualism aided by hedonistic therapeutic self-care. Often our Christianity confirms this restricted way of being, rather than calling us beyond it. It is tailored to make us feel at home with ourselves and in the world: it is our "comfort zone". It may contain elements of protest and longing, but they are often no more than wistfulness, which make no difference to the world or our lives. We know cheap grace is unacceptable because Bonhoeffer said so;[7] but we mostly live in it, under other guises. Cheap grace lets us accommodate uncritically to the ways of the world, rather than pressing upon us the invitation to follow Jesus into God's new world.

Even within the limits of the comforts we shape and guard for ourselves, life is vulnerable to disturbance. Our world can be broken up by a death, some loss, a new person, the intrusion of an old memory, or an unexpected call. Not only undesirable threats of destruction disturb, but good things, like beauty, joy, the sublime, surprise us.[8] The Bible is treasured as a bulwark of social and personal security and comfort, but it is a dangerous text: we can never predict when and how it will bring us into a strange New World.[9]

When this happens, language will mark where the earthquake is breaking as words crack under the strain. That is how it is with theology, speaking of God. We may say, "God", but if we are not shaken by standing in the presence of the holy, are we getting near to speaking truthfully "of God"?[10]

Matthew 18:10

This verse begins with the instruction not to despise little ones. This is a broader and cooler concept than "causing them to stumble": not as concrete and colourful, but no less searching. Despising starts in the heart and mind. It thinks down and against its object, as the Greek *kataphroneo* suggests. It comes to expression in words and actions; it is the driver and the meaning of abuse. It has power to make victims feel they are little or nothing in the eyes of the despiser. Despising assaults the self-esteem and erodes the inner being of the little one. Its evil climaxes when the will and spirit of the victim is brought under the control of the despiser, and despises and degrades herself.[11]

Undervaluing little ones is the first step in taking advantage of their vulnerability and relative weakness. Undervaluing and not noticing them may come from carelessness and idle indifference and insensitivity.[12] Then they are not respected enough to be cared for appropriately. But despising goes far beyond neglect. Sometimes, the despiser laughs at other people's stumbles and then takes pride in his perverse sense of humour. The bully may be a weak little one posing as someone of substance, who finds an even smaller one to be his victim and compensation. A lot of despising falls within the ambit of the prayer: "Father, forgive them, they don't know what they are doing, even though they should."

But some do know. The clever ruthless man, confident in his impunity, grooms young people into being sexually exploited, causing them to stumble from one bad experience to another, extending even to irreparable destruction as persons.[13] The despising is audible in his derogatory vocabulary – his victims are mere "flesh" and "trash". Cynically he turns the word "love" into an instrument of deception and entrapment. To use words so that their beauty, promise and precision are jeopardised is a basic form of despising: it poisons the ground water of human life. Despising people goes along with the perversion of language.[14]

With language perverted, despising can appear to be an acceptable way of seeing life. Sometimes, the despising cloaks itself in what is held to be necessary or normal. It becomes invisible.[15] Despising is not confined to obviously despicable people. A veneer of caring may disguise despising. Paternalism runs the risk of putting people down because it builds its own status and role on the dependence of those who need to be looked after. If it sees nothing more than this dependence, it may fall into despising. Was the Grand Inquisitor a despiser?[16] He cared for people by refusing to risk letting them live in the freedom Christ brought and represented. Thus he diminished them. So, teachers, managers, social workers, parents, pastors and politicians can be despisers. They are not saved by having the best of motives. The warning against despising was given to disciples who were close to Jesus: it is a message for all of us.

Despising is doubly evil because it rates others under their true worth and leads the despiser to over-value himself. Damaging both parties, it makes for an utterly rotten relationship, in which is no truth or hope or friendship. No one is so little as to be looked down on, since Christ died for them.[17] No excellence qualifies anyone to be a despiser, since God the high and holy one dwells only with the humble.[18]

Despising: personal, supra-personal and impersonal

The prime *locus* of despising is in interpersonal relationships between persons and groups. Human life and relations teach us what despising is.[19] Despising takes myriad forms, and life is shot through every day with despising and being despised, as people are tempted to it, suffer it, retaliate and strive to rise above it.

Despising is possible in the world because creatures are limited, vulnerable, insecure and varied. Where there is difference, comparison and competition is inevitable and it can be invidious. Rankings, league tables and hierarchies are useful for some purposes, but they open the door to despising.

Although primarily interpersonal, despising also appears in non-personal forms. The language of despising has a metaphorical capacity to illumine human experience in all its dimensions and contexts, including the non-human and inanimate.

Collisions, losses and put-downs are not always the work of intentional agents; sometimes no human agency can be held responsible for these hurts. Sometimes circumstances are like walls, standing around us, hemming us in. They are blank, faceless, without voices, with no evidence of mind. But they impress our littleness upon us and that is akin to being despised, both as a depressing experience and as a challenge to respond. As the walls close in they "say" to us that we do not count, that all our hopes and values come to nothing and that our self-esteem is futile pretence. They induce a sense of humiliation, unfairness and disempowerment. The poverty in which millions live gives the message, "You don't matter."[20]

Consider death as a despiser. It comes to most people as a natural event in the ordinary course of life and without the action of a human despiser, like a killer or a negligent carer. That I cannot escape death is thus no cause for complaint or grievance against any personal agent. Yet facing death is, for some, at the very least like being despised. It is not only in the Bible that death is seen as the last enemy, provoking fear and complaint.[21] Death brings life to an end. It often appears to crown and confirm the shortfall and unfairness of life, taking away its joy and beauty. It seems to scrap beings, as though on to the rubbish heap; we go through indignity into nothingness. To be brought to nothing – is that not central to the robbery, hurt and injustice felt by anyone who is despised? There is a hostile power at work which has no respect for the worth of beings. Death is the symbol of the despising facing our creaturely vulnerability. By death, we are despised.

To see an active despiser in the natural event of death is admittedly symbolic: a form of personification. But such ways have value for facing realities we must somehow live with. The mythological should not be overplayed, but it is well-grounded in life-experience, and not to be despised.[22]

Seeing death as a despiser goes along with recognising that the physical environment on earth is not a consistently friendly habitat for humanity.[23] Much of it is hostile to human being. The world is ordered and driven by impersonal structures and processes, at least some of them palpably hostile. It is not surprising that some see human being as but the plaything of higher powers, lacking reliability, love or respect.[24] Any theological attempt to ignore the dark side of experience in the world, on the ground that a loving God is wholly in control of all events global and local, leads us into unreality and incompetence for living. There are various plausible interpretations of our human experience. One that cannot be dismissed without consideration is that we are beset by layers of despising eating back into the foundations of value and meaning. To know and believe God in Christ is to make a stand against this manifold despising. It cannot, however, be resisted by refusing to think about it.[25]

In the Bible and Christian faith traditions there are mythologies and meditations coming out of the experience of people who wrestle with multi-dimensional despising. Through the Psalms we meet people who are surrounded by enemies mocking and wishing them ill. These oppressors engineer death, taking pleasure in bringing their despising to success in the destruction of their victims. The world itself still provokes lament, as in this poem:

TSUNAMI THEOLOGY

God together swept out by the wave
No habitation left to stand upon the earth
Sea swallows without comment

smooths memory all away
The children fathers mothers are not

Once little ones quite nothing now
waved away, Tsunami despised
Died with no arms about them
No eyes upon them

And the children who live still?
How can we be children without father, mother?
Rolled still by the wave, trafficked by the sea,
Let down by tectonic fall

Despised by unhomely earth
Busy with its own story [26]

Don't despise

Despising has to be taken seriously if Matthew's text, and indeed the Bible and Christian faith, are not to be reduced to pious evasion. It is necessary to register despising as a terrible reality, causing us to stumble on the path into the kingdom of God. Perhaps others have better examples or analyses to give, but we are indicating a way of reckoning with the terrible nature of despising in its many forms. However, this Gospel text does not explore despising as we have been doing. Rather it simply contradicts and forbids the practice of it. And in so doing it takes us into even more mysterious territory.

Matthew 18:10 starts with a simple warning: "Take care that you don't despise one of these little ones who believe in me." And then it concentrates on how despising is opposed, overcome and put aside by God's affirmation. The reason for not despising little ones is explicitly and disturbingly theological: "The angels of the despised little ones always behold the face of my Father in heaven." In contrast with Matthew 18:6, attention is not focused on the offender and his punishment, but rather on the distress and the hope of the despised one. It approaches despising from within the situation of the despised, rather than the guilt and danger of the despiser.

Being despised is more than being ill-treated by others: it means being brought to a weak loneliness, where one struggles for life. Faith, hope and joy, the stuff of a good life and good relationships, are all lost. Essential worth is undermined; life is cut off. Being despised goes deep into the person, and from there reflects back a darkness which empties the world, life and God of relevance and presence. The final hope of the despised is that God is there for them,[27] but the deep distress of the despised is that the capacity to hold on to that hope is taken away. It seems that God is not there for them; or that God can or will do nothing for them. The rejection of the child, the despising of little ones, is a theological matter not just because Jesus forbids it, but because God, along with the little ones, appears to be overwhelmed by the despising. Thus we come to the question at the foundation of Christian faith and life: what is the reality of God? What is God doing to make and keep human life human?[28]

This is why this verse gives more trouble than verse six: it is easier to pursue the abuser than to protect, comfort and restore the despised. Seeing the abuser is easier than seeing God. It is not in punishing the offender, but in the long journey of the despised towards light and healing, that theology (talk of God) has the hardest work to do.

What help and hope is there for the despised in the strange theology of this text? It says they are not to be despised because, "their angels always behold the face of my [Jesus'] Father who is in heaven." Our first, and even our second, reaction might be to ask what possible practical assistance this represents. The despised and downtrodden on earth need effective affirmation. They want rescue from the power of their enemies who scorn and despise them. They want "a very present help in time of trouble." In the Bible there are stories of God's coming with saving acts of deliverance, bringing people from darkness to light. The witness of the

Bible is echoed by the community of faith, which affirms and rejoices in the great things God is doing in the earth.[29] But this text does not appear to point to the works of God on earth now. Instead we are given the angels in what could be portrayed as some kind of detached heavenly scene.

What difference does their gazing on the Father's face make? "As in heaven, so on earth" is the pattern of Christian praying, but often in practice it seems the link between the two is broken, and heaven is distant and inoperative on earth. The imagery of angels and the face of God builds in distance, waiting and uncertainty to the practice of trusting God. Even if angels behold the Father's face, what help is that to us when we are surrounded by the evil faces of our enemies?[30] Being despised by the enemy is made worse when the helper does not help "right early".[31] The despising puts distance between need and help; even a promise that it will come "some day" leaves the pain of waiting;[32] and in the waiting, doubt eats away at hope and faith.

In wrestling with this distress, it should first be admitted that the confession and celebration of *Christian* faith requires this kind of language. Faith and hope in God cannot be expressed in slick triumphalist affirmation. Language is true to God when, like Jesus, it carries distance, waiting and uncertainty within its positive confession, "clinging to heaven by the hems."[33] Language is not used here to make statements of fact from a secure standpoint above life, but rather to pray within and for life, against its loss. Jesus inducts us into this kind of language, by leading us through teasing signs and parables into the struggles of Gethsemane.

All this is hard to bear. It would be simpler to escape the tension, either by giving up looking for God or by fabricating a cocoon of spiritual peace, an upper room with doors securely closed against the frightening world. But such a half-life is not offered by God in Christ. This text speaks to faith in a positive and encouraging way, but never without distance, waiting and uncertainty. It indirectly witnesses to the vulnerability, even the weakness, of God. Its imagery reflects both God's decisive riposte against despising and

God's exposure to it in company with the despised. The language is unusual, because it avoids the brash simplicities found in conventional conflicts of faith and scepticism. Its idiom is more complex, like "I believe, help thou my unbelief," which is more than, but not incompatible with, "faith seeking understanding."

The face of my Father in heaven

Face reveals the person: it is the primary and most complex set of identity-markers.[34] Face communicates the person to others, by its smiles and frowns and other expressions. So face shapes relationships; before someone speaks, the face may tell whether the other is open or closed to us. Faces generally are (believed to be) managed by the person, so they are instruments that can deceive as well as reveal: smiles need to be interpreted and tested. Some friendly people have naturally forbidding faces, while it is possible to "smile and smile and be a villain."[35]

The faces of powerful people and of those we care about are specially important to us. For the lover, at least in romantic fiction, there is only one face that matters, and life depends on whether that face is turned towards him with a smile that can be trusted. The frown of kings, and all their modern successors, is frightening. The face of him who sits on the throne can be so terrible people ask for rocks to fall, to hide them from it (Revelation 6:16).

The Bible knows of the forbidding, hidden and averted face of God. Not to see the face of God is to be abandoned and without God's blessing (Psalm 10:10-11; 13:1). God sometimes hides his face. The righteous Job asks why God should do this (Job 13:24). For the innocent this hiding means distress and puzzlement. For the sinner it is the fair judgment of God, who both "hides his face from" (Psalm 30:7; 44:24; 102:2; 104:27-30; 143:7;Isaiah 59:2; 64:7; Jeremiah 33:5) and "sets his face against" him (Leviticus 17:10; 20:3,5; 26:17; Jeremiah 44:11; Ezekiel 14:8; 15:7).

On the other side, as in the Aaronic blessing (Numbers 6:24-26; cf. Genesis 32:20; 33:10), seeing the face of God is a sign of favour, joy and encouragement: "The Lord bless you and keep you; the Lord make his face to shine upon you and be gracious to you; the Lord lift up his countenance upon you and give you peace."

Psalm 22[36] is the cry of "a worm and no man, scorned by men and despised by the people" (Psalm 22:6-7) which becomes an exhortation to all who fear God to praise him, "for he has not despised or abhorred the affliction of the afflicted; and he has not hid his face from him, but has heard when he cried to him."

Psalm 27:7-9 outlines a three-movement drama:

> *Thou hast said, Seek ye my face.*
> *My heart says to thee,*
> *Thy face, O Lord, do I seek.*
> *Hide not thy face from me.*

First, God's invitation to seek his face symbolises the readiness of God to bless his creatures and assures us of his welcome. Then, the heart responds eagerly, with an impatient thirst for the living God (Psalm 42:1-3). Yet prayer is still made for God not to hide his face; and still, "My tears have been my food night and day while men say to me continually, Where is your God?" God's invitation is not taken for granted. The face of God is God's generosity, but it is not to be lightly assumed that it is always available. The shining of God's face is God's choice and good will, so the hiding of the face always has to be reckoned with, since respect for God implies recognizing God as the free and gracious Lord. And there are the enemies, who carry the attack forward to the inner citadel of the downcast soul, not merely threatening life, but making mockery of God in his absence.

When we come to the New Testament, we find that God's face shines in Jesus Christ, the image of the invisible God (Colossians 1:15; Hebrews 1:3; 2:9; John 1:14,18; 14:9). It is God who said, "Let light shine out of darkness," who has shone in our hearts to give the light of the knowledge of glory of God in the face of Jesus Christ (2 Corinthians 4:5-6). The face of Jesus Christ is the face of God turned towards us in a judgment which takes effect in generous re-creative justifying grace. It is for us, not against us. It is in beholding this face, in the openness and freedom of the Spirit, that we are made free and changed from glory to glory (2 Corinthians 3:17-18).

The face of God in Christ is the face of the incarnate and crucified God. So, beholding the Father's face yields no simple triumphant rest, for it incorporates us into the life of God as lived in Christ crucified. The real treasure of God is given us, but we have it in earthen vessels, says Paul (2 Corinthians 4:7), as he launches into another of his summaries of what life in Christ is like. Following Jesus, as given to Paul after the resurrection of Jesus, involved bearing the dying of Christ in his mortal body so that the life of Christ might be made manifest. In Christ, the glory of the Father is seen, as it shines upon us; but as the light of Christ the crucified, it includes, and does not immediately cancel, the distance, waiting and uncertainty we have already detected in Matthew 18:10.

Their angels behold the face of my Father in heaven

Although babies are wired to look for a human face, a symbol of the face of God,[37] the despised little one does not directly behold the face of the Father. Being despised makes for distance and blocks vision. To talk of these little ones as though they were themselves standing before the Father with seeing eyes open to his smile would be to overlook the reality of their being despised. Vulnerable to the range of despisings that beset human life, children, along with the rest of us, experience distance, waiting and uncertainty in various ways. It is not by unqualified unbroken immediacy to the face of the Father that children come to know themselves in faith and hope.[38] Even small children discover the puzzle of prayer. Often the most urgent and justifiable of prayers do not get what they ask for. Children who do not give up on God when they discover that prayer does not "work" as expected, only go on by finding ways of living with the waiting, distance and uncertainty, taking the yoke of Christ upon them and finding his rest. That is what growing in faith means.

Much contemporary Christianity pays little attention to doctrines of mediation. Christ as Mediator is rarely the subject of teaching, exploration or meditation.[39] Romantic models of how God loves encourage the attempt to live all the time in a conscious direct personal relation with God. So the mediation of God in Christ through the Holy Spirit is underplayed. The "means of grace" are neglected because they are not needed. Valuing mediation involves acknowledging distance. Without that acknowledgement, there will be no readiness to entertain angels. In their action of representing the despised little ones before the face of the faithful God, angels stand as reminders of the distance.[40] They do not remind us of the distance by making it and guarding it, so that it is a fixed gulf. These angels are not the cherubim and the flaming sword which blocked the way back to the tree of life, when Man was driven out of Eden.[41] A bridge is a mediator inviting meeting and enabling traffic. It makes a connection between one side and the other, but in a way that gives all who use it, a giddy sight of height and depth and length.[42] The chasm is still there, not filled up but bridged.

Some people look to angels, seeking and finding help. Others do not see them and have little expectation of help from them. Yet we are all pointed to them. They do not help us by doing for us what we are given to do. Having faith and hope in God, looking to the Father, praying "Our Father", is all for us to do. But angels represent us at the place where we are not, and so encourage and draw us forward in faith to what we have not yet attained.[43] The angels are there "for those who have no prayers to say, who in despair are dumb."[44]

Angels have largely been eliminated from our thinking.[45] Conventional angels, with their aeronautically impractical wings, fly only on Christmas cards. Some concepts and images of angels have become unthinkable because of changes in culture. The danger is that, with their disappearance, this text evaporates. Letting it go, however, is not the only option. We can enquire whether angels can be understood in the terms that have everyday meaning and value for us.[46] Francis Thompson insisted that "the angels keep their ancient places": they have not disappeared or given up their work. If they are missed, it is because of the way we, with our "estrangéd faces", look away and have no eyes for them. He urges us in our disenchanted and miserable situation ("when so sad thou canst not sadder") to "move a stone and start a wing."[47]

Suppose Matthew 18:10, despite all its ancient colouring, is a practical, contemporary text. If so, we should not read it as though it is pulling us back into a culture we cannot freely inhabit. It is rather an invitation to look for angels who are functionally effective in dealing with real issues in life as it is given to us now. Whatever the imagery through which we picture angels, the important point is to find and appreciate them as load-bearing "ladders" between heaven and whatever bit of earth is ours – for Jacob it was Bethel,[48] for Thompson, Charing Cross.

Looking for angelic function in human life, rather than being tied to old angelic forms alone, extends the range of what we have eyes for in the Bible as well as contemporary life. When Cain murdered his brother Abel – a definitive despising – he shrugged off any responsibility and expected God to be taken in by his cover story: "Why do you expect me to know? Am I my brother's keeper?"[49] Such a denial of responsibility implies and compounds the despising intrinsic to the act of murder. But God had his sources of information: "The voice of your brother's blood is crying to me from the ground." The blood is like the angels of Matthew 18:10, representing Abel to God. The angel-blood was part of and within, rather than above, the earthly event. For a modern detective blood is a trace left at the murder which serves as a source of information about the murderer; in the biblical story, it is the lasting echo of the cry and prayer of the murdered one.[50] The Father in heaven is not short-sighted; he sees the significance of earthly stuff and receives these angels with an open face.

Every Cain tells his story thinking that God can be tricked and the brother does not matter. But God who hears the blood crying from the earth tells back to Cain the true story that Abel can no longer tell for himself. As we hear such cries, we too can tell the story. Then we do not merely tell stories about angels: we get close to being angels ourselves. Of course in sharing in this angelic action, we must not give ourselves airs and graces; the stories angels tell are never about themselves, expressing their wants and feelings, but about despised and excluded others. They are intercessory.[51] To tell an Abel-story truly is to resist the rampant Cain-story. The practice of telling Abel-stories requires identifying with Abel against his despiser. Modelled on this primal story, our stories are outcomes of our hearing the blood crying from the ground, of our looking, listening and taking note. We do more than report what we hear; we enter into it and bear it and thus our story-telling becomes in turn angelic representation to God.

It is not only when murder is done, and blood literally is shed, that this story becomes a relevant model. There are many ways of despising others which do not kill the body, but share the killer's spirit of hate, fear, jealousy and disrespect. It is still common to trivialise events and processes of despising, moving on as though nothing seriously wrong has been done. Shake hands at the end of the match[52] and leave the weak victim to absorb the hurt quietly, letting the ground soak up the blood till it is forgotten. Thus, Cain's realm is wide and strong in its practicable dishonesties. The despised still cry in frustration, struggling to be heard and vindicated. Human communication is always ambiguous, undecided in its attitude and mixed in its effects: some media are in cahoots with Cain, but others look out for and speak up for Abel.

There are now many declarations and conventions on human rights.[53] In the light of this text, they may be seen as functional angels. They speak for the despised, challenging governments and people to "keep" all their brothers and sisters with true respect and practical generosity. Multifarious despisings are noted and rebutted by these many-articled specifications of what is due to each human being. These declarations are designed to be implemented and enforced by legal means, and serve as criteria for the use of power by governments and others. They are making real differences in the way the world is run. But their standards and aspirations are regettably very far from fully realised. They cannot be taken as descriptions of the way the world is. When one billion people lack safe drinking water, it is obvious that the right to life is not universally respected or enjoyed. Human rights declarations are statements of obligation which aspire to something better than what is achieved at present. They are the voice of complaint, like blood crying from the ground. Distance, waiting and uncertainty indwell these declarations. They are like angels standing, with hope and suffering, in the distance between how human beings are and the *Shalom* they desire and are called to.

Recently, many Christians have been trying hard to catch up with the wisdom of the world and its best practice. So they have argued for rights-based Christian practice with children, building on the 1989 UN Convention on the Rights of the Child. But they have generally not understood rights in a realistic or Christian theological perspective, and so have glossed over the agonising frustrating distance between human rights aspirations and what actually happens to people.[54] Christians ought not to dissent from the Convention on the Rights of the Child or hesitate to work for the rights of children; the rights of human beings are not contrary to the right of God. But they should witness to what they and others know: the Convention does not reflect how the world is; it is not even a firm promise of what will shortly be realised by earthly powers; at best it is an agenda for sustained work and prayer. Advocating human rights is a prayer embodied in work which represents the despised before the Father's face.

Always beholding the face of the Father in heaven

Angels are still with us, in modern working-clothes. They are to be seen in those who take up the cause of the despised in the everyday life of the world. But what or who is the final, definitive audience for this advocacy? The text tells us it is "the face of the Father." Does it make sense to interpret human rights declarations as though they are addressed to God? They stand for and with the despised, but do they stand in the presence of the Father? And if they do, what does that mean? What good is it? This question is unavoidably theological. Is theology in this place not an unnecessary burden, inherited clutter undermining clarity and efficiency?

Despising and God

Christians believe human beings live within the calling and promise of God (that is what the doctrines of creation, providence and salvation imply). But this life with God is contradicted whenever human beings are rubbished and despised by deliberate identifiable despisers, bullies, tyrants and exploiters, or by the impersonal indifference and deadliness of the world. The contradiction provokes questions and protests which are directed to where the buck stops or is believed to stop: God. Part of Job's desire was to have it out face to face with God.[55] Why does God allow and tolerate this despising of his creatures? Is not God complicit in the despising, even responsible for it? Is God then a despiser, even the Despiser?[56] Is it true that God is loving, caring, reliable? The way things happen in the world does not encourage faith in God's being, justice or capability.[57] Hard questions like these are at the core of any responsible theology.

Christians believe God is the just Judge of all the earth, but what happens in history cannot be taken as the enactment of his justice. Suffering and defeat can sometimes be accepted as God's punishment for the sins of individuals and nations, but oftentimes the punishment seems out of proportion to the sin. Job in his righteousness refused to accept this explanation of his troubles. The suffering of innocent children cannot be explained or palliated within this framework.

Interpreting the exile as the punitive response of holiness to the sin of the people could not be more than an initial and partial help to people who had to live through its devastation. Moralism, even if theologically based, is not enough to be true to God and humanity. Baruch, Jeremiah's servant, lamented his sorrow and pain.[58] The prophet was given a word of strange comfort for him: the Lord is undoing his work, plucking up the whole land and bringing evil on all flesh. Why or how then should Baruch seek great things for himself? Pause to feel the terror that comes to us in this sort of experience, when we hear that the Lord taking his creation back to chaos.[59] The heart of the terror is not what Baruch suffers and loses, bad though that is. It is not what the Lord is doing in careless indifference but what he is suffering as the land is dismantled. The only comfort, which is no explanation, let alone justification of what is happening, is that Baruch will be given his life as a prize of war wherever he goes. He is required to live bravely within this hard-pressed and unpredictable history. That is his encouragement.

Ezekiel[60] saw the exile as judgment on the people's conduct. They were scattered amongst the nations and wherever they went, they profaned God's name, not by behaving badly but because they gave others the chance to interpret the event so as to belittle God. The name was profaned because others said of them, "These are the people of the Lord, yet they had to go out of his land." What happened made it seem that God could not be faithful in sustaining his election of the people. So God was despised and discredited in the world. In response, God says the people will be gathered from the nations, brought into their own land, cleansed and made faithful, with abundance replacing desolation. All this will be done, not for the people's sake, not as though they were great or deserving, but "for the sake of my holy name," so that through the restored people God's holiness is "vindicated" before the eyes of the nations.

This reading of the devastating event does not put emphasis on explaining why it happened and how it is fair punishment for the people. We are rather asked to see God as the One whose name is profaned, his validity called into question in the world. As the people suffer, so does God. Explanations of why this happened cannot stand on their own for they can never bring peace. They are the prelude to the challenge to be truthful about the complexity and depth of the evil, the destruction of creation and the thwarting of

God's good purpose; to go with God through it towards God's future.

The Bible makes us inheritors of profound traditions of people of faith who not only sought God but held on tenaciously to God, despite the most discouraging of experiences. They cried out for God to turn, show himself, come to them, and rescue. They believed God was good and for them; but experience was dark, as though God's face was turned away.

Faith does not mean pretending that the night is not dark: rather it looks toward the dawn.[61] A prayer for God to arise is situated in the reality of God's present distance, where we wait and bear uncertainty. This kind of faith, very different from what is often offered by Christian devotional and inspirational literature, is given and enabled by the God and Father of our Lord Jesus Christ through the Spirit. There is no God except the One who takes the distance, waiting and uncertainty into God-self.

In the hardest place where Jesus is crucified, the question whether God is the ultimate despiser is explicitly posed in the history of God: "My God, my God, why hast thou forsaken me?"[62] The answer comes from the same place, where Jesus the Son and Servant of God was despised and rejected, "A man of sorrows and acquainted with grief; and as one from whom men hide their faces, he was despised and we esteemed him not" (Isaiah 53:3). If Jesus is the Son and Servant of God, God is revealed and known in his life, which is God's life in humanity. Suffering and shame is not imposed on Jesus by a distant alien God, for it is *God* who was in Christ reconciling the world to himself, as Christ was made sin for us, who knew no sin (2 Corinthians 5:19-21).

This is the one who does not despise the little ones. He rather upholds and vindicates them by taking their part against the enemies, becoming little with them, as little as a seed. His face shines upon them to give them peace, and in so doing, it enters into conflict with despising and judges for the despised against the despiser. In this context the doctrine of justification may be understood in a down-to-earth and dramatic way. Little ones are accused, mocked and undermined by powers that conspire to bring them to nought. But their condemnation cannot stand where God justifies and puts them in the right so that nothing separates them from the love of God in Christ (Romans 5:1-11; 8:31-39). This central element in Paul's theology is an indispensable aid in reading Matthew 18:10.

What Christ did was unnatural and unusual. He gave up protecting himself from being despised, which, in most circumstances, is the right thing for people to do for themselves and certainly for others. He gave his back to the smiters to expose despising for the evil it is, by letting it play itself out to the full in the sight of God and humanity.[63] Confronted by Jesus, when he comes into their hands, the despisers display the petty passion of little, ordinary people, terrified and bemused by the complexities and dangers of their situation. But there is more: their action belongs to the black hole of despising which lurks in the world with the power to bring all things to nothing. This is death, not just an event that brings physical life to an end, but a symbol of all that eats away at hope, value, meaning, confidence in being. God in Christ by the cross exposed despising by being despised.

In the same way and in the same event, God receives the despised, being despised with them, numbered with transgressors, rejected and excluded from society. They know they are despised when they lose meaning and joy in life, are made hopeless, have no friends and no way forward. In Christ, they are not saved by a sudden miraculous switch from misery to glory. They are not immediately received into peace and rest. They find themselves befriended by one who is with them where they are; and their first step in hope is to see in this present Friend even deeper despising. There is darkness over the whole land. But this despising is placed in the perspective of hope in God. "My God, my God, why have you forsaken me?" wrestles with, "Father, into your hands I place my spirit."[64]

The blessing of God, the kingdom of God, signed by God in Jesus, does not have free course in the world; it is contested, blocked, misused. It therefore has to assert itself against opposition and to find its path despite stumbling-blocks, within and without the community of faith. It fights, suffers and dies, and only so may come to victory.[65] The blessing of God imparts abundant life and love, in the faithfulness of God, but only because it goes through all that works against it, all that obscures and blocks it. The blessing of God is not just the free unimpeded flow of goodness, but includes the sharable history of the struggle of God. The blessing is not plenty enjoyed without effort, but is the deepest spiritual and bodily engagement in real questions of life and death. In Christ crucified, the blessing of God corresponds to a holistic, realistic way of being human.

The blessing of God occurs as the justification of sinners, the reconciliation of enemies, the resurrection of the dead, the light of hope for those in the darkness of despair. Its characteristic and fundamental form is the recovery of the lost and the reassertion of the righteousness of God in all the world, against all unrighteousness. The blessing of God for human living is the gift of resilience. Our resilience is called forth, sustained and fulfilled by the resilience which is essential to God in Christ, who goes through death to newness of life, because he could not let his creation go to waste.[66]

One sign of the resilience of God for humanity and of human beings with God is the gift of a child. In dark times a new child comes into danger and discouragement. The fear and sorrow of adults is intensified as they see what the child is likely to suffer. And yet the child is defiant hope and love, desired, intended and welcomed. A child is life now and life in prospect: even in its weakness, it answers the despiser.[67] The cherished words of Isaiah[68] are too often abstracted from real life and lose meaning by being used in comfortable Christmas celebrations. We need to hear them in their original precarious raw recklessness. They came to people who walked in long-term and overwhelming darkness, who were blessed with a great light and a child born, not to be a sentimentalised baby but as the hope of the effective rule of God. The child is Emmanuel, God with us, God present despite and within the distance, waiting and uncertainty. And the child reiterates the call for courageous faith, by which people move towards God, through the distance, waiting and uncertainty.

Do not despise

Matthew 18:10 has led us to consider the phenomenon and extent of despising in human experience and in the mystery of the suffering and the resilience of God. The text itself is not an exploration of despising but is a command not to despise. The command is backed by a reason: there are angels, representing the despised, by beholding the Father's face which shines upon them. The Father is for the despised, even though they may not see or know it. This saying is addressed directly to the despiser. It is for him to learn and to change, to reverse his despising from its roots within himself and to make peace with the Father by respecting and receiving the little one.

The command, "Do not despise," is given to the disciples. It thus takes us back to the beginning: the quest for greatness carries the seeds of despising in it. The cure Jesus gave them was to receive the child they overlooked. Only so would they enter the kingdom of God where the outsider, the poor and the lame are welcome. The disciples needed to change in their whole being, so as to follow and be with Jesus. They were called to share with Jesus in showing the kingdom of God as a public reality, a present promise of welcome. If the disciples despised little ones they could not do this work, even if they were confident of being close to the Lord as his chosen ones. When they are faithful in this mission, enacting the opposite of despising little ones, they are like angels who stand before the Father, beholding his face. In the world they become points where God's light shines.[69]

NOTES

1   "Hell is not good enough for them" and "Let them rot in Hell" are common ways of expressing this. There can be no minimising or excusing the evil of child abuse in any form, or indeed the abuse of any little one. Our point is that

this is not the issue this verse has in view and that quoting and responding emotively to this text is a very inefficient way of exposing and dealing with child abuse.

2   Compare the nothingness of this little child in their sight with the unforgettable portrayal of ultimate marginalisation in Ralph Ellison's *The Invisible Man*, 1952.

3   Leviticus 19:14: "You shall not put a stumbling block before the blind." Deuteronomy 27:18: "Cursed be he who misleads the blind man on the road." The word *scandalon* is used in various ways in the New Testament. It harks back to the rock of offence in Isaiah (8:14; 28:16) and is applied to Christ. At root it has the image of a rock or stone that causes a person to stumble or fall.

4   Ulrich Simon's great, underrated book, *A Theology of Auschwitz*, (1967) includes costly explorations of this difficult truth. "... life without God is nothingness and ... the abolition of man is precisely the earthly experience of a nothingness which has no right of survival." p. 74

5   Aldous Huxley, *Brave New World*, 1932

6   Significantly Peter himself becomes a scandal or stumbling block to Jesus on his road to the cross (Matthew 16:23)

7   Dietrich Bonhoeffer, *Discipleship*, 2001, chapter 1

8   C.S. Lewis, *Surprised by Joy*, 1955, chapters XI, XIV.

9   Karl Barth, "The Strange New World within the Bible," in *The Word of God and the Word of Man*, pp. 28-50

10 Rudolf Otto, *The Idea of the Holy*, 1923; Andrew Shanks, *What is Truth?*, 2001. The hymn, "Father, hear the prayer we offer, not for ease our prayer shall be," speaks to the issue we are concerned with here.

11 Despising is characteristic of the preconditions that make abuse more likely. Despising may be a judgment made in the heart and mind which then leads to action. Or it may not be aware of itself before the act is done and a little one is made to stumble. Even then, the despiser may not admit what he has done and what it reveals about himself. The act may appal observers as well as the victim, while the perpetrator carries on without remorse.

12 This is well-known territory for all who have studied the ways in which "the other" (whether women, ethnic groups, the poor, those with disability and so on) are overlooked and put down, taken beyond marginalisation into invisibility.

13 http:// www.paceuk.info, the website of PACE, Parents Against Child Sexual Exploitation (formerly CROP, the Coalition for the Removal of Pimping)

14 For an extreme example, Viktor Klemperer, *The Language of the Third Reich*, 1957, http://www.timeshighereducation.co.uk/story.asp?storyCode=412045&sectioncode=26; D. Bonhoeffer, *Ethics*,1955, chapter III, Ethics as Formation, section, "the Despiser of Men"; C.S. Lewis, *The Abolition of Man*, 1943; *That Hideous Strength*, 1945

15 Michael Sandel, *What Money Can't Buy: the Moral Limits to Markets*, 2012, is a critique of the ways in which money and markets obscure and supplant value.

16 F. Dostoevsky, *The Brothers Karamazov*; Rowan Williams, *Dostoevsky: Language, Faith and Fiction*, 2008

17 Romans 14:10,16

18 Isaiah 57:15. The mistake is indicated by difference between looking at and looking down on. It is possible to look at little things and little ones without looking down on them. "Looking down on" is a dynamic equivalent of calling anything that God has made unclean (Acts 10:14-15). Matthew 7:1-5. Compare the famous sketch, "I look down on him": http://www.britmovie.co.uk/forums/british-television/88237-john-cleese-

ronnie-barker-ronnie-corbett.html

19 Bob Holman, *Keir Hardie*, 2008, pp. 16-17. This is but one terrible incident in the life of this Christian politician who was "never a child" but a victim of systematic class-based despising from his early days as a poor child labourer.

20 It is recorded that as a young man, Wess Stafford, later CEO of Compassion International, represented a consortium of relief and development agencies in Haiti, the poorest country in the Western Hemisphere. During his four years in Haiti, Wess concluded that the most devastating message that poverty speaks to a child is, "You don't matter."

21 1 Corinthians 15:26,55; Isaiah 25:8 links death not only with tears but with reproach; Hebrews 2:14-15; 12:2: to be shamed is to be despised while to endure death in the spirit of Jesus is to despise the despising.

22 Marilynne Robinson, *Absence of Mind*, 2010. It may be that attempts to dispel the value of myths can in themselves conspire in the whole process of despising as we are describing it. For myths have a power to give value to life and death, in spite of all the physical evidence to the contrary.

23 Barry Dainton, "First stop, Moon", a review of David Deutsch, *The Beginning of Infinity*, TLS, 25:11.2011, p. 28: "The notion that the Earth is a maternally inclined spacefaring vessel is a suspect one ... parts of our planet have many of the attributes of a spaceship, but the power supplies, medical technologies and sanitation systems that render life safe and comfortable have invariably been produced by human effort and scientific ingenuity, not by Mother Nature."

24 W. Shakespeare, *King Lear* (Act IV scene 1)
> He has some reason, else he could not beg.
> I' th' last night's storm I such a fellow saw,
> Which made me think a man a worm. My son
> Came then into my mind, and yet my mind
> Was then scarce friends with him. I have heard more since.
> As flies to wanton boys are we to th' gods.
> They kill us for their sport.

See also Thomas Hardy's *Tess of the D'Urbervilles*: " 'Justice' was done, and the President of the Immortals (in Aeschylean phrase) had ended his sport with Tess."

In the conflict with Gnosticism, Christian orthodoxy made its fundamental decision against this approach. The gnostic saw himself as a being of ultimate worth, lost in a world made by an incompetent Demiurge. The gnostic's aim was to escape the world; he knew himself to be one who was not properly recognised and respected by the powers of the world. The gnostic felt himself unfairly despised because he knew who he was, different, special and superior to the dark ignorant world. So the despised gnostic comforted himself by despising the world, in both the way he saw it and the way he lived in it. Christian faith in a good Creator who loves and makes all things good, despite its enormous difficulties, makes for an alternative view of human existence: we are not essentially despised despisers. Hans Jonas, *The Gnostic Religion: The Message of the Alien God and the Beginnings of Christianity*, 1958

25 Karl Barth, *How My Mind has Changed*, 1966, p. 86, which shows the spirit and theology with which Barth responded to his illness in 1966.

26 This poem was written by Haddon Willmer following the Tsunami in Asia in December 2004.

27 "When my mother and father forsake me, the Lord will take me up." Psalm 27:10

28 The phrase is Paul Lehmann's: *The Decalogue and a Human Future: The Meaning*

of the Commandments for Making and Keeping Human Life Human, 1995. Also, *The Transfiguration of Politics,* 1975 p. 10, p. 44. Philip G.Ziegler and Michael J. Bartel, *Explorations in Christian Theology and Ethics: Essays in conversation with Paul L. Lehmann,* 2009

29 Psalm 46:9: the works of God are desolations in the earth, so that wars cease to the end of the earth; Psalm 104:24 ff.

30 Compare E. Bethge, *Dietrich Bonhoeffer,* 1970, p. 832: Klaus Bonhoeffer in a note made after his trial in 1945: "I am not afraid of being hanged, but I don't want to see those faces again ... so much depravity ... I'd rather die than see those faces again. I have seen the Devil and I can't forget it."

31 Psalm 46:5. The oddity of faith is evident in the two sides of Luke 18:8, following Jesus' story telling us that we ought always to pray and not lose heart: "Will not God vindicate his elect, who cry to him day and night? Will he delay long over them? I tell you, he will vindicate them speedily. Nevertheless, when the Son of man comes, will he find faith on earth?"

32 Revelation 6:9-11

33 Francis Thompson, *In no strange land.* The text of this poem is in note 31, chapter 6. The phrase, "Clinging to heaven by the hems" may be reminiscent of Luke 8:44, where the woman touched the hem of Jesus' garment to be healed. It is an image which speaks of distance and hesitance as well as of faith and determined supplication. .

34 Among the many texts that we have been able to draw on for this chapter are the work of Emmanuel Levinas, *Humanism of the Other,* 2003 and Roger Scruton, *The Face of God,* 2012 and David Ford, *Self and Salvation,* 1999. John M. Hull, "Blindness and the Face of God: Toward a Theology of Disability" in Hans-Georg Ziebertz et al (eds.) *The Human Image of God,* 2000, pp. 215-229 (http://www. johnmhull.biz/Blindness%20and%20the%20Face%20of%20God.html)

35 W. Shakespeare, *Hamlet,* Act 1, scene 5

36 Quoted by Jesus on the cross, Matthew 27:46; Mark 15:34

37 See, for example, James E. Loder, *The Logic of the Spirit,* pp. 118-122

38 We wonder whether, and if so, how far, those who engage in reflecting on children's spirituality build this truth into the process. It seems to be implied that all children are connected in some direct way to the sublime, the "Other", God.

39 D. Bonhoeffer, *Life Together,* 1996, p. 40: " Within the spiritual community there is never, in any way whatsoever, an "immediate" relationship of one to another. However, in the self-centred community there exists a profound, elemental emotional desire for community, for immediate contact with other human souls ..."

Compare also,Thomas Binney's hymn, which is not only no longer sung, but could not be written now: *Eternal Light, eternal light ...*

40 Angelology developed in Jewish faith as the sense of distance from God increased, partly through historic experiences of defeat and exile, being despised amongst the nations, and under the judgment of God.

41 Genesis 3:24

42 Ponder Andrew Parker, who made himself a human bridge inside the capsized Herald of Free Enterprise, enabling 20 people to escape drowning in 1987. This mediation is regarded as heroic not so much because it was successful but because it cannot be contemplated without our sensing the awful gap which, left unbridged, meant death. http://www.thefreelibrary.com/i+saved+20+lives+ but+couldn't+save+my+marriage%3b+tragedy+drove+couple...-a061048229 http://www.kentonline.co.uk/kentonline/home/special_reports/herald_of_free_

enterprise/andrew_parker_-_the_human_step.aspx

43 Philippians 3:12-14. Nik Wallenda, who walked across the Grand Canyon on a tight rope, said: "My faith plays a huge role in my life, and I am very blessed to be where I am. One of the questions I always get is, 'Are you testing your faith / are you testing God?' I don't see it like that at all. I don't believe God keeps me on the wire.

"I believe God gives me a unique ability to walk the wire, but it's up to me whether I train properly. There's a lot of people that have amazing relationships with Christ that lose their lives in a car accident. Does that mean they didn't have a good enough relationship with Jesus? No. Life happens and God created us all in his image, but we're all our own people. We're not robots. We make decisions." http://www.christianitytoday.com/ct/2013/june-web-only/walking-by-faith-across-grand-canyon-tightrope.html?utm_source=ctdirect-html&utm_medium=Newsletter&utm_term=9465739&utm_content=188038575&utm_campaign=2013

44 From the hymn by Timothy Dudley Smith, *Remember, Lord, the world you made* ..., which as a whole, resonates with our argument.

45 George Eliot, *Silas Marner*, 1861, chapter 14: "In the old days there were angels who came and took men by the hand and led them away from the city of destruction. We see no white-winged angels now. But yet men are led away from threatening destruction; a hand is put into theirs, which leads them forth gently towards a calm and bright land, so that they look no more backward; and the hand may be a little child's."

46 This is explored in Jostein Gaarder, *Through a Glass Darkly*, which nicely marks the ambiguous nature of the place and experience of an angel.

47 See chapter 6, note 37 for the whole poem.

48 Genesis 28:17

49 Genesis 4:1-16; Job 16:18-19

50 J.B. Metz, "Communicating a dangerous memory," in Fred Lawrence (ed.), *Communicating a Dangerous Memory*, pp. 37-54

51 Pandita Ramabai's writings on behalf of oppressed girl-children in Western India are characterised by her determination to let the stories speak for themselves.

52 http://www.guardian.co.uk/football/2011/nov/16/sepp-blatter-fifa-race-rows-handshakes. A more serious and widespread form of shameless impenitence about despising is the widespread toleration of rape.

53 Notably, the United Nations Universal Declaration of Human Rights, 1948, the progenitor of a whole family which includes the United Nations Convention on the Rights of the Child, 1989. See also, Clare Mulley, *The Woman who saved the Children: Eglantyne Jebb, Founder of Save the Children*, 2009, p. 307

54 One example of an attempt to relate biblical principles to the 1989 UN Convention on the Rights of the Child is to be found in D. McConnell, *Understanding God's Heart for Children*, 2007. In a chapter titled "Theological Dignity and Human Rights for Children" (pp. 23-31) Dave Scott suggests that rights are a tool, not a paradigm for Christian ministry. The way the book as a whole is organised does not allow the theological questions arising from the disparity between God's nature, and the harsh realities of the world He has created and loves to be explored. They are noted, for example on page 15, by Doug McConnell: "Our experience of living with children living in risky environments mocks the ideals of God's created order," but not pursued.

55 Job 13:13-16; 23:2-7

56 W. Shakespeare, *Macbeth*, V.v.16

57 Hebrews 2:8-9

58 Jeremiah 45

59 Genesis 3:19; Ecclesiastes 3:20; 12:1-8; Isaiah 28:14-22

60 Ezekiel 36:16-32

61 Keith J. White, *In The Meantime*, 2013, reflects on periods of suffering, waiting, grieving and hoping: all in the context where the end is not yet known. The loneliness associated with the night hours and the waiting for the dawn is described pp. 216-217.

62 Psalm 22:1,23-24

63 Isaiah 50:5-6: "I gave my back to the smiters, and my cheeks to those who pluck out the beard; I hid not my face from shame and spitting." The expression, I gave my back ... is not to be minimised. It points to a violent imposition, where the victim is overpowered and robbed. He gives nothing freely, but rather has it taken away. There is however a special set of instances where someone may give himself willingly to suffer. When this is carried through without retaliation, the giving by the sufferer becomes more inspiring and fruitful than the violent and cruel taking of the persecutor. The passion of Christ is a leading example of this kind of triumphant and redemptive action.

64 Matthew 27:46; Mark 15:34; Luke 23:46. These two sayings are not found together in any one Gospel.

65 God battling, not by flesh and blood or bombs and guns, but spiritually in the reality of human living, is a valuable, indispensable perspective of the gospel, This perspective is not to be lost in any competition between theories of atonement defending their exclusive claim to saving truth. Cf G. Aulen, *Christus Victor*; Karl Barth, *Church Dogmatics*, IV.3.1 165-273

66 Athanasius, *On the Incarnation of the Word*, 6: "The thing that was happening was in truth both monstrous and unfitting. It would, of course, have been unthinkable that God should go back upon His word and that man, having transgressed, should not die; but it was equally monstrous that beings which once had shared the nature of the Word should perish and turn back again into non-existence through corruption. It was unworthy of the goodness of God that creatures made by Him should be brought to nothing through the deceit wrought upon man by the devil; and it was supremely unfitting that the work of God in mankind should disappear, either through their own negligence or through the deceit of evil spirits. As, then, the creatures whom He had created reasonable, like the Word, were in fact perishing, and such noble works were on the road to ruin, what then was God, being Good, to do? Was He to let corruption and death have their way with them? In that case, what was the use of having made them in the beginning?"

67 Psalm 8:2

68 Take Isaiah 7–12 as a whole, without cherry picking a few verses such as 7:14-16; 9:2-7; 11:6-9.

69 Matthew 5:16 (following the Beatitudes, "Blessed are the poor in spirit ..."). As in the work of the Russian Orthodox artist Vitali Linitsky who painted Christians as points of light in the wintry darkness.

Conclusion

ND SO A CONVERSATION between us spanning more than a dozen years comes to a close. And likewise, for readers who have stayed the course, the conversation between us and them is all but over. And at the end we ask ourselves, "So what?" or "How should we then live?" It is our belief that theology is not worth the name unless it takes place in the crucible of experience and results in repentance and practical action. We hope there are those among our readers who share this view.

We begin by asking what this book has done to us. What sticks and what do we carry forward? What have we discovered that we did not know before this long labour? What strange new land have we travelled and what have we collected from it?

We have devoted a seemingly excessive amount of time to a snippet from Matthew's Gospel. This has led us to see things in the whole of the Gospel we had not considered deeply before. This book is based on Matthew, but is not exegetical commentary. As New Testament scholars we are severely challenged; with what little knowledge and intelligence we have, we have sought to attend to the text. For us, reading Matthew intensively has been a discipline and liberation, a ground for adventuring. It has imposed itself on us but not in a limiting way. It is like a springboard. Or perhaps, better, like the secure base of a home which makes us fit to venture into the world, irritates us so we want to get out into the world and still welcomes us back to roots and refreshment. We have enjoyed our reading of Matthew, however odd and partial.

We did not know when we started that we would end up with a distinctive treatment of Child Theology. We are uncertain whether this comes from a personal distaste for being conventional, a standing suspicion of what is commonly accepted. Are we just awkward dissidents underneath our respectable appearance? We think there are better reasons for what some may deem our heresies, but we may be mistaken.

Here are some of the key points as we understand them.

▨ **First**, the "child in the midst" of this book is simply the child placed by Jesus and standing beside Jesus (see Chapter 1). This is not a special sort of child, but an ordinary child chosen by Jesus. We see no reason in the text or narrative for imputing particular characteristics or gifts to the child. It is an unknown, unexceptional child, living in a contemporary world that ranked children with the lowest in society. The only clue offered by Jesus is that we should become humble like the little children, and that inevitably means coming down to ground level.

▨ **Second**, child as seen and placed by Jesus signs the kingdom of God, which is a powerful, historically and biblically rooted, but dangerously ambiguous, concept. This was so for the disciples and for the followers of Jesus ever since. It may have come as a surprise to some readers that we believe it was also an ambiguous and far from straightforward concept for Jesus in his own life and journey of faith and faithfulness.

Some may be disturbed by the way in which we have highlighted Jesus in his seeking the kingdom of God, following him through temptation, conflict, suffering and death, so that simple statements of his divinity or human uniqueness are missing. No sacred or habitual orthodoxy should stop us thinking within this disturbance. And our thinking is not presented with a claim to the status of orthodoxy.

Third, in the shortest, but crucial hinge chapter (Chapter Four), we may have produced a novel, or at least rare, exegesis. In it we take the child signing the way into the kingdom of God as another way of stating the terms of Jesus' call to discipleship. We realise that historically child and cross have mostly been separated from each other, as if they were growing alternative Christianities with different values, aspirations and feelings. We argue against seeing them as alternatives that provide followers of Jesus with the chance to choose between them. Rather, for us, the child placed by Jesus reiterates or restates the call to discipleship. The substance remains unchanged, but the child as sign brings us into it by a strange, unsuspected way. In our view much contemporary child-focused Christianity needs to ask itself how far the child serves as an alternative to the call of Jesus, and how far the child represents a faithful version of the same call.

Once we accepted that the child reiterates the call to discipleship in the way of the cross, we were bound to ask how Jesus, according to the text, helps us not only with the clue we have noted – "Humble yourselves as the little children" – but also by saying, "Receive the child in my name." Our wrestling with the concept and practice of humility is evident. We accept the call to be humble, while asking what humility as signed by a child means, what is good about it, and how is it possible. Humility is against the spirit of our age and probably of every age. Humiliation is not a good thing and God is not King by putting down all his creatures and having them grovel. Late in the day, we linked humility with hope in the newness God gives in grace. Have we, we wonder, been led stumbling into the humility that is characteristic of the kingdom where creatures reflect and share in the glory of God?

There is always a danger in theological and religious discourse that the child will be reduced to an idea, a symbol, a focus for the dreams, values and emotions of adults. Just as the cross, when Jesus speaks of it, is hard earthly reality, so the child placed in the midst is a real, actual person. This child stands for any and every child; Jesus says, "Whoever receives one such child in my name receives me." It is always a real child. Children do not come to us as a mass of "childhood". Each child invites and needs a reception that is adequate to the full being of the child, some of which is evident and most of which is hidden, for the child is like a seed, full of life which has yet to be lived. In Chapter Six the theological argument derived from the gospel story converges with practical involvement with children. The gospel meets people in the everyday practice of parenting, education and care. These activities are set within the perspective of God's welcome and hospitality in Christ.

Receiving the child fits with the best of our contemporary aspirations and activities, secular and Christian, that we noted in Chapter One. And yet we know too painfully in our world what Matthew's text speaks of bluntly: little ones are made to stumble; they are despised. Many children are well received when they are babies and go on being appropriately received as they grow older. But many are neglected or ill-treated from the beginning and for many children a happy start becomes a disappointment as they grow up. Many children in dire need are rescued by a plethora of organisations, but there are many more in need who are left unhelped. Those who engage with children, or with any real human concern in the world, will be taken into the darkness which is represented by the despising of little ones. Sometimes they armour themselves against it by their cheerful can-do busyness and their joyful songs and by avoiding the kind of prophetic reflection which keeps its eyes open in the evil day, refusing to sleep in Gethsemane. Sometimes they are overwhelmed in the core of their being and faith.

▓ **Fourth,** when we read of "disciples" in the Gospels we are reading about ourselves as Christians now and therefore it is not surprising that parallels are to be found between their mistaken concepts and ambitions for the kingdom of God and contemporary Christian enterprises, including what is going on in relation to children. We cannot assume that, because we sit this side of the cross and resurrection of Jesus, and of Pentecost, and because we dwell in centuries of tradition formed by various engagements with the New Testament, we are self-evidently better than the disciples at following Jesus as Lord.

The challenge of the sign of the child to our conceptions of greatness remains uncomfortable and remarkably radical. It is clear that ministers, leaders and congregations see numerical progress, wealth and influence as signs of God's blessing; and that many are attracted to global movements and initiatives that see themselves ordained by God to transform the world. Such thinking and assumptions are in a direct line from the prevailing view of the disciples at the time of Jesus.

We have been confronted by the terms in which Jesus called people to be his disciples. We have accepted, without much discussion, that this call is addressed to any of us today who want to be Christian. Whether we should make that move is a matter of disagreement amongst Christians. Just as some argue that gifts like speaking in tongues were for the early church only, so it could be argued that the call to take up the cross only applied to those who could physically follow Jesus on his walk to Jerusalem. We take the view that both cross and Spirit are for today as well as then, since Jesus Christ is the same yesterday, today and for ever.

So we find ourselves in the same crisis the first disciples lived through with Jesus. By following Jesus they were taken into a life they could neither imagine nor manage. They were tempted by the promise of the kingdom of God, frightened and bewildered by the way Jesus was walking towards it, with its unbearable cost. We cannot say that the years we have spent on this book have brought us to a confident accommodation to discipleship, as Jesus calls us to it. The first thing, every day, is to hear the call in the reality of our situation, individually and corporately, and not to tailor it to our sensitivities, convenience or habits. This calls for the courage to say "No" to the self that wants either to be at ease with Jesus or to do without him.

▨ **Fifth**, if the child placed by Jesus is the starting point of the book, the child leads us to take Jesus seriously and to ask, "Who is this?" So we have engaged with this question, not as though we can give a complete systematic Christology, but to refresh and deepen our understanding of Jesus. We have done this by bringing together in our picture of Jesus the child placed in the midst by him, the arguments about the kingdom of God which were arguments Jesus had with himself (temptation), his calling of disciples to share his mission, and his call to them to take up the cross in company with him. The cross is inescapable in a faithful vision and following of Jesus. The significance of the child for disciples is that the call to humility and to become like the children is a restatement of the call to take up the cross and not an alternative way into the kingdom of God. This should be shocking to many Christians today, because in our tender concern for children and our often simplistic affirmation of life (spirituality), we develop an alternative Christianity without the cross for children – and for ourselves.

The book thus poses a choice. We do not claim to have made the choice perfectly. We are aware that our practice and thinking is typical of much contemporary Christianity, which hopes that it can somehow follow Jesus who took up his cross while sharing with children forms of life and religion where anything so divisive and profound as cross is kept out.

▨ **Sixth**, this book is for us an attempt to do Child Theology. Please note that it is not definitive or intended to be so. And we fear that there will be those who will be disappointed because they were expecting a new section in what is understood to be systematic theology. They assume that the child should be an organising concept for a whole system of theology: an extension if you like of books that explore "the child in the Bible". We need to apologise if sometimes we have given the impression that that is what we are seeking and are trying to offer. We are not systematic theologians in any conventional sense, and it is not our intention primarily to contribute another systematic essay.

Our starting point on theology is a broad, open, essentially lay, understanding that theology is talking and thinking about (from, to, with, for) God. There are many ways in which theology may be done, many ways that can be helpful, though none of them can be universal in reach or authority, and none grasps God or even touches God – we are doing well if we point (for example, "Behold the Lamb of God") faithfully. The particular way that this piece of free theology has developed is as an exploratory meditation on a fragment of biblical text (Matthew 18), in a readiness to follow where it leads.

▨ **Seventh**, all this has led us in the direction of writing what is a kind of practical theology. The chapter on reception is where this becomes plain in a down-to-earth everyday way. There is no mistaking the call to each of us to welcome or receive a child in the name of Jesus. But this call and action does not turn away from theology. It is not a chapter which concedes that theological talk is unnecessary or pedantic because what counts is the action of receiving a child, as if this can be done in obedience to Christ with neither theological context nor theological depth of meaning. Rather, following the text, we see that receiving a child is to receive Christ and the One who sent him. The child signs the kingdom of God which operates as human beings receive one another as God in Christ receives them. This is the chain reaction of the yeast in the lump (Matthew 13:33).

Our focus was on a mere ten verses of the Gospel of Matthew, and although we were aware of the proximity of the parable of the one lost sheep, we did not attempt to expound it in this context. Readers will by now see that it can, and perhaps should, be read as an extension of the idea of receiving a child through going out to find and recover the sheep gone astray (Matthew 18:12-14). If so, reception is more than welcoming and treating well the child who is present: it involves caring for the child who is neither in our midst nor seen. Such a child does not confront us, but is "out there" and has to be sought.

At the end of the story (Matthew 18:14) there is a repeat of verse 10, in different language: "It is not the will of my (your) Father that one of these little ones should perish." The message of the gospel is that God seeks, recovers and receives even the lost and the enemy: God forgives rather than being bound to give people what they earn. So the kingdom of God is here, both as a little seed, and also as a vision of new creation.

■ **Eighth,** this is an essay: it is offered as a stimulus to discussion, not as a teaching or a definitive analysis. It is tentative and incomplete. We chance our arm, making points, knowing they are questionable and hoping that the questioning they provoke might be useful. We have used our freedom to write a text which is personal and precarious. Precarious now means uncertain and vulnerable: it is characteristic of any "little one". But the root of the word is the Latin *precarius*, meaning prayer or entreaty. So the contemporary meaning is a secularisation and an impoverishment.

It is worth being reminded that what we label as precarious is a call and occasion of prayer; and that prayer is at home in every place where the earth is moved and the foundations are shaken. Indeed prayer itself is not a simple security untouched and distanced from that shaking: an escape from the precariousness of human being in the world. It is at its heart "the living of these days." How often do we teach prayer and seek it as the solution to problems and the power to get beyond the uncertainties and incapabilities that distress us? That we should seek such relief by being raised to peace above the troubled world is not surprising and has a certain justification, but it does not secure what we want here and now. We are called to live with the doubleness of the precarious, the uncertainty and the praying together.

What we have written is not a confessional statement of what the Child Theology Movement stands for, but is written within the vision of what CTM is: a fellowship of thinking and active disciples exploring the gospel seed and sign of the child placed in the midst by Jesus. This book has already been stimulated and encouraged within fellowship of the kind which is represented by, but not restricted to, CTM. It is now handed over, not to be judged kindly or adversely but to be used according to the best critical and constructive capabilities of readers. It leaves much to be completed and much to be bettered.

We have not concluded the book with a rousing call to action, to yet more action, on behalf of children in the world. Instead we have pursued our fragile theological search to the end by looking for God in the darkness and in new light. If we follow in this way, it will be God in Christ who calls. Our work can be no more than to point to God, and to pass on his call.

SELECTED BIBLIOGRAPHY

Books

Aries, Philippe, *Centuries of Childhood*, 1965, Vintage Books

Arnold, Johann Christoph, *A Little Child Shall Lead Them*, 1997, Plough/IVP

Athanasius, *On the Incarnation of the Word*, tr. Penelope Lawson, http://www.spurgeon.org/~phil/history/ath-inc.htm

Aulen, Gustav, *Christus Victor*, 1931, SPCK

Bakke, O.M., *When Children Became People: the Birth of Childhood in Early Christianity*, 2005, Augsburg

von Balthasar, Hans Urs, *Unless You Become Like This Child*, 1991, Ignatius

Barth, Karl, *The Word of God and the Word of Man*, n.d., Hodder and Stoughton

Barth, Karl and Thurneysen, Eduard, *God's Search for Man*, 1935, T&T Clark

Barth, Karl, *Letter to a Pastor in a Marxist Land*, 1959, Association Press

Barth, Karl, *How My Mind Has Changed*, 1969, St Andrew Press

Barth, Karl, *The Christian Life*, 1981, T&T Clark

British Council of Churches, *The Child in the Church*, 1976

British Council of Churches, *Understanding Christian Nurture*, 1981

Bergler, Thomas E., *The Juvenilisation of American Christianity*, 2012, Eerdmans

Berryman, Jerome W., *The Complete Guide to Godly Play* (Volume One), 2002, Living the Good News

Berryman, Jerome W., *Children and the Theologians: Clearing the Way for Grace*, 2009, Morehouse

Bonhoeffer, Dietrich, *The Cost of Discipleship*, 1959, SCM

... *Discipleship*, 2001, Fortress

... *Letters and Papers from Prison*

... *Ethics*, 1955, SCM

... *Life Together*, 1996, Fortress

Brannen, Julia, "Children and Agency in Academic and public Policy Discourses," in *Children and Social Exclusion*, ed. Keith J. White, 1999, NCVCCO

Brennan, Patrick McKinley (ed.), *The Vocation of the Child*, 2008, Eerdmans

Brueggemann, Walter, *Old Testament Theology: An Introduction*, 2008, Abingdon

Bunge, Marcia J., *The Child in Christian Thought and Practice*, 2001, Eerdmans

... *The Child in the Bible*, 2008, Eerdmans

... *Children, Adults, and Shared Responsibilities: Jewish, Christian, and Muslim Perspectives* (Cambridge University Press, 2012)

Consultative Group on Ministry among Children, *Unfinished Business: Children and the Churches*, 2001, CCBI

Collier, John (ed.), *Toddling to the Kingdom*, 2009, CTM

Copsey, Kathryn, *From the Ground Up: Understanding the Spiritual World of the Child*, 2005, Bible Reading Fellowship

Cunningham, Hugh, *The Invention of Childhood*, 2006, BBC

Dallaire, Roméo, *Shake Hands with the Devil: The Failure of Humanity in Rwanda*, 2004, Arrow

Darling, John, *Child-Centered Education and its Critics*, 1994, Paul Chapman/Department of Education and Science

Dickens, Charles, *David Copperfield*, 1850

... *Oliver Twist*, 1839

Donovan, Vincent, *Christianity Rediscovered*, 2003, Orbis

Dostoevsky, Fyodor, *The Brothers Karamazov*, 1880

Eliot, George, *Silas Marner*, 1861

Ellison, Ralph, *The Invisible Man*, 1952, (2001, Penguin Modern Classics)

Ford, David, *Self and Salvation*, 1999, Cambridge

Gaarder, Jostein, *Through A Glass, Darkly*, 1998, Phoenix

Grenz, Stanley J., *Theology for the Community of God*, 1994, Broadman and Holman

Griffiths, Jay, *Kith: The Riddle of the Childscape*, 2013, Hamish Hamilton

Griffiths, Mark, *One Generation from Extinction*, 2009, Monarch

Hay, D. and Nye, R., *The Spirit of the Child*, 1998, Fount

Herzog, Kristin, *Children and Our Global Future: Theological and Social Challenges*, 2005, Pilgrim Press

Heniger, Alice Minnie Herts, *The Kingdom of the Child*, 1918, E.P. Dutton,

Hobbes, Thomas, *Leviathan*, 1651

Holman, Bob, *Keir Hardie, Labour's Greatest Hero?*, 2008, Lion

Hughes, David, *The Lent Jewels*, 2003, Arrow

Hughes, Gerard W., *God of Surprises*, 1985, Darton, Longman and Todd

Huxley, Aldous, *Brave New World*, 1932, Penguin

Jarman, David and Van Oss, Celia, *Childhood's Pattern: Christian Childhoods Explored*, 1985, Firethorn

Jarrett-Macauley, Delia, *Moses, Citizen & Me*, 2005, Granta Books

Jenks, Chris, *The Sociology of Childhood: Essential Readings*, 1982, Batsford

Jensen, David H., *Graced Vulnerability: A Theology of Childhood*, 2005, Pilgrim Press

Jeyaraj, Jesudason (ed.), *Children at Risk: Issues and Challenges*, 2009, ISPCK

Jonas, Hans, *The Gnostic Religion: The Message of the Alien God and the Beginnings of Christianity*, 2001, Beacon

Kempis, Thomas á, *The Imitation of Christ*, 1441

Kilbourn, Phyllis, *Shaping the Future, Girls and Our Destiny*, 2008, William Carey Library

... *Children in Crisis: A New Commitment*, 1996, MARC

Klemperer, Viktor, *The Language of the Third Reich*, 1957, Continuum

Kraybill, Donald, *The Upside-Down Kingdom*, 1978, Herald Press

Lamont, Ronni, *Understanding Children Understanding God*, 2007, SPCK

Lausanne Movement, The, *The Cape Town Commitment*, 2011, Lausanne Movement

Layard, Richard & Dunn, Judy, *A Good Childhood: Searching for Values in a Competitive Age*, 2009, Penguin

Lehmann, Paul, *The Decalogue and a Human Future: The Meaning of the Commandments for Making and Keeping Human Life Human*, 1994, Eerdmans

Levinas, Emmanuel, *Humanism of the Other*, 2003, University of Illinois

Lewis, C.S., *The Silver Chair*, 1953, Geoffrey Bles

Loder, James E., *The Logic of the Spirit*, 1989, Josey-Bass

McBride, James, *Miracle at Sant'Anna*, 2002, Hodder and Stoughton

McConnell, D., *Understanding God's Heart for Children*, 2007, Authentic

MacDonald, George, *Unspoken Sermons*, 1886, Longman, Greens and Co

McDonnell, F. and Akallo, G., *Girl Soldier: A Story of Hope for Northern Uganda's Children*, 2007, Baker Books

McFadyen, Alistair, *Bound to Sin: Abuse, Holocaust and the Christian Doctrine of Sin*, 2000, Cambridge University Press

Macleod, George F., *Only One Way Left*, 1956, The Iona Community

Magdalen, Sister, *Conversations with Children: Communicating our Faith*, 2001, Stavropegig Monastery of St John the Baptist Essex

Marshall, Kathleen and Parvis, Paul, *Honouring Children: The Human Rights of the Child in Christian Perspective*, 2004, St Andrew Press

Marty, Martin E., *The Mystery of the Child*, 2007, Eerdmans

Mbali, Zolile, *The Churches and Racism: A Black South African Perspective*, 1987, SCM

Mercer, Joyce Ann, *Welcoming Children*, 2005, Chalice

Miles, Glenn and Wright, Josephine-Joy (ed.), *Celebrating Children: Equipping People Working with Children and Young People Living in Difficult Circumstances Around the World*, 2003, Paternoster

Miller, Bonnie, *Let the Children Come: Re-imagining Childhood from a Christian Perspective*, 2003, Jossey-Bass

Moltmann, J., *The Crucified God*, 1974, SCM

Mulley, Clare, *The Woman who Saved the Children: A Biography of Eglantyne Jebb, Founder of Save the Children*, 2009, One World

Newbigin, Lesslie, *The Gospel in a Pluralist Society*, 2004, SPCK

Nouwen, Henri J.M., *Adam: God's Beloved*, 1997, Orbis

Oppenheimer, Helen, *Finding and Following: Talking with Children about God*, 1994, SCM

Otto, Rudolf, *The Idea of the Holy*, 1917

Pakenham, Frank (Lord Longford), *Humility*, 1969, Harper Collins

Pohl, Christine D., *Making Room: Recovering Hospitality as a Christian Tradition*, 1999, Eerdmans

Pollock, J.C., *The Good Seed*, 1959, Hodder and Stoughton

Prevette, Bill, *Child, Church and Compassion: Towards Child Theology in Romania*, 2012, Regnum

Rahner, Karl, "Ideas for a Theology of Childhood," *Theological Investigations*, Volume 8, 1971

Rawson, Beryl, *Children and Childhood in Roman Italy*, 2003, OUP

Richards, Anne and Privett, Peter (ed.), *Through the Eyes of a Child*, 2009, Church House Publishing

Robinson, John, *Nobody's Child: an Unwanted Boy Who Found Hope*, 2003, Monarch

Robinson, Marilynne, *Absence of Mind*, 2010, Yale University Press

Rousseau, J-J., (trans. Barbara Foxley), *Émile*, 1912, Everyman

Ruether, Rosemary Radford, *Christianity and the Making of the Modern Family*, 2001, SCM

Simon, Ulrich, *A Theology of Auschwitz*, 1967, Gollancz
Saward, John, *The Way of the Lamb: The Spirit of Childhood and the End of the Age*, 1999, T&T Clark
Scruton, Roger, *The Face of God*, 2012, Continuum
Shanks, Andrew, *What is Truth? Towards a Theological Poetics*, 2001, Routledge
Shier-Jones, Angela (ed.), *Children of God: Towards a Theology of Childhood*, 2007, Epworth
Sims, David A., *The Child in American Evangelicalism and the Problem of Affluence: a Theological Anthropology of the Affluent American-Evangelical Child in Late Modernity*, 2009, Pickwick
So, Damon, *The Forgotten Jesus and the Trinity You Never Knew*, 2010, Wipf & Stock
Sölle, Dorothee, *Christ the Representative*, 1967, SCM
... *Suffering*, 1975, Fortress Press
Sprange, Harry, *Children in Revival*, 2002, Christian Focus Publications
Spufford, Francis, *The Child that Books Built*, 2002, Faber
Stafford, Wess, *Too Small to Ignore: Why Children are the next Big Thing*, 2005, WaterBrook
Taylor, John V., *Kingdom Come*, 2012, SCM
Thatcher, Adrian, *Theology and Families*, 2006, Blackwell
Titmuss, Richard, *The Gift Relationship: From Human Blood to Social Policy*, 1970 (1997, New Press)
UN Convention on the Rights of the Child, 1989, www.unicef.org/crc/
Vanstone, W.H., *The Stature of Waiting*, 1982, DLT
Velasco, Joey, *They Have Jesus: the Stories of the Children of the Hapag*, 2006, Kenosis
Volf, Miroslav, *Exclusion and Embrace*, 1996, Abingdon Press
Weber, Hans-Ruedi, *Jesus and the Children*, 1994, John Knox Press
White, Keith J., *"Child Theology as a Seed" in Toddling Forward*, 2010, CTM Australia 2010
... (ed.), *Now and Next*, 2011, Compassion
... *In the Meantime*, 2013, WTL
... *The Growth of Love*, 2008, Bible Reading Fellowship
Williams, Niall, *As it is in Heaven*, 1999, Picador
Williams, Rowan, *Lost Icons*, 2003, T&T Clark
... *Dostoevsky: Language, Faith and Fiction*, 2011, Baylor University Press
Willmer, Haddon, *Experimenting Together: One Way of Doing Child Theology*, 2007, CTM
Winnicott, D.W., *The Child, the Family, and the Outside World*, 1973, Penguin
Wolff Pritchard, Gretchen, *Offering the Gospel to Children*, 1992, Cowley Publications
Woodhead, M. and Montgomery, H., *Understanding Childhood*, 2003, Wiley
Wright, N.T., *Jesus and the Victory of God*, 1996, SPCK
Wullshläger, Jackie, *Inventing Wonderlands*, 1995, Methuen
Young, Frances, *Face to Face*, 1985, (Revised edition, 1991), Epworth
Zuck, Roy B, *Precious in His Sight: Childhood and Children in the Bible*, 1996, Baker Books

Papers

Berlin, Isaiah, "The Originality of Machiavelli,"
http://berlin.wolf.ox.ac.uk/published_works/ac/machiavelli.pdf

Brewer, Sandy, "From Darkest England to The Hope of the World: Protestant Pedagogy and the Visual Culture of the London Missionary Society," *Material Religion: The Journal of Objects, Art and Belief*, Volume 1, Number 1, January 2005, pp. 98-124

Bunge, Marcia "Theologies of Childhood and Child Theologies," *Dharma Deepika*, Vol. 12, No. 2 Issue 28, July-December 2008, pp. 33-53

Carroll, John T., "Children in the Bible", *Interpretation*, Volume 55, No 2, April 2001, pp. 121-134

Devries, Dawn, "Towards of Theology of Childhood", *Interpretation*, Volume 55, No 2, April 2001, pp. 161-173

Finney, Charles, "The Child-Like Spirit an Essential Condition of Entering Heaven," *The Oberlin Evangelist*. 1852,
http://www.gospeltruth.net/1852OE/520526_child_like_spirit.htm

Gundry-Volf, Judith, "To Such Belongs the Reign of God," *Theology Today*, Vol. 56, No 4, pp. 469-480

Hull, John M., "Blindness and the Face of God: Toward a Theology of Disability," in *The Human Image of God*, Hans-Georg Ziebertz et al (eds.), 2000, Brill, pp. 215-229

Metz, J.B. "Communicating a Dangerous Memory," in Fred Lawrence (ed.), *Communicating a Dangerous Memory*, 1987, Scholars Press, pp. 37-54,
http://www.loneranresource.com/pdf/books/9/Lawrence,_Fred_-_Communicating_a_Dangerous_Memory.pdf

Moltmann, J., "Child and childhood as Metaphors of Hope", *Theology Today*, Volume 56, No 4, January 2000, pp. 593-603

White, Keith J., "Child Theology is Born", read to the Annual Forum of the Christian Child Care Forum in London on 5th February 2002.

White, Keith J., "Insights into Child Theology Through the Life and Work of Pandita Ramabai," *Dharma Deepika*, Vol. 12, No. 2 Issue 28, July-December 2008, pp. 77-93

Willmer, Haddon, "Child Theology and Christology in Matthew 18:1-5," *Dharma Deepika*, Vol. 12, No. 2 Issue 28, July-December 2008, pp. 68-76

Willmer, Haddon, "Otto Dibelius and Dietrich Bonhoeffer," in *Studies in Church History*, volume 15, 1978, pp. 443-452

Willmer, Haddon, "The Justification of the Godless: Heinrich Vogel and German Guilt", in *Protestant Evangelicalism: Britain, Ireland, Germany and America 1750 to c. 1950, Essays in Honour of W.R. Ward*, ed. Keith G. Robbins (Studies in Church History, Subsidia 7, 1990)

Willmer, Haddon, " 'Vertical' and 'Horizontal' in Paul's Theology of Reconciliation in the Letter to the Romans," in *Transformation*, Vol. 24, Nos 3 and 4, 2007

Willmer, Haddon, "Ant and Sparrow in Child Theology," *Faith and Thought*, April 2013, pp. 20-31, Victoria Institute

William Wordsworth, *Ode: Intimations of Immortality from Recollections of Early Childhood*, 1804

CTM Publications
(see www.childtheologymovement.org)

Consultation Reports

Penang One Report of Consultation (2002)
Cape Town Report of Consultation (2004)
Houston Report of Consultation (2004)
Penang Two Report of Consultation (2004)
Cambridge Report of Consultation (2004)
Prague (Praha) Report of Consultation (2005)
Penang Three Report of Consultation (2006)
Sao Paulo Report of Consultation – Portuguese and English (2006)
Penang Three Report of Consultation (2006)
Addis Ababa Report of Consultation (2006)
Australasia Report of Consultation (2007)
Nepal Report of Consultation (2008)
South Asia Report of Consultation (2008)
South India Report of Consultation(2011)

Booklet Series

Tan, Sunny, *Child Theology for the Churches in Asia: An Invitation*, London: CTM, 2007
White, Keith J. and Haddon Willmer, *An Introduction to Child Theology*, London: CTM, 2008
Willmer, Haddon, *Experimenting Together: One Way of Doing Child Theology*, London: CTM, 2007
Grobbelaar, Jan, *Child Theology and the African Context*, London: CTM, 2012

Index
to Bible References

Old Testament

New Testament

Index

ACKNOWLEDGEMENTS

What do you have you that you did not receive?

1 CORINTHIANS 4:7

W̲E ARE AWARE that this book is rooted in a multifarious humus of personal and cultural indebtedness, much of it beyond memory and precise accounting. There are people who have contributed to our work who are "known only to God." We acknowledge them in a general but not perfunctory thanksgiving. Rather, in sensing our unlisted sources, we find ourselves with them, once again, before God, who besets us before and behind, laying his hand upon us, giving knowledge which "is too wonderful for me; it is high, I cannot attain it" (Psalm 139).

But within the knowledge of God, which for us is largely a mixture of Unknown and Known Unknowns, there are some Known Knowns: groups and individuals who can be named with gratitude for their contribution to our work.

We start with the Child Theology Movement: several hundred people across the world have shared in Child Theology Movement consultations which have spurred and encouraged us. There is a list of these consultations in the Bibliography. The trustees of CTM have been patient and unwavering in their support: Shiferaw Michael, Wendy Strachan, Marcia Bunge, Sunny Tan, Viktor Nakah, D.J. Konz and David Sims.

Then there are those who have responded to presentations of Child Theology made in other contexts. These include the Victoria Institute, the UK Christian Childhood Forum, Now and Next, the symposium on James E. Loder, and seminars in several seminaries. We are grateful to churches and denominations in different continents that have invited us to explore Child Theology with them.

The Child Theology Movement itself has roots in other movements and has developed in conversation with them. These include Viva and the Cutting Edge conferences, Holistic Child Development, Compassion International, World Vision International, the Asian Graduate School of Theology, the Lutheran Church in Finland, CTM Australia, and many friends and colleagues in India.

Children have been present in our lives, in our work and in our imaginations all through. There is a probably insoluble issue within Child Theology that concerns the appropriate place of actual children in the contemporary process of theological reflection. We have both been blessed by the presence of real children in our respective lives throughout the writing of the book. And we have sought to be inclusive of children by the use of imagination. Readers will be aware that we do not wish to saddle children with burdens that should properly be borne by adults.

Thanks to some who have read the text and in other ways engaged closely with us in the development of the book, especially John Collier, Donald Rutherford, Bill Prevette and Tony Cantale.

Last but not least we thank our respective wives, Ruth and Hilary, for their unfailing patience and eloquent frustration as they sought to encourage us to rein in our conversation and produce an agreed text over a period of many years.

Lightning Source UK Ltd.
Milton Keynes UK
UKHW041344211118
332683UK00001B/52/P